Psychotherapy and Existentialism

Selected Papers on Logotherapy

by

VIKTOR E. FRANKL

with contributions by

James C. Crumbaugh

Hans O. Gerz

Leonard T. Maholick

A Clarion Book
Published by Simon and Schuster

IN MEMORIAM
RUDOLPH ALLERS

A Clarion Book
Published by Simon and Schuster
Rockefeller Center, 630 Fifth Avenue
New York, New York 10020
All Rights Reserved
including the right of reproduction
in whole or in part in any form
Copyright © 1967 by Viktor E. Frankl
Published by arrangement with Washington Square Press, Inc.

SECOND PAPERBACK PRINTING
SBN 671-20056-9

Manufactured in the United States of America
Printed by Deven Lithographers, Inc., Long Island City, N.Y.
Bound by Electronic Perfect Binders, Inc., Brooklyn, N.Y.

Acknowledgments

The author wishes to express his appreciation to the following for permission to reprint, in whole or in part, articles appearing within this collection.

American Journal of Psychotherapy—for "Paradoxical Intention: A Logotherapeutic Technique," *American Journal of Psychotherapy,* Vol. 14, No. 3 (July 1960), 520-535.

The Christian Century Foundation—for "The Will to Meaning," Copyright, ©, 1964, Christian Century Foundation. Here reprinted from *The Christian Century,* Vol. 71 (April 22, 1964), 515-517, as a section of "The Philosophical Foundations of Logotherapy."

Dr. James C. Crumbaugh and Dr. Leonard T. Maholick—for their article "An Experimental Study in Existentialism: The Psychometric Approach to Frankl's Concept of *Noögenic* Neurosis."

Dr. and Mrs. Joseph Fabry—for their translation of "Psychotherapy, Art, and Religion."

Dr. Hans O. Gerz—for his article "The Treatment of the Phobic and the Obsessive-Compulsive Patient Using Paradoxical Intention sec. Viktor E. Frankl."

Group Psychotherapy, J. L. Moreno, M.D., editor, Beacon House, Inc., publisher—for "Group Psychotherapeutic Experiences in a Concentration Camp," *Group Psychotherapy,* Vol. 7 (1954), 1, 81–90.

International Journal of Neuropsychiatry—for "The Treatment of the Phobic and the Obsessive-Compulsive Patient Using Paradoxical Intention sec. Viktor E. Frankl, *Journal of Neuropsychiatry,* Vol. 3, No. 6 (July-August 1962), 375–387.

The Jewish Echo—for "In Memoriam," *The Jewish Echo,* Vol. 5, No. 6, 11.

Journal of Clinical Psychology—for "An Experimental Study in Existentialism: The Psychometric Approach to Frankl's Concept of Noögenic Neurosis," *Journal of Clinical Psychology,* Vol. 20, No. 2 (April 1964), 200–207.

Journal of Existentialism, Libra Publishers, Inc.—for "Beyond Self-Actualization and Self-Expression," *Journal of Existential Psychiatry,* Vol. 1, No. 1 (Spring 1960), 5–20; "Dynamics, Existence and Values," *Journal of Existential Psychiatry,* Vol. 2, No. 5 (Summer 1961), 5–16, here reprinted in revised form as "Dynamics and Values"; "Existential Dynamics and Neurotic Escapism," *Journal of Existential Psychiatry,* Vol. 4 (1963), 27–42.

Journal of Individual Psychology—for "The Spiritual Dimension in Existential Analysis and Logotherapy," *Journal of Individual Psychology,* Vol. 15 (1959), 157–165, here reprinted in revised and abridged form as "Existential Analysis and Dimensional Ontology."

Journal of Religion and Health—for "Psychiatry and Man's Quest for Meaning," *Journal of Religion and Health,* Vol. 1, No. 2 (January 1962), 93–103.

Motive Magazine—for "Existential Escapism," *Motive Magazine,* January-February 1964, here reprinted in abridged form as "Logotherapy and the Challenge of Suffering."

Review of Existential Psychology and Psychiatry—for "Logotherapy and the Challenge of Suffering," *Review of Existential Psychology and Psychiatry,* Vol. 1 (1961), 3–7, here reprinted in abridged form as "Logotherapy and Existence."

Universitas, Dr. H. W. Bähr, editor, Wissenschaftliche Verlagsgesellschaft M. B. H., Stuttgart, English Language Edition—for "Collective Neuroses of the Present Day," *Universitas,* Vol. 4 (1961), 3, 301–315; "Existential Dynamics and Neurotic Escapism," *Universitas,* Vol. 5 (1962), 3, 273–286.

Father Adrian L. VanKaam—for "The Philosophical Foundations of Logotherapy" and "Logotherapy and Existence."

Foreword

This volume consists mainly of a number of my papers in the field of logotherapy published during recent years. I have selected for reprinting those essays which I believe will provide the clearest and most direct understanding of the principles of logotherapy and their therapeutic applications—essays which both complement the broader discussion of logotherapy available in my other works and provide further discussion of specific aspects of this system.

All too often readers have attempted to obtain access to the literature listed in bibliographies and have found that most of the papers referred to have appeared in professional journals with only a relatively small circulation. I would hope, then, that this collection will serve as an introduction or as a sourcebook for the wide variety of persons who have been interested in logotherapy.

I have chosen to present the articles more or less as they were originally presented or printed, rather than to rework them into a highly structured book. Yet, just as each paper offered the opportunity to introduce new ideas or material into print at the time of its publication, so such a collection as this offers the opportunity for the regrouping of new material with old, fresh ideas with familiar. This is not to say, however, that I have chosen to collate all material on a given topic. After all, each paper formed a basic whole, and it did not seem wise to destroy this original wholeness for the sake of an artificial one. Similarly, most of the papers were read to an audience, and for didactic reasons I have chosen to abstain from editing or revising them heavily. That is to say, I chose to allow the conversational tone to remain.

Certainly these decisions entailed the risk of partial overlap, since only at the cost of restructuring each essay to fit within a fully structured volume would it have been possible to eliminate each and every instance of repetition. What is more important, repetition may well serve a didactic purpose and finally prove helpful to the reader—particularly since the repetitions refer to the basic tenets of logotherapy and occur within different contexts within each essay as the subject is viewed from different angles.

Hence, wherever it seemed both preferable and possible, I have maintained the original title and unity of each article. In those cases in which minimal collation of relevant material proved advisable, I have changed the titles to fit the essays as they now stand.

A few words of clarification may be needed to justify the title of the book, *Psychotherapy and Existentialism.*

Logotherapy represents one of the schools in the field of psychotherapy, and, more specifically, is considered by various authors to fall under the category of what they call "existential psychiatry." As early as the thirties I introduced the term *Existenzanalyse* as an alternative designation and denotation of logotherapy—a word which I had coined in the twenties. When American writers began to publish papers on *Existenzanalyse,* they translated the word as "existential analysis." However, they used the same term to cover the teachings of the late Ludwig Binswanger who, in the forties, had started to call his teachings *Daseinsanalyse.* Thus existential analysis became an ambiguous notion. In order not to add to the confusion aroused by this ambiguity, I decided to use only the term "logotherapy," and to refrain as much as possible from using its synonym, existential analysis, as a translation of *Existenzanalyse*.

As to existential psychiatry, or for that matter existential-ism in its most inclusive and encompassing sense, it is safe to say that there are as many existentialisms as there are existentialists. In the framework of this book, some will be sided with while others will be criticized. The latter is particularly true of those who are not aware that they really misconstrue and misuse phrases which they borrow from the nomenclature of the true existentialists.

At the conclusion of this foreword it is my strongly felt desire to say thanks to all those who have offered their valuable advice and assistance in editing my writings even prior to their appearance in this book. I hope it will not be an offense in their eyes if they find themselves simply listed without their services being properly and separately appraised. I herewith gladly express my gratitude, appreciation, and indebtedness to Gordon W. Allport, Heinz L. Ansbacher, Joseph B. Fabry, the late Emil A. Gutheil, Eleanore M. Jantz, Paul E. Johnson, Melvin A. Kimble, Daniel J. Kurland, Robert C. Leslie, Lester C. Rampley, Randolph J. Sasnett, Donald F. Tweedie, Jr., Adrian L. VanKaam, George Vlahos, Werner Von Alvensleben, Rolf H. Von Eckartsberg, Mrs. Walter A. Weisskopf, Antonia Wenkart, and Julius Winkler.

Vienna, 1967   VIKTOR E. FRANKL

Contents

Foreword   *vii*

  I: The Philosophical Foundations of Logotherapy   1
 II: Existential Dynamics and Neurotic Escapism   19
III: Beyond Self-Actualization and Self-Expression   37
 IV: Logotherapy and Existence   53
  V: Dynamics and Values   59
 VI: Psychiatry and Man's Quest for Meaning   71
VII: Logotherapy and the Challenge of Suffering   87
VIII: Group Psychotherapeutic Experiences in a
       Concentration Camp   95
 IX: In Memoriam   107
  X: Collective Neuroses of the Present Day   113
 XI: Existential Analysis and Dimensional Ontology   133
XII: Paradoxical Intention: A Logotherapeutic
       Technique   143
XIII: Psychotherapy, Art, and Religion   165
XIV: An Experimental Study in Existentialism:
       The Psychometric Approach to Frankl's
       Concept of Noögenic Neurosis   183

XV: The Treatment of the Phobic and the Obsessive-
    Compulsive Patient Using Paradoxical
    Intention Sec. Viktor E. Frankl   199
    Bibliography   223
    About the Author   230
    Index of Names   231
    Index of Subjects   232

Psychotherapy and Existentialism

The Philosophical Foundations of Logotherapy[1]

I

According to a statement made by Gordon W. Allport, logotherapy is one of those schools in this country to which the label "existential psychiatry" is applied. As Aaron J. Ungersma has pointed out in his book *The Search for Meaning: A New Approach in Psychotherapy and Pastoral Psychology,* logotherapy is actually the only school within the vast field of existential psychiatry which has succeeded in developing what one might be justified in calling a psychotherapeutic technique. Donald F. Tweedie, Jr., in his volume *Logotherapy and the Christian Faith,* observes that this fact will elicit the interest of the typical American, whose outlook is traditionally pragmatic.

However this might be, logotherapy exceeds and surpasses existential analysis, or ontoanalysis, to the extent that it is essentially more than analysis of existence, or being, and involves more than a mere analysis of its subject. Logotherapy is concerned not only with being but also with meaning—not only with *ontos* but also with *logos*—and this feature may well account for the activistic, therapeutic orientation of logotherapy. In other words, logotherapy is not only analysis but also therapy.

---

[1]Paper read before the Conference on Phenomenology, Lexington, Kentucky, April 4, 1963.

As is the case in any type of therapy, there is a theory underlying its practice—a *theoria*, i.e., a vision, a *Weltanschauung*. In contrast to many other therapies, however, logotherapy is based on an explicit philosophy of life. More specifically, it is based on three fundamental assumptions which form a chain of interconnected links:

1. Freedom of Will;
2. Will to Meaning;
3. Meaning of Life.

THE FREEDOM OF WILL

Man's freedom of will belongs to the immediate data of his experience. These data yield to that empirical approach which, since Husserl's days, is called phenomenological.[2] Actually only two classes of people maintain that their will is not free: schizophrenic patients suffering from the delusion that their will is manipulated and their thoughts controlled by others, and alongside of them, deterministic philosophers. To be sure, the latter admit that we are experiencing our will as though it were free, but this, they say, is a self-deception. Thus the only point of disagreement between their conviction and my own refers to the question of whether or not our experience is conducive to truth.

Who should be the judge? To answer this question, let us take as a starting point the fact that not only abnormal people such as schizophrenics but even normal persons can, under certain circumstances, experience their will as something which is not free. They can do so if we have them take a small dose of lysergic acid diethylamide (LSD). Soon they start suffering from an artificial psychosis in which, according to published research reports, they experience themselves as automata. In other words, they arrive at the

---

[2]Phenomenology, as I understand it, speaks the language of man's prereflective self-understanding rather than interpreting a given phenomenon after preconceived patterns.

"truth" of determinism. However, it is high time to ask ourselves whether or not it is probable that truth is accessible to man only after his brain has been poisoned. A strange concept of *aletheia:* that truth can only be disclosed and uncovered through a delusion, that *logos* can only be mediated through *patho-logos!*

Needless to say, the freedom of a finite being such as man is a freedom within limits. Man is not free from conditions, be they biological or psychological or sociological in nature. But he is, and always remains, free to take a stand toward these conditions; he always retains the freedom to choose his attitude toward them. Man is free to rise above the plane of somatic and psychic determinants of his existence. By the same token a new dimension is opened. Man enters the dimension of the noetic, in counterdistinction to the somatic and psychic phenomena. He becomes capable of taking a stand not only toward the world but also toward himself. Man is a being capable of reflecting on, and even rejecting, himself. He can be his own judge, the judge of his own deeds. In short, the specifically human phenomena linked with one another, self-consciousness and conscience, would not be understandable unless we interpret man in terms of a being capable of detaching himself from himself, leaving the "plane" of the biological and psychological, passing into the "space" of the noölogical. This specifically human dimension, which I have entitled noölogical,[3] is not accessible to a beast. A dog, for example, after wetting the carpet may well slink under the couch but this would not yet be a sign of bad conscience; it is some sort of anticipatory anxiety—namely, fearful anticipation of punishment.

The specifically human capacity for self-detachment is mobilized and utilized for therapeutic purposes in a special logotherapeutic technique called paradoxical intention. A

[3] *Cf.* V. E. Frankl, "The Concept of Man in Logotherapy," *Journal of Existentialism*, 4: 53 (1965).

clear and concise illustration of paradoxical intention may be seen in the following case:

The patient was a bookkeeper who had been treated by many doctors and in several clinics without any therapeutic success. When he came to my clinic, he was in extreme despair, admitting that he was close to suicide. For some years, he had suffered from a writer's cramp which had recently become so severe that he was in danger of losing his job. Therefore only immediate short-term therapy could alleviate the situation. In starting treatment my associate recommended to the patient that he do just the opposite from what he usually had done; namely, instead of trying to write as neatly and legibly as possible, to write with the worst possible scrawl. He was advised to say to himself, "Now I will show people what a good scribbler I am!" And at that moment in which he deliberately tried to scribble, he was unable to do so. "I tried to scrawl but simply could not do it," he said the next day. Within forty-eight hours the patient was in this way freed from his writer's cramp, and remained free for the observation period after he had been treated. He is a happy man again and fully able to work.

A sound sense of humor is inherent in this technique. This is understandable since we know that humor is a paramount way of putting distance between something and oneself. One might say as well, that humor helps man rise above his own predicament by allowing him to look at himself in a more detached way. So humor would also have to be located in the noetic dimension. After all, no animal is able to laugh, least of all at himself.

The basic mechanism underlying the technique of paradoxical intention perhaps can best be illustrated by a joke which was told to me some years ago: A boy who came to school late excused himself to the teacher on the grounds that the icy streets were so slippery that whenever he moved one step forward he slipped two steps back again. Thereupon the teacher retorted, "Now I have caught you in a lie—if this were true, how did you ever get to school?"

Whereupon the boy calmly replied, "I finally turned around and went home!"

I am convinced that paradoxical intention is in no way a procedure which simply moves on the surface of a neurosis; rather it enables the patient to perform on a deeper level a radical change of attitude, and a wholesome one at that. However, there have been attempts to explain the undeniable therapeutic effects obtained by this logotherapeutic technique on psychodynamic grounds.[4] One of the doctors on my staff at the Vienna Poliklinik Hospital, a fully trained Freudian, presented to the Viennese Psychoanalytic Society, the oldest in the world, a paper on paradoxical intention explaining its successes exclusively in psychodynamic terms. While he was preparing the paper, it happened that he was consulted by a patient suffering from a severe agoraphobia and tried paradoxical intention upon her. But, unfortunately, after one session she was free from any complaints and it was very difficult for him to get her to return for more sessions in order to find out the psychodynamics underlying the cure!

THE WILL TO MEANING

Now let us turn to the second basic assumption: will to meaning. For didactic reasons the will to meaning has been counterposed by way of a heuristic oversimplification both to the pleasure principle, which is so pervasive in psychoanalytic motivational theories, and to the will to power, the concept which plays such a decisive role in Adlerian psychology. I do not weary of contending that the will to pleasure is really a self-defeating principle inasmuch as the more a man would actually set out to strive for pleasure the less he would gain it. This is due to the fundamental fact that pleasure is a by-product, or side

---

[4]*Cf.* V. E. Frankl, *The Doctor and the Soul: From Psychotherapy to Logotherapy* (2d ed.; New York: Alfred A. Knopf, Inc., 1965), p. 236.

efec., of the fulfillment of our strivings, but is destroyed and spoiled to the extent to which it is made a goal or target. The more a man aims at pleasure by way of a direct intention, the more he misses his aim. And this, I venture to say, is a mechanism etiologically underlying most cases of sexual neurosis. Accordingly, a logotherapeutic technique based on this theory of the self-thwarting quality of pleasure intention yields remarkable short-term results, and this technique has been used effectively even by psychodynamically oriented therapists on my staff. One of them, to whom I have assigned the responsibility for treatment of all sexually neurotic patients, has used this technique exclusively—in terms of a short-term procedure which has been the only one indicated in the given setting.

In the last analysis, it turns out that both the will to pleasure and the will to power are derivatives of the original will to meaning. Pleasure, as we have said above, is an effect of meaning fulfillment; power is a means to an end. A certain amount of power, such as economic or financial power, is generally a prerequisite for meaning fulfillment. Thus we could say that while the will to pleasure mistakes the effect for the end, the will to power mistakes the means to an end for the end itself.

We are not really justified, however, in speaking of a *will* to pleasure or power in connection with psychodynamically oriented schools of thought; they assume that man aims for the goals of his behavior unwillingly and unwittingly and that his conscious motivations are not his actual motivations. Erich Fromm, for instance, only recently spoke of "the motivating forces which make man act in certain ways, the drives which propel him to strive in certain directions."[5] As for myself, however, it is not conceivable that man be really driven to strivings; I would say either that he is striving or that he is driven. *Tertium non datur.* Ignoring this difference

[5] *Beyond the Chains of Illusion* (New York: Simon & Schuster, Inc., 1962), p. 38.

or, rather, sacrificing one phenomenon to another, is a procedure unworthy of a scientist. To do so is to allow one's adherence to hypotheses to blind one to facts. One such distortion is the assumption that man "is lived by" his instincts. Since the man quoted here is Sigmund Freud, for the sake of justice, another of Freud's statements which is not so well known must be added. In a book review he wrote for the *Wiener Medizinische Wochenschrift* in 1889, he says: "Reverence before the greatness of a genius is certainly a great thing. But our reverence before facts should exceed it."

Freud, and consequently his epigones, have taught us always to see something behind, or beneath, human volitions: unconscious motivations, underlying dynamics. Freud never took a human phenomenon at its face value; or, to adopt the formulation used by Gordon W. Allport, "Freud was a specialist in precisely those motives that cannot be taken at their face value."[6] Does this, however, imply that there are no motives at all which should be taken at their face value? Such an assumption is comparable to the attitude of the man who, when he was shown a stork, said, "Oh, I thought the stork didn't exist!" Does the fact that the stork has been used to hide the facts of life from children in any way deny that bird's reality?

The reality principle is, according to Freud's own words, a mere extension of the pleasure principle; one which serves the pleasure principle's purpose. One could just as well say that the pleasure principle itself is a mere extension working in the service of a wider concept called the homeostasis principle and serves *its* purposes. Ultimately, the psychodynamic concept of man presents him as a being basically concerned with maintaining or restoring his inner equilibrium, and in order to do so, he is trying to gratify his drives and satisfy his instincts. Even in the perspective in which man has been portrayed by Jungian psychology,

[6]*Personality and Social Encounter* (Boston: Beacon Press, 1960), p. 103.

human motivation is interpreted along this line. Just think of archetypes. They, too, are mythical beings (as Freud called the instincts). Again man is seen as bent on getting rid of tensions, be they aroused by drives and instincts claiming their gratification and satisfaction, or by archetypes urging their materialization. In either case, reality, the world of beings and meanings, is debased and degraded to a pool of more or less workable instruments to be used to get rid of various stimuli such as irritating superegos or archetypes. What has been sacrificed, however, and hence totally eliminated in this view of man, is the fundamental fact which lends itself to a phenomenological analysis—namely, that man is a being encountering other beings and reaching out for meanings to fulfill.

And this is precisely the reason why I speak of a will to meaning rather than a need for meaning or a drive to meaning. If man were really driven to meaning he would embark on meaning fulfillment solely for the sake of getting rid of this drive, in order to restore homeostasis within himself. At the same time, however, he would no longer be really concerned with meaning itself but rather with his own equilibrium and thus, in the final analysis, with himself.

It may now have become clear that a concept such as self-actualization, or self-realization, is not a sufficient ground for a motivational theory. This is mainly due to the fact that self-actualization, like power and pleasure, also belongs to the class of phenomena which can only be obtained as a side effect and are thwarted precisely to the degree to which they are made a matter of direct intention. Self-actualization is a good thing; however, I maintain that man can only actualize himself to the extent to which he fulfills meaning. Then self-actualization occurs spontaneously; it is contravened when it is made an end in itself.

When I was lecturing at Melbourne University some years ago, I was given as a souvenir an Australian boomerang. While contemplating this unusual gift, it occurred to me that in a sense it was a symbol of human existence. Generally, one assumes that a boomerang returns to the hunter; but actually, I have been told in Australia, a boomerang only comes back to the hunter when it has missed its target, the prey. Well, man also only returns to himself, to being concerned with his self, after he has missed his mission, has failed to find a meaning in his life.

Ernest Keen, one of my assistants during a teaching period at the Harvard Summer Session, devoted his doctoral dissertation to demonstrating that the shortcomings of Freudian psychoanalysis have been compensated for by Heinz Hartmann's ego psychology, and the deficiencies of ego psychology, in turn, by Erikson's identity concept. However, Keen contends, a last link was still missing, and this link is logotherapy. In fact, it is my conviction that man should not, indeed cannot, struggle for identity in a direct way; he rather finds identity to the extent to which he commits himself to something beyond himself, to a cause greater than himself. No one has put it as cogently as Karl Jaspers did when he said: "What man is, he ultimately becomes through the cause which he has made his own."

Rolf Von Eckartsberg, also a Harvard assistant of mine, has shown the insufficiency of the role-playing concept by pointing out that it avoids the very problem behind it—the problem of choice and value. For again there is a problem: *Which* role to adopt, *which* cause to advocate? We are not spared decision-making.

The same holds for those who teach that both man's ultimate destination and primary intention is to develop his potentialities. Socrates confessed that he had within himself the potentiality to become a criminal, but decided to turn away from materializing this potentiality, and this decision, we might add, made all the difference.

But let us now ask the real purpose of the assertions: Should man just try to live out his inner potentialities, or—as it is also put—to express himself? The hidden motive behind such notions is, I believe, to lessen the tension aroused by the gap between what a man is and what he ought to become; the tension between the actual state of affairs, and the ideal one which he is to materialize; the tension between existence and essence, or as one could say as well, between being and meaning. In fact, preaching that man need not worry about ideals and values since they are nothing but "self-expressions" and that he should therefore simply embark on the actualization of his own potentialities is good news. Man is told, as it were, that he need not reach out for the stars, to bring them down to earth, for everything is all right, is already present, at least in the form of potentialities to actualize.

Pindar's imperative—Become what you are—is then deprived of its imperative quality and transmuted into the indicative statement that man has been all along what he should become! Man, therefore, need not reach out for the stars, to bring them down to earth, for *the earth is itself a star!*

The fact remains that the tension between being and meaning is ineradicable in man. It is inherent in being human, and therefore indispensable to mental well-being. Thus, we have started from man's meaning orientation, i.e., his will to meaning, and now we have arrived at another problem; namely, his meaning confrontation. The first issue refers to what man basically *is:* oriented toward meaning; the second refers to what he *should be:* confronted with meaning.

However, it makes no sense to confront man with values which are seen merely as a form of self-expression. All the less would it be the right start to have him see in values "nothing but defense mechanisms, reaction formations, or rationalizations of his instinctual drives," as two outstanding psychoanalytically oriented workers in the field have defined them. My own reaction to this theorizing is that I would not be willing to live for the sake of my "defense mechanisms," much less to die for the sake of my "reaction formations."

On the other hand, in a given case and setting, the indoctrination of a patient along the lines of psychodynamic interpretations may well serve the purpose of what I should like to call *existential rationalization*. If a person is taught that his concern about an ultimate meaning to his life is no more than, say, a way of coming to terms with his early childhood Oedipal situation, then his concern can be analyzed away, along with the existential tension aroused by it.

Logotherapy takes a different stand. Logotherapy does not spare the patient a confrontation with the specific meaning which he has to carry out and which we have to help him find. Professor Tweedie has referred to what once happened in my office when an American doctor in Vienna asked me to tell him the difference between logotherapy and psychoanalysis in one sentence. Thereupon, I invited him first to tell me what he regarded as the essence of psychoanalysis. When he replied: "During psychoanalysis, the patient must lie down on a couch and tell you things that sometimes are very disagreeable to tell," I jokingly retorted: "Now, in logotherapy the patient may remain sitting erect, but must hear things that sometimes are very disagreeable to hear."

The otherness of the other being should not be blurred in existential thinking, as Erwin Straus has so rightly stressed; and this also holds true for meaning. The meaning which a being has to fulfill is something beyond himself, it is never just himself. Only if this otherness is retained by meaning, can meaning exert upon a being that demand quality which yields itself to a phenomenological analysis of our experience of existence. Only a meaning which is not just an expression of the being itself represents a true challenge. You remember the story in the Bible: When the Israelites wandered through the desert God's glory went before in the form of a cloud; only in this way was it possible for the Israelites to be guided by God. Imagine, on the other hand, what would have happened if God's presence, the cloud, had dwelled in the midst of Israelites; rather than leading them the right way, this cloud would have clouded everything, and the Israelites would have gone astray.

In other words, meaning must not coincide with being; meaning must be ahead of being. Meaning sets the pace for being. Existence falters unless it is lived in terms of transcendence toward something beyond itself. Viewed from this angle, we might distinguish between people who are pacemakers and those who are peacemakers: the former confront us with meanings and values, thus supporting our meaning orientation; the latter alleviate the burden of meaning confrontation. In this sense Moses was a pacemaker; he did not soothe man's conscience but rather stirred it up. Moses confronted his people with the Ten Commandments and did not spare them confrontation with ideals and values. Peacemakers, on the other hand, appease people; they try to reconcile them with themselves. "Let's face facts," they say. "Why worry about your shortcomings? Only a minority live up to ideals. So let's forget them; let's care for peace of mind, or soul, rather than those existential meanings which just arouse tensions in human beings."

What the peacemakers overlook is the wisdom laid down in Goethe's warning: "If we take man as he is, we make him worse; if we take him as he ought to be, we help him become it."

Once meaning orientation turns into meaning confrontation, that stage of maturation and development is reached in which freedom—that concept so much emphasized by existentialist philosophy—becomes responsibleness. Man is responsible for the fulfillment of the specific meaning of his personal life. But he is also responsible *before* something, or *to* something, be it society, or humanity, or mankind, or his own conscience. However, there is a significant number of people who interpret their own existence not just in terms of being responsible to something but rather to some*one,* namely, to God.[7]

Logotherapy, as a secular theory and medical practice, must restrict itself to factual statements, leaving to the patient the decision as to how to understand his own being-responsible: whether along the lines of religious beliefs or agnostic convictions. Logotherapy must remain available for everyone; I would be obliged to adhere to this by my Hippocratic oath, if for no other reason. Logotherapy is applicable in cases of atheistic patients and usable in the hands of atheistic doctors. In any case, logotherapy sees in responsibleness the very essence of human existence. Capitalizing on responsibleness to this extent, a logotherapist cannot spare his patient the decision for what, and to what, or to whom, he feels responsible.

A logotherapist is not entitled consciously to influence the patient's decision as to how to interpret his own responsibleness, or as to what to embrace as his personal meaning. Anyone's conscience, as anything human, is subject to error; but this does not release man from his obligation to obey it—existence involves the risk of error. Man must risk committing himself to a cause not worthy of his commitment. Perhaps my commitment to the cause of logotherapy is erroneous. But I prefer to live in a world in which man has the right to make choices, even if they are wrong choices, rather than a world in which no choice at all is left to him. In other words, I prefer a world in which, on the one hand, a phenomenon such as Adolf Hitler can occur,

[7]I personally doubt whether, within religion, truth can ever be distinguished from untruth by evidence which is universally acceptable to man. It seems to me that the various religious denominations are something like different languages. It is not possible, either, to declare that any one of them is superior to the others. Similarly, no language can justifiably be called "true" or "false," but through each of them truth—the one truth—may be approached as if from different sides, and through each language it is also possible to err, and even to lie.

and on the other hand, phenomena such as the many saints who have lived can occur also. I prefer this world to a world of total, or totalitarian, conformism and collectivism in which man is debased and degraded to a mere functionary of a party or the state.

THE MEANING OF LIFE

We have now reached the point of the third basic assumption: After discussing freedom of will and will to meaning, meaning itself becomes the topic.

While no logotherapist *prescribes* a meaning he may well *describe* it. By this I mean describing what is going on in a man when he experiences something as meaningful, without applying to such experiences any preconceived pattern of interpretation. In short, our task is to resort to a phenomenological investigation of the immediate data of actual life experience. In a phenomenological way, the logotherapist might widen and broaden the visual field of his patient in terms of meanings and values, making them loom large, as it were. In the course of a growing awareness, it might then finally turn out that life never ceases to hold and retain a meaning up to its very last moment. This is due to the fact that, as a phenomenological analysis can show us, man not only finds his life meaningful through his deeds, his works, his creativity, but also through his experiences, his encounters with what is true, good, and beautiful in the world, and last but not least, his encounter with others, with fellow human beings and their unique qualities. To grasp another person in his uniqueness means to love him. But even in a situation in which man is deprived of both creativity and receptivity, he can still fulfill a meaning in his life. It is precisely when facing such a fate, when being confronted with a hopeless situation, that man is given a last opportunity to fulfill a meaning—to realize even the highest value, to fulfill even the deepest meaning—and that is the meaning of suffering.[8]

Let me summarize. Life can be made meaningful in a threefold way: first, through *what we give* to life (in terms of our creative works); second, by *what we take* from the world (in terms of our experiencing values); and third, through *the stand we take* toward a fate we no longer can change (an incurable disease, an inoperable cancer, or the like). However, even apart from this, man is not spared facing his human condition which includes what I call the tragic triad of human existence; namely, pain, death, and guilt. By pain, I mean suffering; by the two other constituents of the tragic triad, I mean the twofold fact of man's mortality and fallibility.

Stressing these tragic aspects of man's life is not as superfluous as it may seem to be at first sight. In particular, the fear of aging and dying is pervasive in the present culture, and Edith Weisskopf-Joelson, professor of psychology at Duke University, has claimed that logotherapy might help counteract these particularly widespread American anxieties. As a matter of fact, it is my contention, and a tenet of logotherapy, that life's transitoriness does not in the least detract from its meaningfulness. The same holds for man's fallibility. So there is no need to reinforce our patients' escapism in the face of the tragic triad of existence.

And now let me come back for a moment to suffering. You may have heard the story which I so much like to tell my audiences because it proves to be so helpful in "making the meaning of suffering loom." An old doctor consulted me in Vienna because he could not get rid of a severe depression caused by the death of his wife. I asked him, "What would have happened, Doctor, if you had died first, and your wife

[8]It goes without saying that suffering can be meaningful only if the situation cannot be changed—otherwise we would not be dealing with heroism but rather masochism.

would have had to survive you?" Whereupon he said: "For her this would have been terrible; how she would have suffered!" I then added, "You see, Doctor, such a suffering has been spared her, and it is you who have spared her this suffering; but now you have to pay for it by surviving and mourning her." The old man suddenly saw his plight in a new light, and reevaluated his suffering in the meaningful terms of a sacrifice for the sake of his wife.

Even if this story is well known to you, what is unknown is a comment which was given by an American psycho-analyst some months ago. After hearing this account, he stood up and said, "I understand what you mean, Dr. Frankl; however, if we start from the fact that obviously your patient had only suffered so deeply from the death of his wife because unconsciously he had hated her all along. . . ."

If you are interested in hearing my reaction, here it is: "It may well be that after having the patient lie down on your couch for five hundred hours, you will have brainwashed and indoctrinated him to the point where he confesses, 'Yes, Doctor, you are right, I have hated my wife all along, I have never loved her at any time. . . .' But then," I told him, "you would have succeeded in depriving that old man of the only precious treasure he still possessed, namely, this ideal marital life they had built up, their true love . . . while I succeeded, within a minute, in bringing about a significant reversal of his attitude, or let me frankly say, in bringing consolation."

A person's will to meaning can only be elicited if meaning itself can be elucidated as something which is essentially more than his mere self-expression. This implies a certain degree of objectiveness, and without a minimum amount of objectiveness meaning would never be worth fulfilling. We do not just attach and attribute meanings to things, but rather find them; we do not invent them, we detect them. (No more than this is meant when I speak of the objectiveness of meaning.) On the other hand, however, an unbiased investigation would also reveal a certain subjectiveness inherent in meaning. The meaning of life must be conceived in terms of the specific meaning of a personal life in a given situation. Each man is unique and each man's life is singular; no one is replaceable nor is his life repeatable. This twofold uniqueness adds to man's responsibleness. Ultimately, this responsibleness derives from the existential fact that life is a chain of questions which man has to answer by answering for life, to which he has to respond by being responsible, by making decisions, by deciding which answers to give to the individual questions. And I venture to say that each question has only one answer—the right one!

This does not imply that man is always capable of finding the right answer or solution to each problem, of finding the true meaning to his existence. Rather, the contrary is true; as a finite being, he is not exempt from error and, therefore, has to take the risk of erring. Again, I quote Goethe who once said: "We must always aim at the bull's eye—although we know that we will not always hit it." Or, to put it more prosaically: We have to try to reach the absolutely best—otherwise we shall not even reach the relatively good.

While speaking of the will to meaning, I referred to meaning orientation and meaning confrontation; while speaking of the meaning of life, I now must refer to meaning frustration, or existential frustration. This represents what could be called the collective neurosis of our time. The dean of students at a major American university has told me that in his counseling work he is continually being confronted by students who complain about the meaninglessness of life, who are beset by that inner void which I have termed the "existential vacuum." Moreover, not a few instances of suicide among students are attributable to this state of affairs.

What is needed today is to complement, not to

supplement or substitute, the so-called depth-psychology with what one might call height-psychology. Such a psychology would do justice to man's higher aspects and aspirations, including their frustrations. Freud was enough of a genius as to be aware of the limitations of his system, such as when he confessed to Ludwig Binswanger that he had "always confined" himself "to the ground floor and basement of the edifice."[9]

A height-psychologist in the sense outlined above has said that what is needed is a "basis of convictions and beliefs so strong that they lifted individuals clear out of themselves and caused them to live, and die, for some aim nobler and better than themselves," and that one should teach students that "ideals are the very stuff of survival."[10]

And who is this height-psychologist that I have just quoted? The speaker was not a logotherapist, nor a psychotherapist, a psychiatrist or a psychologist, but the astronaut Lt. Col. John H. Glenn, Jr.—a "height"-psychologist, indeed. . . .

---

[9]Ludwig Binswanger, *Sigmund Freud: Reminiscences of a Friendship* (New York: Grune & Stratton, Inc., 1957), p. 96.

[10]This is neither idealism nor materialism; it is simply realism. I am the sort of realist that Goethe was when he said: "When we take man as he is, we make him worse; but when we take man as if he were already what he should be, we promote him to what he can be." If I measure the blood pressure of a patient and find it slightly increased, and I then tell the patient about it, I actually do not tell him the truth, for he will then become anxious and the blood pressure will increase even more. If I tell him, in reverse, that he need not worry, I do not tell him a lie, for he will be calmed and his blood pressure will become normal.

Existential Dynamics and Neurotic Escapism[1]

II

Ever more frequently psychoanalysts report that they are confronted with a new type of neurosis that is characterized mainly by loss of interest and by lack of initiative. They complain that in such cases conventional psychoanalysis is not effective. Time and again the psychiatrist is consulted by patients who doubt that life has any meaning. This condition I have called "existential vacuum." As to the frequency of this phenomenon, I refer to a statistical survey made among my students at the University of Vienna: Only 40% of the students (German, Swiss, and Austrian) who attended my lectures held in German stated that they knew from their own experience that feeling of ultimate absurdity, while not 40 but 81% of the students (American) who attended my lectures held in English professed to the same experience. From these percentages we must not draw the conclusion that the existential vacuum is predominantly an American disease, but rather that it is apparently a concomitant of industrialization.

The existential vacuum seems to issue from man's twofold loss: the loss of that instinctual security which surrounds an animal's life, and the further, more recent loss of those traditions which governed man's life in former times. At

[1]Paper read before the Conference on Existential Psychiatry, Toronto, Canada, May 6, 1962.

present, instincts do not tell man what he has to do, nor do traditions direct him toward what he ought to do; soon he will not even know what he really wants to do and will be led by what other people want him to do, thus completely succumbing to conformism.

Is psychotherapy prepared to deal with the present need? Above all, I consider it dangerous to press man's search for a meaning into stereotype interpretations such as "nothing but defense mechanisms" or "secondary rationalizations." I think that man's quest for, and even his questioning of, a meaning to his existence, i.e., his spiritual aspirations as well as his spiritual frustrations, should be taken at face value and should not be tranquilized or analyzed away.[2] Therefore, I cannot share Freud's opinion as he stated it in a letter to Princess Bonaparte: "The moment a man questions the meaning and value of life he is sick."[3] I rather think that such a man only proves that he is truly a human being. I remember how my science teacher in high school once explained that life, in the final analysis, was nothing but a process of oxidation. At this I jumped up and passionately asked: "If that is so, then what meaning does life have?" It might well be that with this question I actualized spiritual self-hood for the first time.

Rather than being merely a "secondary rationalization" of instinctual drives, the striving to find a meaning in life is a primary motivational force in man. In logotherapy we speak in this context of a will to meaning in contradistinction to both the pleasure principle and the will to power principle. Actually, "pleasure" is not the goal of human strivings but

---

[2]A patient of mine, a university professor in Vienna, was referred to my clinic because he was tormenting himself about the meaning of his life. It turned out that he suffered from a recurrent endogenous depression; however, it was not during the phases of his psychic illness that he doubted the meaning of his life, but during the intervals when he was healthy.

[3]*Letters of Sigmund Freud*, ed. Ernst L. Freud (New York: Basic Books, Inc., 1960).

rather a by-product of the fulfillment of such strivings; and "power" is not an end but a means to an end. Thus, the "pleasure principle" school mistakes a side effect for the goal, while the "will to power" school mistakes a means for the end.

Psychotherapy tries to make the patient aware of what he really longs for in the depth of his self. In making something conscious, however, logotherapy does not confine itself to the instinctual unconscious, but is also concerned with man's spiritual aspirations: It tries to elicit his striving for a meaning to life, and it tries also to elucidate the meaning of his existence. In other words, we have to deepen our patients' self-understanding not only on the subhuman, but on the human level as well. The time has come to complement the so-called depth-psychology with what one might call height-psychology.

In logotherapy the patient is, indeed, confronted with meanings and purposes and is challenged to fulfill them. At this point the question might be raised whether the patient is not overburdened with such a confrontation. However, in the age of the existential vacuum, the danger lies much more in man's not being burdened enough. Pathology results not only from stress, but also from relief of stress which ends in emptiness. A lack of tension created by the loss of meaning is as dangerous a threat in terms of mental health as is too high a tension. Tension is not something to be avoided indiscriminately. Man does not need homeostasis at any cost, but rather a sound amount of tension such as that which is aroused by the demand quality (*Aufforderungscharakter*) inherent in the meaning to human existence. Like iron filings in a magnetic field, man's life is put in order through his orientation toward meaning. Thereby a field of tension is established between what man is and what he ought to do. In this field existential dynamics, as I call it, is operating. By this dynamics man is pulled rather than pushed; instead of being determined by meaning, he decides whether his life is to be structured by the demand quality of a meaning to his existence.

Much in the same way as man needs the pulling force of gravity (at least in his usual way of life), he needs the pulling force emanating from the meaning to his existence. He needs the call and the challenge to actualize this meaning. The impact of existential dynamics as it appears in the logotherapeutic concept of "meaning orientation" was pointed out by Kotchen when he found a significantly positive correlation between meaning orientation and mental health.[4] Furthermore, Davis, McCourt, and Solomon have shown that hallucinations occurring during sensory deprivation could not be obviated simply by providing the subject with sensory perceptions but only by restoring a meaningful contact with the outer world.[5] Finally, Pearl Schroeder has reported that clients rating high on responsibility showed more improvement in therapy than individuals who had a low sense of responsibility.[6]

A strong meaning orientation might also have a life-prolonging, or even a lifesaving effect. As to the former, let me remind you of the fact that Goethe worked seven years on the completion of the second part of *Faust*. Finally, in January 1832, he sealed the manuscript; two months later he died. I dare say that during the final seven years of his life he biologically lived beyond his means. His death was overdue, but he remained alive up to the moment his work was completed and meaning fulfilled. As to the lifesaving effect of meaning orientation, I refer to my clinical and

---

[4]Theodore A. Kotchen, "Existential Mental Health, An Empirical Approach," *Journal of Individual Psychology*, 16: 174 (1960).

[5]John M. Davis, William F. McCourt, and Philip Solomon, "The Effect of Visual Stimulation on Hallucinations and other Mental Experiences During Sensory Deprivation," *The American Journal of Psychiatry*, 116: 889 (1960).

[6]Pearl Schroeder, "Client Acceptance of Responsibility and Difficulty of Therapy," *Journal of Consulting Psychology*, 24: 467 (1960).

metaclinical experiences gathered in the living laboratory of the concentration camps.[7]

In emphasizing the beneficial and decisive influence of meaning orientation on mental health preservation or restoration, I am far from depreciating such valuable assets of psychiatry as electro convulsive treatments (ECT), tranquilizing drugs, or even lobotomy. As early as 1952, even before the "March to Miltown" began, I had developed the first tranquilizer in Continental Europe. And several times during my clinical work I have diagnosed indications for lobotomy, in some cases even performed it myself, without finding any reason later to regret the surgery. Nor must we deprive the patient, in severe cases of endogenous depression, of the relief which ECT can give. I consider it a misconception to say that in such cases the guilt feelings should not be shocked away because authentic guilt is underlying them. In a sense, every one of us has become guilty during the course of his life; this existential guilt is simply inherent in the human condition. A patient suffering from endogenous depression only experiences it in a pathologically distorted way. That does not allow us to infer that existential guilt is the cause of endogenous depression. Endogenous depression only brings about an abnormal awareness of this guilt. Just as the emergence of a reef from the sea at low tide does not cause low tide, but is caused by it, guilt feelings appearing during an endogenous depression—an emotional low tide—are not the cause of the depression. Moreover, a confrontation of a patient with his existential guilt during a depressive state may very well intensify his tendency to self-accusation to such an extent that it eventually provokes suicide.

This is different in a neurotic depression. Here the

[7]An extended presentation and analysis of these experiences may be found in *Man's Search for Meaning: An Introduction to Logotherapy* (Boston: Beacon Press, 1962; paperback edition, New York: Washington Square Press, Inc., 1963), a revised and expanded edition of *From Death-Camp to Existentialism* (Boston: Beacon Press, 1959). [Editor's note.]

typically neurotic escapism must be removed. This escapism not only refers to guilt but also to the two other constituents of what I call the tragic triad of human existence, namely, pain and death. Man has to accept his finiteness in its three aspects: He has to face the fact (1) that he has failed; (2) that he is suffering; and (3) that he will die. Thus, after having dealt with guilt, let us turn to pain and death.

It is a tenet of logotherapy that meaning can be found in life not only through acting or through experiencing values but also through suffering. This is why life never ceases to have and to retain a meaning to the very last moment. Even facing an ineluctable fate, e.g., an incurable disease, there is still granted to man a chance to fulfill even the deepest possible meaning. What matters, then, is the stand he takes in his predicament. Life can be made meaningful (1) by what we give to the world in terms of our creation; (2) by what we take from the world in terms of our experience; and (3) by the stand we take toward the world, that is to say, by the attitude we choose toward suffering.

Let me illustrate what I mean:

Once, an elderly general practitioner consulted me because of his severe depression. He could not overcome the loss of his wife who had died two years before and whom he had loved above all else. Now how could I help him? What should I tell him? Well, I refrained from telling him anything, but instead confronted him with the question, "What would have happened, Doctor, if you had died first, and your wife would have had to survive you?" "Oh," he said, "for her this would have been terrible; how she would have suffered!" Whereupon I replied, "You see, Doctor, such a suffering has been spared her, and it is you who have spared her this suffering; but now, you have to pay for it by surviving and mourning her." He said no word but shook my hand and calmly left my office. Suffering ceases to be suffering in some way at the moment it finds a meaning, such as the meaning of a sacrifice.

Of course, this was not therapy in the proper sense since, first of all, his despair was not a disease and, secondly, I could not change his fate—I could not revive his wife. But I at least succeeded in changing his attitude toward his unalterable fate so that from this time on he could at least see a meaning to his suffering. Logotherapy insists that man's main concern is not to seek pleasure or to avoid pain, but rather to find a meaning to his life. Thus we see that man is ready to suffer if only he can be satisfied that his suffering has a meaning.

As logotherapy teaches, human freedom is in no way a freedom from conditions but rather the freedom to take a stand toward conditions. Therefore, choosing a stand toward suffering means exerting freedom. In doing so, man, in a sense, transcends the world and his predicament therein. Let me try to illustrate this with an experience I had during my first days at the concentration camp in Auschwitz. The odds of surviving there were no more than one in twenty. Not even the manuscript of a book which I had hidden in my coat seemed likely ever to be rescued. This manuscript was the first version of my book *The Doctor and the Soul: An Introduction to Logotherapy* that was later, in 1955, published in translation by Alfred A. Knopf, Inc., in New York. At the concentration camp I had to surrender my clothes with the manuscript. Thus I had to overcome the loss of my spiritual child, as it were, and had to face the question of whether this loss did not make my life void of meaning. An answer to this question was given to me soon. In exchange for my clothes I was given the rags of an inmate who had already been sent to the gas chamber; in a pocket I found a single page torn from a Hebrew prayer book. It contained the main Jewish prayer *Shema Yisrael*, i.e., the command "Love thy God with all thy heart, and with all thy soul, and with all thy might," or, as one might interpret it as well, the command to say "yes" to life despite whatever one has to face, be it suffering or even dying. A life, I told myself, whose meaning stands or falls on whether one can publish a manuscript would, ultimately, not be worth living. Thus in that single page which replaced the many pages of my manuscript I saw a symbolic call henceforth to live my thoughts instead of merely putting them on paper.

Here I should like to report the following case:

The mother of two boys was admitted to my clinic after an attempt at suicide. One of her sons was crippled with infantile paralysis and could be moved around only in a wheel chair, while her other son had just died at the age of eleven. My associate, Dr. Kocourek, invited this woman to join a therapeutic group. While he was conducting a psychodrama in this group I happened to step into the room just as this mother was telling her story. She was rebellious against her fate, she could not overcome the loss of her son, but when she tried to commit suicide together with the crippled son who was left it was the latter who prevented her from suicide. For him life had remained meaningful. Why not so for his mother? How could we help her to find a meaning?

I asked another woman in the group how old she was. Upon her reply that she was thirty I retorted: "No, you are not thirty but instead eighty now and lying on your death bed. You are looking back upon your life, a life which was childless but full of financial success and social prestige." I then invited her to imagine what she would feel in such a situation. "What will you think of it? What will you say to yourself?" Let me quote her answer from the tape that recorded that session: "Oh, I married a millionaire; I had an easy life full of wealth; and I lived it up! I flirted with men. I teased them! But now, I am eighty; I have no children of my own. Looking back as an old woman, I cannot see what all that was for; actually, I must say, my life was a failure!"

Then I invited the mother of the crippled son to imagine herself in the same situation. Again I quote from the tape: "I wished to have children and this wish has been granted to me; one boy died, the other, however, the crippled one, would have been sent to an institution if I had not taken over his care. Though he is crippled and helpless, he is after all my boy. And so I have made a fuller life possible for him; I have made a better human being out of my son." At this moment she burst into tears but continued: "As for myself, I can look back peace-fully on my life; for I can say my life was full of meaning, and I have tried hard to fulfill it; I have done my best—I have done the best for my son. My life was no failure!" Anticipating a re-view of her life as if from her death bed, she suddenly was able to see a meaning to her life, a meaning which even included all of her sufferings. By the same token it had become clear to her that even a life of short duration like that of her dead boy could be so rich in joy and love that it contained more meaning than some life that lasts eighty years.

Through a right and upright way of suffering man transcends the dimension of success and failure as it prevails in the present-day business world. A businessman moves

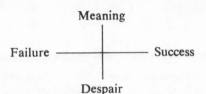

between the poles of success and failure. *Homo patiens,* however, rises above this dimension; he moves between the poles of meaning and despair which lie in a line perpendicular to that of success and failure. What do I mean by this? One might enjoy a life full of pleasure and power and yet be caught in the feeling of its ultimate meaninglessness. Just remember the patient whose recorded evaluation of her life I quoted first. Conversely, it is conceivable that a man has to face a situation beyond hope, and yet he may fulfill the very meaning of his life. He might be deprived of wealth and health and yet be willing and able to suffer, be it for the sake of a cause to which he is commit-ted, be it for the sake of a loved one, or for the sake of God. Remember here the patient whom I quoted last. Such an achievement, to be sure, is a stumbling block and foolishness to the materialists, and is only understandable in terms of the diagram sketched above.

Through his freedom a human being is not only able to detach himself from the world, but he is also capable of self-detachment. In other words, man can take a stand toward himself; as a spiritual person he can choose an attitude toward his own psychological character. The following story is a good illustration of this specifically human capacity for self-detachment. During World War I a Jewish military doctor in the Austrian army was sitting next to a colonel when heavy shooting began. Teasingly, the colonel said: "Just another proof that the Aryan race is superior to the Semitic one! You are afraid, aren't you?" "Sure, I am afraid," was the doctor's answer. "But who is superior? If you, my dear colonel, were as afraid as I am, you would have run away long ago." Fear and anxiety as such do not count. What matters is our attitude toward facts rather than the facts themselves. This also applies to the facts of our inner life.

The specifically human capacity for self-detachment is also mobilized by a special logotherapeutic technique which I have called "paradoxical intention." Hans O. Gerz, Clinical Director of the Connecticut Valley Hospital, has had remarkable results in applying this technique.[8] In this context I like to quote Professor Tweedie who says in his book on logotherapy: ". . . logotherapy, contrary to many so-called existential psychotherapies, has an explicit therapeutic procedure to offer."[9]

Today the exercising of one's freedom is sometimes hampered by what I call a crippling pandeterminism which is so pervasive in psychology.[10] The doctor's pandeterminism plays into the hands of the patient's fatalism,

---

[8]See Chapter XV, p. 200.

[9]Donald F. Tweedie, Jr., *Logotherapy and the Christian Faith: An Evaluation of Frankl's Existential Approach to Psychotherapy* (Grand Rapids, Mich.: Baker Book House, 1961).

[10]Paul E. Johnson, "Logotherapy: A Corrective for Determinism," *Christian Advocate*, 5: 12 (1961).

thus reinforcing the latter's neurosis.[11] There is, for instance, the contention that a person's religious life is wholly conditioned by his early childhood experiences—that his concept of God is formed according to his father image. In order to obtain a more accurate information on this correlation, I had my staff at the Vienna Poliklinik Hospital screen the patients that visited its outpatient clinic in a day. This screening showed that twenty-three patients had a positive father image, thirteen a negative one. But only sixteen of the subjects with a positive father image and only two of the subjects with a negative father image had let themselves be fully determined through these images in their respective religious developments. Half of the total number screened developed their religious concepts independent from their father images. Thus half of the subjects displayed what education has made out of them, the other half exhibited what, by way of decision, they had made out of themselves. A poor religious life cannot always be traced back to the impact of a negative father image (seven of the screened subjects). Nor does even the worst father image necessarily prevent one from establishing a sound relation to God (eleven of the subjects).

Here I am prepared to meet an objection on the part of the theologians, since one might say that succeeding in building up one's religious belief in spite of unfavorable educational conditions is unconceivable without the intervention of divine grace: If man is to believe in God, he has to be helped by grace. But one should not forget that my investigation moves within the frame of reference of psychology or rather anthropology, that is to say, on the human level. Grace, however, dwells in the suprahuman dimension and, therefore, appears on the human plane only as a projection. In other words, what on the natural plane takes on the appearance of being man's decision might well

---

[11]Godfryd Kaczanowski, "Frankl's Logotherapy," *The American Journal of Psychiatry*, 117: 563 (1960).

be interpreted on the supranatural plane as the sustaining assistance of God. Logotherapy, as the secular practice and theory which it is, refrains, of course, from leaving the boundaries of medical science. It can open the door to religion, but it is the patient, not the doctor, who must decide whether he wants to pass through that door.[12]

In any case, we should beware of interpreting religion merely in terms of a resultant of psychodynamics, i.e., on the ground of unconscious motivation. If we did, we would miss the point and lose sight of the authentic phenomenon. Either man's freedom of decision for or against God is respected, or indeed, religion is a delusion and education an illusion.

What threatens man is his guilt in the past and his death in the future. Both are inescapable, both must be accepted. Thus man is confronted with the human condition in terms of fallibility and mortality. Properly understood, it is, however, precisely the acceptance of this twofold human finiteness which adds to life's worthwhileness, since only in the face of guilt does it make sense to improve, and only in the face of death is it meaningful to act.

It is the very transitoriness of human existence which constitutes man's responsibleness—the essence of existence. If man were immortal, he would be justified in delaying everything; there would be no need to do anything right now. Only under the urge and pressure of life's transitoriness does it make sense to use the passing time. Actually, the only transitory aspects of life are the potentialities; as soon as we have succeeded in actualizing a potentiality, we have transmuted it into an actuality and, thus, salvaged and rescued it into the past. Once an actuality, it is one forever. Everything in the past is saved from being transitory. Therein it is irrevocably stored rather than irrecoverably

---

[12]Ferdinand Birnbaum, "Frankl's Existential Psychology from the Viewpoint of Individual Psychology," *Journal of Individual Psychology*, 17: 162 (1961).

lost. Having been is still a form of being, perhaps even its most secure form.

What man has done cannot be undone. I think that this implies both activism and optimism. Man is called upon to make the best use of any moment and the right choice at any time, be it that he knows what to do, or whom to love, or how to suffer. This means activism. As to optimism, let me remind you of the words of Lao-tse: "Having completed a task means having become eternal." I would say that this holds true not only for the completion of a task, but for our experiences, and last but not least, for our brave sufferings as well.

Speaking figuratively one might say that the pessimist resembles a man who observes with fear and sadness how the wall calendar from which he daily tears a sheet grows thinner and thinner with the passing days. However, a person who takes life in the sense suggested above is like a man who removes each leaf and files it carefully after having jotted down a few diary notes on it. He can reflect with pride and joy on all the richness set down in these notes, on all the life he has already lived to the full.

Even in advanced years one should not envy a young person. Why should one? For the possibilities a young person has, or for his future? No, I should say that, instead of possibilities in the future, the older person has realities in the past—work done, love loved, and suffering suffered. The latter is something to be proudest of—although it will hardly raise envy.

It was Edith Weisskopf-Joelson of Duke University who, in her paper on logotherapy, pointed to the possibility that this school may counteract the fear of aging and of suffering which she considers an unhealthy trend in the present-day culture of the United States.[13] I cannot conclude my paper without quoting another personality

[13]Edith Weisskopf-Joelson, "Logotherapy and Existential Analysis," *Acta Psychotherapeutica*, 6: 193 (1958).

who, on the other side of the Atlantic, has found my teaching worthy of support. Martin Heidegger, during a visit at my home, had discussed my optimistic views on the past presented here. In order to show how much he agreed with me, he wrote in my guest book the following lines:

> *Das Vergangene geht;*
> *Das Gewesene kommt.*

In English this would read:

> What has passed, has gone;
> What is past, will come.

Imagine what consolation the logotherapeutic attitude to the past would bring to a war widow who has only experienced, say, two weeks of marital bliss. She would feel that this experience can never be taken from her. It will remain her inviolable treasure, preserved and delivered into her past. Her life can never become meaningless even if she might remain childless. By the way, the assumption that procreation is the only meaning of life contradicts and defeats itself; something that by itself is meaningless can never be made meaningful merely by perpetuating it.

It is not the least task of psychotherapy to bring about reconciliation and to bring consolation: Man has to be reconciled to his finiteness, and he also has to be enabled to face the transitoriness of his life. With these efforts psychotherapy indeed touches the realm of religion. There is common ground enough to warrant mutual rapprochement. Bridging, however, does not mean merging. There still remains the essential difference between the respective aims of psychotherapy and religion. The goal of psychotherapy,

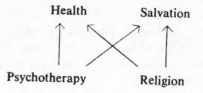

of psychiatry and, quite generally, of medicine, is health. The goal of religion, however, is something essentially different: salvation. So much for the difference of goals. The results achieved, however, are another matter. Although religion may not aim at mental health it might result in it. Psychotherapy, in turn, often results in an analogous by-product; while the doctor is not, and must not be, concerned with helping the patient to regain his belief in God, time and again this is just what occurs, unintended and unexpected as it is.

How, then, does this occur in the actual situation? Let me return to the logotherapeutic group session, or logodrama, which I mentioned before. During the discussion of the meaning of suffering I asked the whole group whether an ape which is punctured many times in order to develop poliomyelitis serum is able to grasp the meaning of its suffering. Unanimously the group replied, "Of course it would not! For with its limited intelligence it cannot enter the world of man, i.e., that world in which its suffering would be understandable." I then pressed on with the following: "And what about man? Are you sure that the human world is the terminal point in the evolution of the cosmos? Is it not conceivable that there is still another dimension, a world beyond man's world; a world in which the question of an ultimate meaning to man's suffering is answered?"

By its very nature this ultimate meaning exceeds man's limited intellectual capacity. In contrast to those existential writers who declare that man has to stand the ultimate absurdity of being human, it is my contention that man has to stand only his incapacity to grasp the ultimate meaning on intellectual grounds. Man is only called upon to decide between the alternatives of "ultimate absurdity or ultimate meaning" on existential grounds, through the mode of existence which he chooses. In the "How" of existence, I would say, lies the answer to the question for its "Why."

Thus, the ultimate meaning is no longer a matter of intellectual cognition but of existential commitment. One might as well say that a meaning can be understood but that the ultimate meaning must be interpreted. An interpretation, however, involves a decision. Reality is intrinsically ambiguous since it admits of a variety of interpretations. Man, in choosing one of these interpretations, finds himself in a situation similar to the one in a projective test. To illustrate this, let me relate the following experience.

Shortly before the United States entered World War II, I was called to the American Consulate in Vienna to receive my immigration visa. My old parents expected me to leave Austria as soon as the visa was given. However, at the last moment I hesitated: The question of whether I should leave my parents beset me. I knew that any day they could be taken to a concentration camp. Shouldn't I stay with them? While pondering this question I found that this was the type of dilemma which made one wish for a hint from Heaven. It was then that I noticed a piece of marble lying on a table at home. When I asked my father about it, he explained that he had found it on the site where the National Socialists had burned down the largest Viennese synagogue. My father had taken this marble piece home because it was a part of the tablets which contained the Ten Commandments. The piece showed one engraved and gilded Hebrew letter. My father explained that this letter is the abbreviation for only one of the Commandments. Eagerly I asked, "Which one is it?" The answer was: "Honor thy father and thy mother: that thy days may be long upon the land." So I stayed with my father and my mother upon the land and decided to let the American visa lapse.

Acknowledging this piece of marble as a hint from Heaven might well be the expression of the fact that already long before, in the depth of my heart, I had decided to stay. I only projected this decision into the appearance of the marble piece. Much the same way would it be self-expression if one saw nothing but $CaCO_3$ in it—although I would call this rather a projection of an existential vacuum. . . .

Man cannot avoid decisions. Reality inescapably forces man to decide. Man makes decisions in every moment, even unwittingly and against his will. Through these decisions man decides upon himself. Continually and incessantly he shapes and reshapes himself. Thomas Aquinas' *"agere sequitur esse"* is but half the truth: Man not only behaves according to what he is, he also becomes what he is according to how he behaves. Man is not a thing among others—things determine each other—but man is ultimately self-determining. What he becomes—within the limits of endowment and environment—he has made himself. In the living laboratories of the concentration camps we watched comrades behaving like swine while others behaved like saints. Man has both these potentialities within himself. Which one he actualizes depends on decision, not on conditions. It is time that this decision quality of human existence be included in our definition of man. Our generation has come to know man as he really is: the being that has invented the gas chambers of Auschwitz, and also the being who entered those gas chambers upright, the Lord's Prayer or the *Shema Yisrael* on his lips.

Beyond Self-Actualization
and Self-Expression[1]

III

According to McGregor "all human behavior is directed toward the satisfaction of needs."[2] Murelius identifies the satisfaction of needs with the reduction of tension.[3] Thus, when Knickerbocker says that "existence may be seen as a continual struggle to satisfy needs, relieve tensions, maintain equilibrium,"[4] we can conclude that both the satisfaction of needs and the reduction of tensions amount to the maintenance of an equilibrium, in other words, the maintenance of homeostasis. This conclusion is supported by Charlotte Buhler: "From Freud's earliest formulations of the pleasure principle, to the latest present version of the discharge of tension and homeostasis principle (as for example presented in Rapaport's model), the unchanging end-goal of all activity all through life was conceived of as the reestablishment of the individual's equilibrium."[5]

[1] Paper read before the Conference on Existential Psychotherapy, Chicago, December 13, 1959.

[2] D. McGregor, "The Staff Function in Human Relations, "*Journal of Social Issues*, 4: 5 (1948).

[3] O. Murelius, "Ethics and Psychology," *American Journal of Psychotherapy*, 12: 641 (1958).

[4] I. Knickerbocker, "Leadership: A Conception and Some Implications," *Journal of Social Issues*, 4: 23 (1948).

[5] Charlotte Buhler, "Basic Tendencies of Human Life, Theoretical and Clinical Considerations," in *Sein und Sinn*, ed. R. Wisser, Anniv. Vol. for Prof. von Rintelen (in press).

Gordon W. Allport, however, objects to such a view of man: "Motivation is regarded as a state of tenseness that leads us to seek equilibrium, rest, adjustment, satisfaction, or homeostasis. From this point of view personality is nothing more than our habitual modes of reducing tension. This formulation falls short of representing the nature of propriate striving. The characteristic feature of such striving is its resistance to equilibrium: Tension is maintained rather than reduced."[6] Maslow's criticism seems to me to point in the same direction when he says: "Homeostasis, equilibrium, adaptation, self-preservation, defense, and adjustment are merely negative concepts and must be supplemented by positive concepts."[7]

However, in my opinion, these criticisms do not go far enough. They do not yet reach the essential point, or it is better to say, the essential shortcomings of the views of man which interpret him as a being for whom reality serves as nothing but a mere means to the end of "satisfying needs, reducing tensions, and/or maintaining equilibrium." From such a perspective, man is considered in what I call a monadologistic[8] way, and his tie with the world in which he exists is disregarded.

In a monadologistic view of man there is no place for any true encounter between man on the one hand and the world and its objects on the other. The objects in the world are no longer seen in their objective essence but, instead, only as more or less useful tools for the maintenance of homeostasis. There is no room left for anything such as commitment to a

---

[6]Gordon W. Allport, *Becoming, Basic Considerations for a Psychology of Personality* (New Haven: Yale University Press, 1955).

[7]A. H. Maslow, *Motivation and Personality* (New York: Harper & Row, Publishers, 1954), p. 367.

[8]This term refers to one of the main works of Leibniz, "Monadology," in which he speaks of "monads" as the prime factors of reality. I would define monads as spiritual atoms without any "windows" leading to the outer world and, therefore, without any connection with the other monads.

cause for its own sake or participation with a partner for the partner's sake. Instead, causes and partners are devaluated to the level of mere means to an end—the end of restoring certain conditions in the subject's psychic system. As means, they appear to the subject to have no *value* in themselves but to be only of *use* to him.

This brings to mind a well-known phenomenon observed in cases of sexual neurosis. We often hear such patients speak of "masturbating on a woman," by which they mean that they sometimes "use" their partners simply for the purpose of reducing sexual tension. As we see, this clearly corresponds to that view of man which we have previously referred to as "monadologistic." It must not be forgotten, however, that such cases are neurotic and, hence, abnormal. The normal approach of man to the world is never primarily that of a means-end relationship.

Rather, such a view, centered around the means-end relationship, corresponds to what is observed in animals which have been exposed to certain artificial conditions. I refer now to the self-stimulation experiments as described by Olds and Milner, Brady, and Werner. They implanted electrodes in the brains of rats, and under certain conditions, i.e., when the electrodes were localized in certain nerve centers of the hypothalamus and the rhinencephalon, the closing of the circuit resulted in a behavior which could be explained only as need satisfaction. Moreover, the animals, when given the opportunity to press a lever which closed the circuit, soon began to do so continuously. The most impressive aspect of this experiment, however, seems to me to be the observation of the experimenters that the animals then completely neglected real food and real sexual partners. It was thus evidenced by the experiments that, as soon as the objects in one's world are considered merely as means to the end of need satisfaction, they may be neglected or even omitted altogether. One need attend to them no longer; closing the electrical circuit suffices.

As Jung rightly points out, the foregoing holds true only for experimental animals in such an artificial situation, not under normal circumstances. This proves that even an animal is not normally, or at least not primarily, interested in the restoration of that psychic condition which is called satisfaction. A fortiori, much less is man. According to logotherapeutic concepts, man is not primarily interested in any psychic conditions of his own, but rather is oriented toward the world, toward the world of potential meanings and values which, so to speak, are waiting to be fulfilled and actualized by him. In logotherapy we speak of a "will to meaning,"[9] and contrast it to the pleasure principle (which we could also call a "will to pleasure") and, on the other hand, to the so-called "will to power."

As it is generally accepted, the pleasure principle includes avoidance of displeasure. In this way, it nearly coincides with the principle of reducing tensions. However, we must ask ourselves whether anything like a will to pleasure in the sense of a primary tendency to be found in man really exists. Now, in my opinion—and in accordance with some observations of Kant and Max Scheler—pleasure is primarily and normally not an aim but an effect, let us say a side effect, of the achievement of a task. In other words, pleasure establishes itself automatically as soon as one has fulfilled a meaning or realized a value. Moreover, if a man really attempted to gain pleasure by making it his target, he would necessarily fail, for he would miss what he had aimed at. This can be easily demonstrated in those cases of sexual neurosis in which our patients are thwarted in obtaining sexual pleasure precisely because they attempt to attain it directly. The more a man sets out to demonstrate his potency or a woman her ability to experience orgasm, the less they will be able to do so. I dare say that not a few cases

---

[9] V. E. Frankl, "The Will to Meaning," *The Journal of Pastoral Care*, 12: 828 (1958).

of sexual neurosis could be traced back to such a starting point.

Something analogous holds true for some other human phenomena also, e.g., that phenomenon which is described by the famous best seller's title, *Peace of Mind*. We can go a step farther by asserting that "pursuit of happiness" amounts to a self-contradiction: The more we strive for happiness, the less we attain it. Peace of mind also must content itself with being a side effect, for it is self-destroying as an intention. We can illustrate this with that specific kind of peace of mind which is associated with a good conscience. A man who is striving for a condition in which he can rightly say, "I possess a good conscience" would already represent a case of Pharisaism. A really good conscience can never be reached by grasping for it, but solely by doing a deed for the sake of a cause, or for the sake of the person involved, or for God's sake. A good conscience is one of those things which can be brought about only as an unintended side effect and is destroyed at the moment that it is sought after directly. (Note the sort of a man who is directly striving for good health. To the degree in which he does so, he has already fallen ill, i.e., displaying that nervous illness called hypochondria.) This can be stated in a simple formula: The aims of both the hedonistic philosophy of the Epicureans and the quietistic philosophy of the Stoics, i.e., happiness and peace of mind (or, as the latter was called by the ancient Greeks, *ataraxia*), cannot possibly be the real aim of human behavior, and they cannot for the a priori reason that they elude man exactly to the same degree that he strives for them.

It seems to me that the present increasing tendency to become addicted to tranquilizing drugs is a sign that contemporary man has been more and more seduced to a belief in the illusion that he can strive for happiness, or for peace of mind. He cannot even strive for "peace of soul," for this kind of peace, which apparently means the (re-)

establishment of a good conscience, eludes him as soon as it has become a matter of intention instead of remaining a matter of effect.

In the framework of the psychodynamic interpretation of conscience, man strives for moral behavior only for the sake of getting rid of the stimulus of a bad conscience or, to stick to psychodynamic terminology, the stimulus of a discontented superego. Obviously, such a view of man's moral behavior misses the point of true morality, which begins only when man has begun to act for the sake of something or someone, but not for his own sake, that is, for the sake of having a good conscience or of getting rid of a bad one.

To return to the question before us, that is, whether or not the homeostasis principle is actually that by which man is guided, we can refer to a simple and well-known fact which, in my opinion, demonstrates that homeostasis can never be the ultimate aim in life. What would be the result if man had the opportunity to satisfy completely each of his needs and drives? Assuredly, the results of such an experiment would in no way consist of an experience of deepest fulfillment, but on the contrary, of a frustrating inner void, of a desperate feeling of emptiness, or to use a logotherapeutic term, of the awareness of one's existential vacuum. This is the result of the frustration of the will to meaning mentioned above. Inasmuch as we may define as existential whatever is connected not only with man's existence but also with the meaning of man's existence, we can speak of existential frustration which is an important concept in logotherapy.

Today, man's existential vacuum is of primary and steadily increasing importance. This is understandable when we consider the twofold loss which man has sustained since he became a true human being. I refer to the fact that at the beginning of human history man was deprived of the basic animal instincts in which animal behavior is imbedded and by which it is secured. Such security is now, like

Paradise, forever closed to man. In addition to this, however, man has suffered another more recent loss. The traditions which supported his behavior are now rapidly diminishing, at least in regard to their morally obligative quality. The average man of today scarcely feels any obligation to them.

A cross-sectional survey was conducted by my staff at the Vienna Poliklinik Hospital of the patients in both the neurological and the psychotherapeutic outpatient wards, as well as the medical personnel and nursing staff of the same institution. This survey revealed that 55% of the persons screened showed a more or less marked degree of existential frustration and/or vacuum. More than half of them experienced a loss of the feeling that life is meaningful.

Logotherapy teaches that this existential vacuum, along with other causes, can also result in neurotic illness. In the frame of reference of this school, such neuroses are termed, in contrast to psychogenic neuroses (i.e., neuroses in the narrower sense of the word), noögenic neuroses. Noögenic neuroses have a different etiology from psychogenic neuroses for they originate in a different dimension of the personality. They originate in the noëtic dimension rather than the psychic. In other words, in cases of noögenic neuroses we are dealing with psychological illnesses which are not, as with psychogenic neuroses, rooted in conflicts between different drives, or clashes of psychic components such as the so-called id, ego, and superego. They are rather rooted in collisions between different values, or in the unrewarded longing and groping of man for that hierarchically highest value—an ultimate meaning to his life. To put it simply, we are dealing with the frustration to man's struggle for a meaning to his existence—a frustration of his will to meaning. It goes without saying that in all of those cases in which neurotic symptoms can be traced back to existential frustration, logotherapy is indicated as the appropriate psychotherapeutic method of treatment.

It should be noted that when we speak of the meaning of one's existence, we specifically refer to the *concrete* meaning of personal existence. By the same token, we could speak of a mission in life, indicating that every man has a mission in life to carry out. Each human being is unique both in his essence (*Sosein*) and his existence (*Dasein*) and thus is neither expendable nor replaceable. In other words, he is a particular individual with his unique personal characteristics who experiences a unique historical context in a world which has special opportunities and obligations reserved for him alone.

Of course it is never the task of the therapist to give a meaning to the life of the patient. It is up to the patient himself to find the concrete meaning to his existence. The therapist merely assists him in this endeavor. That he must find the meaning implies that this meaning is to be discovered and not invented. It implies that the meaning of one's life is, in a certain sense, objective.

Unfortunately, this objectivity is frequently neglected by some of those writers who call themselves existentialists. Though they never weary of repeating ad nauseam that man is "being in the world," they seem to forget that meaning is also "in the world" and thus not merely a subjective factor. It is more than a mere self-expression, or a projection of the self *into* the world.

Here we touch the problem of that aspect of the self, frequently referred to nowadays in psychological literature, called self-actualization. According to Piotrowski, K. Goldstein "fights and argues against a prevalent theory of motivation which assumes that the basic motive is reduction of tension and thus reestablishment of equilibrium. He argues against homeostasis as a theory of motivation. He argues against the idea that the goal of drives is an elimination of the disturbing tension which they produce. Thus, he argues against Freud's pleasure principle and the tension-release theory. . . . To Goldstein, an individual whose chief goal is merely to maintain his level of adjustment is manifesting a sign of illness. . . . Self-expression or self-realization is the ultimate motive in states of health."[10] Charlottee Buhler asserts, "The concept of self-realization has gone through many variations from Nietzsche and Jung to Karen Horney, Erich Fromm, Kurt Goldstein, Frieda Fromm-Reichmann, Abraham Maslow, Carl Rogers, and others who seem to be searching for an all-encompassing theory of life's ultimate goal. With again another connotation, it appears in the context of existentialist thinking."[11]

Elkin critically comments, with special regard to Horney and Fromm, that "their conceptions have taken on mystical connotations. This recalls Jung's conception of the self whose mystical connotations closely parallel those found in eastern religion."[12] My criticism, however, comes from a different direction. The main mistake of appointing self-realization as "the ultimate motive" is that it again devaluates the world and its objects to mere means to an end. As a matter of fact, A. H. Maslow explicitly contends that "the environment is no more than means to the person's self-actualizing ends."[13]

So now we must pose the crucial question of whether or not man's primary intention, or even his ultimate destination, could ever be properly described by the term self-actualization. I would venture a strictly negative response to this question. It appears to me to be quite obvious that self-actualization is an effect and cannot be the object of intention. Mirrored in this fact is the fundamental

---

[10]Z. A. Piotrowski, "Basic Human Motives According to Kurt Goldstein," *American Journal of Psychotherapy*, 13: 553 (1959).

[11]Charlotte Buhler, "Theoretical Observations About Life's Basic Tendencies," *American Journal of Psychotherapy*, 13: 561 (1959).

[12]H. Elkin, "On the Origin of the Self," *Psychoanalysis and the Psychoanalytic Review*, 45: 57 (1958–1959).

[13]A. H. Maslow, *Motivation and Personality* (New York: Harper & Row, Publishers, 1954), p. 117.

anthropological truth that self-transcendence is one of the basic features of human existence. Only as man withdraws from himself in the sense of releasing self-centered interest and attention will he gain an authentic mode of existence. This rule finds its clinical application (and clinical validation) in the logotherapeutic techniques of de-reflection and paradoxical intention.[14]

Charlotte Buhler was, in my opinion, quite right in her assertion that "what they [the representatives of the self-actualization principle] really meant was the pursuit of potentialities."[15] Since self-actualization refers to the fulfillment of the available possibilities, or potentialities, within the subject, one might well call it potentialism. Here the life task of the individual is conceived of as the actualizing of potentialities which will fulfill his personality to the greatest possible degree. Therefore, the degree of self-actualization depends on the number of potentialities realized. But what would be the result if a man should merely actualize the potentials within himself? An answer comes to mind in the case of Socrates. He confessed to the potentiality within him to become a criminal and, therefore, if he had succeeded in fully developing his potentialities, the great defender of law and justice would have been a common law breaker!

The potentialities of life are not indifferent possibilities; they must be seen in the light of meaning and values. At any given time only one of the possible choices of the individual fulfills the necessity of his life task. Herein is involved the challenge of each life situation—the challenge to responsibility. Man must make his choice concerning the mass of present potentials: which will be condemned to non-being and which will be actualized and thus rescued for eternity. Decisions are final, for the only really transitory

---

[14]V. E. Frankl, *The Doctor and the Soul: From Psychotherapy to Logotherapy* (2d ed.; New York: Alfred A. Knopf, Inc., 1965), pp. 253ff.
[15]See note 5.

aspects of life are the potentialities. When a potentiality is actualized, it is actualized forever and can never be destroyed. Man, therefore, must face the responsibility for these immortal "footprints in the sands of time." He must decide, for weal or for woe, what will be the monument of his existence.

Potentialism involves an attempt to avoid this burden of responsibility. Under the pressure of time and in the face of life's transitoriness, man is often beguiled into believing that he can escape the necessity of making responsible choices. His efforts, however, are in vain, for wherever he turns he is confronted with the exigencies of life and the demand to make meaningful and valuable and, thus, existential commitments.

At the same time there is an indispensable value problem involved; for the choice in question is a choice of the only potentiality, among many possibilities, which is worth actualizing. Thus the problem really just begins when potentialism ends. The potentialist attempts to evade this axiological problem but, though he may postpone it, he never really can rid himself of it.

A close examination of such escapism reveals that the potentialist finds the tension between what is (*Sein*) and what should be (*Sein-sollen*) intolerable. However, this tension cannot be eradicated, even by potentialism, for it is inherent in human existence. There is no conceivable human condition in which man may be relieved of the tension between what he has done and, on the other hand, what he should have done or must yet do. As a finite being, man never perfectly completes his life task. When he is willing and able to shoulder the burden of this incompleteness, he is acknowledging this finiteness. This acceptance of finiteness is the precondition to mental health and human progress, while the inability to accept it is characteristic of the neurotic personality. Thus the homeostasis principle, of which we spoke previously, is by no means a normal phenomenon but rather a neurotic one. It is the neurotic individual who cannot abide the normal tension of life—whether physical, psychic, or moral.

In addition to this unbridgeable gap between what is and what should be in human existence, there is yet another polarity to be considered. This is the rift between the subject and the object of cognition. This rift is also ineradicable, though many an author speaks of having "overcome" it. Such a statement is questionable, for such an achievement would be tantamount to overcoming *la condition humaine*—the insurmountable finitude of being human. Even Heidegger, the leading spirit of existential philosophy, neither thought nor taught that true cognition could be achieved beyond the duality of subject and object. I am not a theologian and, thus, do not intend to speak in this connection of "hybris"; but I believe that man should not attempt to overcome the twofold tension of human existence but, instead, to undergo it. An apt, though perhaps a trifle crude, metaphor sets forth the matter succinctly: Modern philosophy should not dump out the baby (the cognitive object) along with the bathwater (Cartesian dualism).

To be sure, the subject by its cognitive acts is capable of approaching the object and thereby establishing that cognitive closeness to the things in the world which I have called "being with" (*Beisein*) the object.[16] Thus it is the remarkable achievement of cognition that the subject attains the object across the gap which separates them. However, the object which is reached by the subject is still an object and does not through the cognitive process become a part of the subject itself.[17] Any theory which obscures the

---

[16]V. E. Frankl, *Der unbedingte Mensch, Metaklinische Vorlesungen* (Wien: Deuticke, 1949), pp. 27ff. (English edition, New York: Washington Square Press, Inc., in preparation).

[17]The reader will be interested in a similar statement in the writings of Erwin Straus. Erwin W. Straus, in *Existence*, ed. Rollo May, Ernest Angel, and Henri F. Ellenberger (New York: Basic Books, Inc., 1958), p. 147.

objectivity of the object and disregards its intrinsic otherness through the assumption that the world is a mere self-expression and nothing but a projection of the subject is a theory which misses the point.

A complete eradication of the subject-object differentiation would not be commendable even if it were possible. Each cognitive act of man is based indispensably upon the polar field of tension between the subject and the object. The essential dynamic which constitutes human cognition has its source in this tensional situation between man and that "world" which he "is in" (to use a popular existential expression). In logotherapy, this dynamics, in contrast to psychodynamics, is referred to as noödynamics.

To ignore the noödynamic tension between subject and object is to ignore the objectivity of the world. Any philosophy or psychology which, by its careful investigation of psychic phenomena in their richness and fullness, deserves to be called a "phenomenological approach" must acknowledge the primordial fact that every true cognitive act implies the objectivity of the object. So, what is called the object, or to speak more generally, the world, is essentially more than a mere self-expression of the subject. To speak of the world as a mere "design" of the cognitive subject is to do injustice to the full phenomenon of the cognitive act which is the self-transcendence of existence toward the world as an objective reality. It is true that man cannot grasp more than a subjective segment as it is cognitively cut out of the world, or in other words, he can only make a subjective selection from the full spectrum of the world; nevertheless, he is always making a subjective selection from an objective world.

The point of view, however, adopted by some of the existentialist writers blurs the objectivity of the object. It might be called a kaleidoscopic epistemology. When one peers into a kaleidoscope, he does not look through it, but instead, observes a certain constellation of different colored bits of glass which are a part of the kaleidoscope. Is not this the same as the epistemological theory of such authors? To them man is a being who, in all his cognitive acts and efforts, can never reach a real world. His world is but a design projected by himself and mirroring the structure of his being. Just as the kaleidoscopic observation depends on how the little pieces of glass have been thrown, this kaleidoscopic epistemology presents a world design (*Weltentwurf*) wholly dependent upon man's "thrownness" (*Geworfenheit*)—a simple reflection of his subjective condition and structure.

The extent to which such subjectivism misses the point of true human cognition becomes obvious as soon as one recalls the fundamental truth that only insofar as a person is capable of ignoring and forgetting himself is he able to recognize anything in and of the world. Only as he moves to the periphery of his attention can he become properly aware of objects beyond himself. This can be illustrated in the case of the eye which sees itself, or something in itself (e.g., a *mouche volante*), only when there is a visual defect. The more the eye sees itself, the less the world and its objects are visible to it. The ability of the eye to see is dependent upon its inability to see itself. Admittedly, finite human cognition cannot become completely free of the subjective moments which are inherent in its activity, but this does not alter the fact that the more cognition actually becomes mere self-expression and a projection of the knowing subject's own structure, the more it becomes involved in error. In other words, cognition is true cognition only to the extent to which it is the contrary of mere self-expression, only to the extent to which it involves self-transcendence.

It appears, in conclusion, that those theories of man which are based upon the reduction of his tension as in homeostasis theory, or the fulfillment of the greatest number of immanent possibilities as in self-actualization, when weighed, are found wanting. It is the contention of the author that an adequate view of man can only be properly formulated when it goes beyond homeostasis, beyond self-actualization, to that sphere of human existence in which man chooses what he will do and what he will be in the midst of an objective world of meanings and values.[18]

---

[18]V. E. Frankl, "Philosophie und Psychotherapie, Zur Grundlegung einer Existenzanalyse," *Schweizerische medizinische Wochenschrift*, 69: 707 (1939).

Logotherapy and Existence[1]

IV

There has been considerable progress in the development of psychotherapy during the last few years inasmuch as the older psychodynamic concept of man as a being mainly concerned with need satisfaction is slowly but noticeably being superseded by the new anthropological view of man as a being whose aim in life is now conceived of as self-actualization and the realization of his own potentialities. We can also say that the category of necessities (in the sense of man's being fully determined by instinctual drives and conditioned by social circumstances) has been replaced more and more by another category, i.e., potentialities to be fulfilled. In other words, we can speak of a current reinterpretation of the human being.

The whole phenomenon of human existence, however, is ineffable and cannot be circumscribed except by a sentence, the sentence: "I am."[2] This "I am" had first been interpreted in terms of "I must" (i.e., I am forced by certain conditions and determinants, drives and instincts, hereditary and environmental factors and impacts), whereas in the

---

[1] An abridgment of a paper read before the American Conference on Existential Psychotherapy, New York, February 27, 1960.

[2] As soon as a phrase is started by "I am" we expect it to continue. "I am" sounds like only half a sentence. The question *what* "I am" still remains open. This *what*, however, goes beyond existence in that it refers to essence.

following period the "I am" was understood in terms of an "I can" (i.e., I am able to actualize this or that aspect of myself).

A third concept, however, is still lacking. For if we want to obtain an appropriate view of human reality in its full dimensionality we must go beyond both necessities and possibilities and bring in—in addition to the "I must" and "I can" aspects of the total "I am" phenomenon—that dimension which can be referred to as the "I ought." What "I ought" to do, however, is in each instance to fulfill the concrete meaning which challenges me in each situation of my life. In other words, at the moment when we bring in the "I ought," we complement the subjective aspect of human existence, *being*, with its objective counterpart, which is *meaning*.

Only after we have done so does the present trend of emphasizing self-actualization become justified. When self-actualization is made an end in itself and is aimed at as the objective of a primary intention, it cannot be attained. Man would founder in such an attempt to seek directly that which is brought about as a side effect. For only to the extent that man has fulfilled the concrete meaning of his personal existence will he also have fulfilled himself.

This is in no way contradictory to the theory of self-actualization as presented by Abraham Maslow. He seems to me to have taken this into account, for instance, when he says:

> It is possible to call my subjects more objective in all senses of the word than average people. They are more problem-centered than ego-centered . . . strongly focused on problems outside themselves. It may be a task that they feel is their responsibility, duty, or obligation. These tasks are nonpersonal or unselfish.[3]

So, Maslow would certainly agree if I venture the statement

---

[3] A. H. Maslow, *Motivation and Personality* (New York: Harper & Row, Publishers, 1954), pp. 211, 213.

that self-actualization is neither the primary intention nor (to envisage the same thing from a more objective angle and not from the subject's viewpoint) the ultimate destination of man but rather an outcome or by-product.

Thus, we can see that when speaking of man's "being in the world" we should not deny that there is also a "meaning in the world." Only when we have taken this meaning into full account have we supplemented the subjective aspect of human existence with its objective correlate. Not before then have we become aware of existence as being expanded in a polar field of tension between the self and the world.

No concept of the world is adequate, then, as long as it is understood in terms of mere projection or self-expression. If, above all, the meaning in the world to be fulfilled by man and the values therein to be realized by him were no more than his "secondary rationalization, sublimations, and reaction formations," nobody would be justified in expecting man to live up to his obligations. As a matter of fact, such pseudo-values totally lack any obligative quality when they are understood merely as a mirroring of processes which go on in the individual in an impersonal way or merely as projections and expressions of the inner structure of the subject. The world must be seen as essentially more than that. We have to take into account the objectivity of the world which alone presents a real challenge to the subject. However, it would not be enough if we simply refrained from regarding the world and its objects, including values and meanings and their challenge to us, as mere self-expression; we should also beware of regarding the world as a mere instrument serving purposes of our own, an instrument for the satisfaction of instinctual drives, for reestablishing an inner equilibrium, for restoring homeo-stasis, or as a means to the end of self-actualization. This would mean degrading the world and again destroying the objective relation of man to the world he "is in." I dare say, man never, or at least not normally and primarily, sees

in the partners whom he encounters and in the causes to
which he commits himself merely a means to an end; for
then he would have destroyed any authentic relationship to
them. Then they would have become mere tools; they would
be of use for him, but by the same token, they would have
ceased to have any value, that is to say, value in itself.

When we speak of meaning, however, we should not
disregard the fact that man does not fulfill the meaning of
his existence merely by his creative endeavors and
experiential encounters, or by working and loving. We must
not overlook the fact that there are also tragic experiences
inherent in human life, above all that "tragic triad"—if I may
use this term—which is represented by the primordial facts of
man's existence: suffering, guilt, and transitoriness.

Of course, we can close our eyes to these "existentials."
The therapist, also, can escape from them and retreat into
mere somato- or psycho-therapy.[4] This would be the case,
for instance, when the therapist tries to tranquilize away the
patient's fear of death or to analyze away his feelings of
guilt. With special regard to suffering, however, I would say
that patients never really despair because of any suffering in
itself. Instead, their despair stems in each instance from a
doubt as to whether suffering is meaningful. Man is ready
and willing to shoulder any suffering as soon and as long as
he can see a meaning in it.

Ultimately, however, this meaning cannot be grasped by
merely intellectual means, for it supersedes essentially—or to

---

[4]Here psychotherapy is meant in the narrower sense of the term, as
against that wider concept which also brings in the human dimension
of the *noetic* in contrast to the *psychic*. This wider psychotherapeutic
approach is called logotherapy, and within its framework we speak of
dimensions (as differentiated from discrete levels) of being and distinguish a biological, a psychological, and the distinctly human dimension.
In German there is a distinction between *geistig* and *geistlich*, the former
indicating the human dimension and the latter indicating the religious
one. In English, however, we have only the word "spiritual," with its
religious connotations, and so logotherapy, being an essentially secular
approach, has coined the term "noölogical" for this dimension.

speak more specifically, dimensionally—man's capacity as a finite being. I try to indicate this fact by the term "super-meaning." This meaning necessarily transcends man and his world and, therefore, cannot be approached by merely rational processes. It is rather accessible to an act of commitment which emerges out of the depth and center of man's personality and is thus rooted in his total existence. What we have to deal with is not an intellectual or rational process, but a wholly existential act which perhaps could be described by what I call *Urvertrauen zum Dasein*, "the basic trust in Being."

Aware now that the meaning of being, or the logos of existence, essentially transcends man's mere intellectuality, we will understand that "logo"-therapy is as far removed from being a process of "logical" reasoning as from being merely moral exhortation. Above all, a psychotherapist—and the logotherapist included—is neither a teacher nor a preacher, nor should he be compared with, say, a painter. By this I wish to say that it is never up to a therapist to convey to the patient a picture of the world as the therapist sees it; but rather, the therapist should enable the patient to see the world as it is. He therefore resembles an ophthalmologist more than a painter. Also, in special reference to meanings and values, what matters is not the meaning of man's life in general. To look for the general meaning of man's life would be comparable to asking a chess player: "What is the best move?" There is no such thing as "the best move" apart from the one that is best within the context of a particular situation of a particular game. The same holds for human existence inasmuch as one can search only for the concrete meaning of personal existence, a meaning which changes from man to man, from day to day, from hour to hour. The awareness of this concrete meaning of one's existence is not at all an abstract one, but it is, rather, an implicit and immediate dedication and devotion which neither cares for verbalization nor even needs it. In psychotherapy, of course, it can be evoked by the posing of provocative questions in the frame of a maieutic dialogue in the Socratic sense. What comes to light, then, is that the ultimate questions of human existence are on the lips of every man and that these questions are continually confronting the therapist. It is not necessary, however, to enter into sophisticated debates with the patients.

"Logos" is deeper than logic.

Dynamics and Values[1]

V

Psychoanalysis, especially in its former, early stages of development, has often been blamed for its so-called pansexualism. I doubt whether in previous times, or even in Freud's time, this reproach has ever been legitimate. Certainly during the most recent history of psychoanalysis one can scarcely find any evidence of pansexualism in the strict sense of the term.

However, there is something different that seems to me to be an even more erroneous assumption underlying psychoanalytic theory—and, unfortunately, psychoanalytic practice—which we may call "pandeterminism." By this I mean any view of man which disregards or neglects the intrinsically human capacity of free choice and interprets human existence in terms of mere dynamics.[2]

Man, as the finite being he basically is, will never be able to free himself completely from the ties which bind him to the various realms wherein he is confronted by unalterable conditions. Nevertheless, there is always a certain residue of

---

[1] Lecture sponsored by the University of Chicago, October 22, 1960.

[2] The word "dynamism" often serves as no more than a euphemistic substitution for the term "mechanism." However, I do not believe that even the orthodox Freudian psychoanalysts have remained or will remain forever the "incorrigible mechanists and materialists" which they were once designated by a clear-cut statement made by no less a person than Sigmund Freud himself.

59

freedom left to his decisions. For within the limits—however restricted they may be—he can move freely; and only by this very stand which he takes toward whatever conditions he may face does he prove to be a truly human being. This holds true with regard to biological and psychological as well as sociological facts and factors. Social environment, hereditary endowment, and instinctual drives can limit the scope of man's freedom, but in themselves they can never totally blur the human capacity to take a stand toward all those conditions.

Let me illustrate this by a concrete example. Some months ago I was sitting with a famous American psychoanalyst in a Viennese coffeehouse. As this was a Sunday morning and the weather was fine I invited him to join me on a mountain-climbing trip. He refused passionately, however, pointing out that his deep aversion to climbing was due to early childhood experiences. As a boy his father had taken him on walking trips of long duration, and he soon began to hate such expeditions. Thus he wanted to explain to me the infantile conditioning process that prevented him from sharing my enthusiasm for scaling steep rocky walls. Now, however, it was my turn to confess; and I began reporting to him that I, too, was taken on weekend trips by my father and hated them because they were fatiguing and annoying. But in spite of all that, I went on to become a climbing guide in an Alpine club.

Whether any circumstances, be they inner or outer ones, have an influence on a given individual or not, and in which direction this influence takes its way—all that depends on the individual's free choice. The conditions do not determine me, but I determine whether I yield to them or brave them. There is nothing conceivable that would condition a man wholly, i.e., without leaving to him the slightest freedom. Man is never fully conditioned in the sense of being determined by any facts or forces. Rather man is ultimately self-determining. He determines not only his fate but also his own self, for man is not only forming and shaping the course of his life but also his very self. To this extent man is not only responsible[3] for what he does but also for what he is, inasmuch as man does not only behave according to what he is but also becomes what he is according to how he behaves. In the last analysis, man has become what he has made out of himself. Instead of being fully conditioned by any conditions, he is constructing himself. Facts and factors are nothing but the raw material for such self-constructing acts, and a human life is an unbroken chain of such acts. They present the tools, the means, to an end set by man himself.

To be sure, such a view of man is just the reverse of that concept which claims that man is a product or effect of a chain of diverse causes. On the other hand, our assertion of human existence as a self-creating act corresponds to the basic assumption that a man does not simply "be," but always decides what he will be in the next moment. At each moment the human person is steadily molding and forging his own character. Thus, every human being has the chance of changing at any instant. There is the freedom to change, and no one should be denied the right to make use of it. We can never predict a human being's future except within the larger frame of a statistical survey referring to a whole group. The individual personality itself is essentially unpredictable. The basis for any predictions would be represented by biological, psychological, or sociological influences. However, one of the main features of human existence is the capacity to emerge from and rise above all such conditions—to transcend them. By the same token, man is ultimately transcending himself. The human person transcends himself insofar as he reshapes his own character.

---

[3]Of course, man's responsibleness is as finite as his freedom. For example, I am not responsible for the fact that I have gray hair; however, I am certainly responsible for the fact that I did not go to the hairdresser to have him tint my hair—as a number of ladies might have done under the same "conditions."

Let me cite the following case. It concerns Dr. J., the only man I have ever encountered in my whole life whom I would dare to characterize as a satanic being. At the time I knew him, he was generally called "the mass murderer of Steinhof," the name of the large mental hospital in Vienna. When the Nazis had started their euthanasia program, he held all the strings in his hands and was so fanatic in the job assigned to him that he tried not to let one single psychotic individual escape the gas chamber. The few patients who did escape were, paradoxically, Jews. It happened that a small ward in a Jewish home for aging people remained unknown to Dr. J.; and though the Gestapo which supervised this institution had strictly forbidden the admission of any psychotic patients, I succeeded in smuggling in and hiding such patients there by issuing false diagnostic certificates. I manipulated the symptomatology in these cases so as to indicate aphasia instead of schizophrenia. I also administered illegal metrazol shocks. Thus these Jewish patients could be rescued, whereas even the relatives of Nazi party functionaries were "mercy"-killed. When I came back to Vienna—after having myself escaped from being sent to the gas chamber in Auschwitz—I asked what had happened to Dr. J. "He had been imprisoned by the Russians in one of the isolation cells of Steinhof," they told me. "The next day, however, the door of his cell stood open and Dr. J. was never seen again." Later I was convinced that, like others, he had by the help of his comrades found his way to South America. More recently, however, I was consulted by a former high-ranking Austrian diplomat who had been imprisoned behind the Iron Curtain for many years, first in Siberia, and then in the famous Ljubljanka prison in Moscow. While I was examining him neurologically, he suddenly asked me whether I happened to know Dr. J. After my affirmative reply he continued: "I made his acquaintance in Ljubljanka. There he died, at about forty, from cancer of the urinary bladder. Before he died, however, he showed himself to be the best comrade you can imagine! He gave consolation to everybody. He lived up to the highest conceivable moral standard. He was the best friend I ever met during my long years of prison!"

This is the story of Dr. J., "the mass murderer of Steinhof." How can you dare to predict the behavior of man! What you may predict are the movements of a machine, of an apparatus, of an automaton. More than that, you may even try to predict the mechanisms or "dynamisms" of the human psyche as well; but man is more than psyche: Man is spirit. By the very act of his own self-transcendence he leaves the plane of the merely biopsychological and enters the sphere of the specifically human, the noölogical dimension. Human existence is, in its essence, noëtic. A human being is not one thing among others: Things are determining each other, but man is self-determining. In actuality, man is free and responsible, and these constituents of his spirituality, i.e., freedom and responsibility, must never be clouded by what is called the reification or depersonalization of man.

By the process of reification or depersonalization the subject is made an object. The human person, when being dealt with merely in terms of a psychic mechanism ruled by the law of cause and effect, loses his intrinsic character as a subject who is ultimately self-determining (according to a statement of Thomas Aquinas the person is *dominium sui actus*). In this way an essential characteristic of human existence, freedom of will, has been totally overlooked in any exclusively psychodynamic interpretation of the human being. The subject who "wills" has been made an object that "must"!

However, freedom, in the last analysis (phenomenological analysis, that is), is the subjective aspect of a total phenomenon and, as such, is still to be completed by its objective aspect, responsibility. The freedom to take a stand, as emphasized above, is never complete if it has not been converted and rendered into the freedom to take responsibility. The specifically human capacity to "will" remains empty as long as it has not yet been complemented by its objective counterpart, to will what I "ought." What I ought, however, is the actualization of values, the fulfillment of the concrete meaning of my personal existence. The world of meanings and values may rightly be termed *logos*. Then, *logos* is the objective correlate to the subjective phenomenon called human existence. Man is free to be responsible, and he is responsible for the realization of the meaning of his life, the *logos* of his existence.

But we have still to pose the question in what regard or to what extent the values to be actualized or the meanings to be fulfilled have any "objective" character. Now, what we mean by this term "objective" is that values are necessarily more than a mere self-expression of the subject himself. They are more than a mere expression of one's inner life, whether in the sense of sublimations or secondary rationalizations of one's own instinctual drives as Freudian psychoanalysis would explain them, or in the sense of inherent archetypes of one's collective unconscious as Jungian psychology would assume (they, too, are mere self-expressions—namely, of mankind as a whole). If meanings and values were just something emerging from the subject himself—that is to say, if they were not something that stems from a sphere beyond man and above man—they would instantly lose their demand quality. They could no longer be a real challenge to man, they would never be able to summon him up, to call him forth. If that for the realization of which we are responsible is to keep its obligative quality, then it must be seen in its objective quality.[4]

_____

[4]This pertains also to that entity to which we are responsible: If the conscience—or that Being of whom this conscience is experienced to be the voice—is reduced to a superego (thus being interpreted in terms of an introjection of one's father image, or its projection) the obligative quality of such an instance would evaporate.

This objective quality inherent in meanings and values and accounting for their obligative quality can no longer be recognized if we see in them "nothing but" a subjective design, or even a projection of instincts or archetypes. Thus we can understand that alongside the reification and depersonalization of the human person (i.e., alongside the *objectification of existence*), another process takes place (i.e., a subjectification of meaning and values), the *subjectification of logos.*

It was psychoanalysis that brought about this twofold process, inasmuch as an exclusively psychodynamic interpretation of the human person must result in an objectification of something that is intrinsically subjective; whereas at the same time, an exclusively psychogenetic interpretation of meaning and values must result in the subjectification of something that is intrinsically objective.

One of the great merits and achievements of *ontoanalysis*[5] seems to me to be that it offers a corrective to the first aspect of the twofold mistake committed by psychoanalysis as delineated above. This newer school of thinking has helped to reinstate the human person as a phenomenon that eludes any attempt to grasp its essence in terms of a fully conditioned and wholly predictable thing among and like other things. Thus, the fully subjective quality, among others, is being reclaimed by ontoanalysis as against psychoanalysis.

However, the other aspect of the same process, the depreciation of the objective quality of meaning and values, the subjectification of the objective, has not yet been rectified. By ontoanalysis the *subjective,* i.e., existence, was

---

[5]Ludwig Binswanger and Erwin W. Straus, "The Existential Analysis School of Thought," in *Existence*, ed. Rollo May, Ernest Angel, and Henri F. Ellenberger (New York: Basic Books, Inc., 1958). *Cf.* Jordan M. Scher, "The Concept of the Self in Schizophrenia," *Journal of Existential Psychiatry*, 1: 64 (1960).

resubjectified. It is *logotherapy*[6] that has taken for its own
task and purpose the *reobjectification of the objective,* i.e.,
logos! Only in this way will the unabridged phenomenon of
the human being in its double aspect be restored: existence
in its subjectivity, and *logos* in its objectivity. We can
diagram the matter thus:

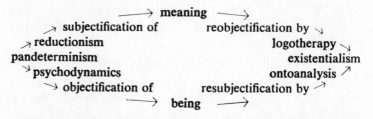

For logotherapy, however, meaning is not only an "ought"
but also a "will": Logotherapists speak of man's "will to
meaning." This logotherapeutic concept should not leave
with the reader the impression that he is dealing with just an
idealistic hypothesis. Let us recall the results of experiments,
reported by J. M. Davis, William F. McCourt, and P.
Solomon, referring to the effects of visual stimulation on
hallucinations during sensory deprivation. The authors
finally come to the following conclusion: "Our results are
consistent with the hypothesis which emphasizes the
parameter of meaning. Hallucinations occur as a result of
isolation from meaningful contact with the outside world.
What the brain needs for normal functioning *is* a continuous
*meaning*ful contact with the outside world."[7]

This had been noted long before by logotherapists. We
have known the detrimental impact of what we call a man's
"existential vacuum," i.e., the result of the frustration of the

---

[6]Paul Polak, "Frankl's Existential Analysis," *American Journal of
Psychotherapy,* 3: 617 (1949), and Donald F. Tweedie, Jr., *Logotherapy
and the Christian Faith: An Evaluation of Frankl's Existential Approach
to Psychotherapy* (Grand Rapids, Mich.: Baker Book House, 1961).
[7]"The Effect of Visual Stimulation on Hallucinations and Other Mental
Experiences During Sensory Deprivation," *The American Journal of
Psychiatry,* 116: 887 (1960).

above-mentioned "will to meaning." The feeling of a total and ultimate meaninglessness of one's life often results in a certain type of neurosis for which logotherapy has coined the term "noögenic" neurosis; that is to say, a neurosis the origin of which is a spiritual problem, a moral conflict, or the existential vacuum. But other types of neuroses are also invading this vacuum! No psychotherapy can be completed, no neurosis of whatsoever kind can be completely and definitely overcome, if this inner void and emptiness in which neurotic symptoms are flourishing has not been filled up by supplementary logotherapy, be it applied unconsciously or methodically.

By this I do not want to give the impression that the existential vacuum in itself represents a mental disease: Doubting whether one's life has a meaning is an existential despair, it is a spiritual distress rather than a mental disease. Thus logotherapy in such cases is more than the therapy of a disease; it is an assignment to all counseling professions. The search for a meaning to one's existence, even the doubt whether such a meaning can be found at all, is something human and nothing pathological.

From the above it can easily be seen how much mental health is based on the presence of an adequate state of tension, similar to that which arises from the unbridgeable gap between what a man has achieved and what he should accomplish. The cleavage between what I am and what I ought to become is inherent in my being human and, therefore, indispensable to my mental well-being. Therefore, we should not be timid and hesitant in confronting man with the potential meaning to be actualized by him, nor in evoking his will to meaning out of its latency. Logotherapy attempts to make both events conscious to man: (1) the meaning that, so to speak, waits to be fulfilled by him, as well as (2) his will to meaning. that, so to speak, waits for a task, nay, a mission to be assigned to him. Inasmuch as logotherapy makes the patient aware of both facts, it represents an essentially analytical procedure for it makes something conscious; not anything psychic, however, but something noëtic, not only the subhuman, but the human itself.

To be charged with the task to fulfill the unique meaning assigned to each of us is nothing to be avoided and feared. The homeostasis principle, however, that underlies the dynamic interpretation of man maintains that his behavior is basically directed toward the gratification and satisfaction of his drives and instincts, toward the reconciliation of the different aspects of his psyche such as id, ego, and superego, and toward adaptation and adjustment to society, toward his own bio-psycho-sociological equilibrium. But human existence is essentially self-transcendence. By the same token, it cannot consist in self-actualization; man's primary concern does not lie in the actualization of his self, but in the realization of values and in the fulfillment of meaning potentialities which are to be found in the world rather than within himself or within his own psyche as a closed system.

What man actually needs is not homeostasis, but what I call noödynamics, i.e., that kind of appropriate tension that holds him steadily oriented toward concrete values to be actualized, toward the meaning of his personal existence to be fulfilled. This is also what guarantees and sustains his mental health; escaping from any stress situation would even precipitate his falling prey to the existential vacuum.

What man needs is not a tensionless state but the striving and struggling for something worth longing and groping for. What man needs is not so much the discharge of tensions as it is the challenge of the concrete meaning of his personal existence that must be fulfilled by him and cannot be fulfilled but by him alone. The tension between subject and object does not weaken health and wholeness, but strengthens them. In neurotic individuals, this is not less so, but even more valid. Integration of the subject presupposes direction toward an object. If architects want to strengthen a decrepit arch, they *increase* the load that is laid upon it, for thereby the parts are joined more firmly together. So, if therapists wish to foster their patients' mental health, they should not be afraid to increase the burden of one's responsibility to fulfill the meaning of his existence.

Psychiatry and Man's Quest for Meaning[1]

VI

A psychiatrist today is confronted more and more with a new type of patient, a new class of neurosis, a new sort of suffering, the most remarkable characteristic of which is the fact that it does not represent a disease in the proper sense of the term. This phenomenon has brought about a change in the function—or should I say mission?—of present-day psychiatry. In such cases, the traditional techniques of treatment available to the psychiatrist prove themselves to be less and less applicable.

I have called this phenomenon, which the psychiatrist now has to deal with so frequently, "the existential vacuum." What I mean thereby is the experience of a total lack, or loss, of an ultimate meaning to one's existence that would make life worthwhile. The consequent void, the state of inner emptiness, is at present one of the major challenges to psychiatry. In the conceptual framework of logotherapeutic teaching, that phenomenon is also referred to as "existential frustration" or the frustration of "the will to meaning."

By the latter concept, logotherapy denotes what it regards as the most fundamental motivational force in man. Freudian psychoanalysis centers its motivational theory on

[1]Opening paper read before the Seminar on Logotherapy, Harvard Summer School, 1961.

the pleasure principle[2] or, as one might call it, the "will to
pleasure," whereas Adlerian individual psychology focuses
on what is generally called the "will to power." In contrast to
both theories, logotherapy considers man to be primarily
motivated by a search for a meaning to his existence, by the
striving to fulfill this meaning and thereby to actualize as
many value potentialities as possible. In short, man is
motivated by the will to meaning.

In former days, people frustrated in their will to meaning
would probably have turned to a pastor, priest, or rabbi.
Today, they crowd clinics and offices. The psychiatrist, then,
frequently finds himself in an embarrassing situation; he
now is confronted with human problems rather than with
specific clinical symptoms. Man's search for a meaning is not
pathological, but rather the surest sign of being truly
human. Even if this search is frustrated, it cannot be
considered a sign of disease. It is spiritual distress, not
mental disease.

How should the clinician respond to this challenge?
Traditionally, he is not prepared to cope with this situation
in any but medical terms. Thus he is forced to conceive of
the problem as something pathological. Furthermore, he
induces his patient to interpret his plight as a sickness to be
cured rather than as a challenge to be met. By so doing, the
doctor robs the patient of the potential fruits of his spiritual
struggle.

The doctor should not let himself be seduced by the still
prevalent reductionism into devaluating man's concern for
meaning and values to "nothing but" a defense mechanism,
a reaction formation, or a rationalization. The "nothing-butness"[3] of human phenomena is indeed one of the foremost

---

[2]According to Freud, the reality principle is nothing but an extension of,
and ultimately operates in the service of, the pleasure principle.

[3]It is true that most of the writers in the field of existentialism are used
to introducing and applying a terminology which is somewhat reminis-
cent of neologisms, a frequent symptom in cases of schizophrenia. I
once presented to the audience in a lecture of mine two quotations, one

features of the reductionist image of man. But would it be wise to base therapy on, or even to start therapy with, Freud's assumption, for example, that philosophy is "nothing more" than a form of sublimation of repressed sexuality?[4] A sound philosophy of life, I think, may be the most valuable asset for a psychiatrist to have when he is treating a patient in ultimate despair. Instead of stubbornly trying to reduce meaning and values to their alleged psychodynamic roots, or to deduce them from psychogenetic sources, the psychiatrist should take these phenomena at face value and not press them into a Procrustean bed of preconceived ideas regarding their function and origin. Preserving the humanness of human phenomena is precisely what the phenomenological approach, as propounded by Husserl and Scheler, has attempted to do.

Certainly, both the meaning of human existence and man's will to meaning are accessible only through an approach that goes beyond the plane of merely psychodynamic and psychogenetic data. We must enter, or better, we must follow man into the dimension of the specifically human phenomena that is the spiritual dimension of being. To avoid any confusion that might arise from the fact that the term "spiritual" usually has a religious connotation in English, I prefer to speak of noëtic in contrast to psychic phenomena and of the noölogical in contrast to

---

taken from Martin Heidegger and the other from a schizophrenic patient. I then invited the audience to assign the words to the man, and it turned out that the majority mistook the words of one of the greatest philosophers of all times for the words of the severely disturbed patient, and vice versa. However, this does not speak against Heidegger but rather against man's capacity to verbalize through the medium of everyday words the experience of a world hitherto unknown, either the world of a new philosophy or that in which a schizophrenic patient is doomed to live. The common denominator is not the expression of a psychotic crisis but rather a crisis of semantic expression.

[4]Ludwig Binswanger, *Sigmund Freud: Reminiscences of a Friendship* (New York: Grune & Stratton, Inc., 1957), p. 9.

the psychological dimension. The noölogical dimension is to be defined as that dimension in which the specifically human phenomena are located.

Through a merely psychological analysis, the human phenomena are, as it were, taken out of the noölogical space and leveled down to the psychological plane. Such a procedure is called psychologism.[5] It entails no less than the loss of a whole dimension. Moreover, what is lost is the dimension that allows man to emerge and rise above the level of the biological and psychological foundations of his existence. This is an important issue, for transcending these foundations and thereby transcending oneself signifies the very act of existing. *Self-transcendence,* I would say, is the essence of existence; and existence, in turn, means the specifically human mode of being. To the extent to which this mode of being exceeds the psychological frame of reference, the appropriate and adequate approach to existence is not psychological but existential.

This holds true even for therapy. Logotherapy is that psychotherapy which centers on life's meaning as well as man's search for this meaning. In fact, *logos* means "meaning." However, it also means "spirit." And logotherapy takes the spiritual or noölogical dimension fully into account. In this way, logotherapy is also enabled to realize—and to utilize—the intrinsic difference between the noetic and psychic aspects of man. Despite this ontological difference between the noetic and psychic, between spirit and mind, the anthropological wholeness and oneness is not only maintained by our multidimensional concept of man, but even supported by it. Speaking of man in terms of his spiritual, mental, and bodily levels, or layers, may well prompt one to assume that each of these aspects can be

---

[5]Insofar as psychoanalysis is more or less linked to abnormal phenomena such as neuroses and psychoses, it tends to deal with the spiritual aspirations of man not only in psychological but also in pathological terms. Thus the pitfall of psychologism is increased by the fallacy that I have termed "pathologism."

separated from the others. Nobody, however, can claim that viewing a human being in his manifold dimensions would destroy the wholeness and oneness inherent in man.

There is a practical implication involved in our "dimensional ontology." I refer to the specific capacity of man to detach himself from himself. Through his emergence into the noölogical dimension, man becomes able to detach himself from his psychological condition. This specifically human capacity for self-detachment is mobilized by logotherapy particularly against pathological events within the psychological dimension, such as neurotic and psychotic symptoms. In spite of the emphasis that it places upon responsibleness as an essential quality of being human, logotherapy is far from holding man responsible for neurotic, or even psychotic, symptoms. However, it does hold him accountable for his attitude toward these symptoms. For it regards man as free and responsible; it considers this freedom not to be freedom from conditions but rather freedom to take a stand, to choose a stand toward conditions. What is called paradoxical intention is a logotherapeutic technique designed to make use of the human capacity for noö-psychic detachment.

A multidimensional view enables us to avoid not only psychologism but also noölogism. Spiritualism is no less a one-sided world view than materialism. Monism, be it spiritual or material, does not so much disclose the alleged oneness of the world as it betrays the one-sidedness of its own view.

An example of flagrant noölogism would be the contention of some psychiatrists that a patient suffering from endogenous depression not only feels guilty, but really is guilty—"existentially guilty"—and that this is why he is depressed. I regard endogenous depression as somatogenic rather than noögenic—or even psychogenic—in origin. This somatogenic psychosis in turn engenders an abnormal awareness of the guilt that is normally linked to the "human condition." One could compare this to a reef that emerges during low tide. No one could claim that the reef causes the low tide. Likewise, the guilt has not caused the psychotic depression but, on the contrary, the depression—an emotional low tide, as it were—has caused the guilt to be felt so acutely. But imagine the potential effect of confronting the psychotic patient with such a spiritualistic, even moralistic, interpretation of his illness in terms of "existential guilt."[6] It would just offer additional content to the patient's pathological tendency toward self-accusations, and suicide might well be his response.

In itself, the existential vacuum is not anything pathological. Nonetheless, it may eventuate in a neurotic illness for which logotherapy has coined the term "noögenic neurosis." This neurosis is not the result of instinctual conflicts or clashes between the claims of ego, id, and superego, but rather it is the effect of spiritual problems and existential frustration. What is required in such cases is a psychotherapy that focuses on both spirit and meaning—i.e., logotherapy. However, logotherapy, as a psychotherapeutic approach and procedure, is also applicable in psychogenic, and even somatogenic, neuroses. As an example of the latter, hyperthyroidism brings about an inclination to anxiety states which the patient often responds to in terms of what is called "anticipatory anxiety." That is to say, he is afraid of the recurrence of anxiety, and the very expectation of such an attack precipitates it again and again. Increasingly, the patient is caught in a feedback mechanism between the primary somatic condition and the secondary psychic reaction. This vicious circle must be attacked on its somatic as well as on its psychic side. In order to achieve the latter, one must use logotherapy, more specifically paradoxical intention, which "takes the wind out of the sails" of

---

[6]How would one explain that existential guilt in a given case appears only, say, from February until April of 1951, from March until June of 1956, without becoming pathogenic at any other time?

anticipatory anxiety; tranquilizing drugs accomplish the other requirement, namely, the removal of the somatic foundation and basis of the whole disorder. According to the observation of the author, masked tetany frequently results in claustrophobias just as mild hyperthyroidism does in agoraphobias. And it happens that the first tranquilizer ever brought out in Continental Europe (it was developed by the author as early as 1952, before the "March to Miltown" had begun) has proved itself to be the most effective drug treatment of choice in cases of somatogenic phobias.

Again and again, however, it turns out that the feedback mechanism called anticipatory anxiety thrives in the existential vacuum. Filling this vacuum prevents the patient from having a relapse. Refocusing him on meaning and purpose and decentering him away from obsession and compulsion cause these symptoms to atrophy. In such cases, the source of pathology is psychological or even biological; but the resource of therapy, the therapeutic agent, is noölogical. As Edith Weisskopf-Joelson puts it, "Logotherapy can also be used as nonspecific therapy, i.e., neuroses which are caused by psychosexual disturbances during childhood can be relieved by spiritual therapy during adulthood."[7]

We do not regard logotherapy as a specific therapy in every case. That is why in psychogenic neuroses logotherapy serves as a supplement to, rather than a substitute for, psychotherapy in the usual sense of the word. The question arises of whether or not therapies that are considered specific really are so. As for psychoanalysis, Joseph Wolpe recently presented "a survey of follow-up studies comprising 249 patients whose neurotic symptoms have either ceased or improved markedly after psychotherapy of various kinds other than psychoanalysis." Wolpe concluded that "this evidence [only four relapses (1.6%)] contradicts the

---

[7]Edith Weisskopf-Joelson, "Logotherapy and Existential Analysis," *Acta Psychotherapeutica*, 6: 701–703 (1955).

psychoanalytic expectation of inferior durability of recoveries obtained without psychoanalysis and does away
with the chief reason for regarding analysis as the treatment
of choice for neurotic suffering." "In other words," he adds,
"what psychoanalytic theory holds to be necessary for
enduring recovery is in fact not necessary. Does this imply
that what the theory proposes as the basis of neurosis is in
fact not the basis?"[8] At least, I should say, this demonstrates
that psychoanalysis is not as specific as the psychoanalysts
think it is. It has been pointed out for a long time by many
writers in the field that one and the same case allows a
variety of theoretical interpretations. Different techniques
based upon these interpretations, however, obtain the same
therapeutic results. Whatever may turn out to be the crucial
agent, if different methods produce approximately the same
therapeutic results, it cannot be the technique which ac-
counts for these results in the first place. What is important,
apparently, is the human relationship between the doctor
and the patient. The personal encounter or, in Jaspers' term,
the "existential communication" seems to matter. "The
warm, subjective, human encounter of two persons," Carl R.
Rogers says, "is more effective in facilitating change
than is the most precise set of techniques growing out of
learning theory or operant conditioning."[9] In another place,
Rogers states: "Personality change is initiated by attitudes
which exist in the therapist, rather than primarily by his
knowledge, his theories, or his techniques. . . . It may be a
new way of experiencing, experiencing in a more immediate, more fluid way, with more acceptance which is the
essential characteristic of therapeutic change, rather than,
for example, the gaining of insight or the working through of

---

[8]Joseph Wolpe, "The Prognosis in Unpsychoanalyzed Recovery from
Neurosis," *The American Journal of Psychiatry*, 118: 35 (1961).

[9]Carl R. Rogers, "Two Divergent Trends," in *Existential Psychology*,
ed. Rollo May (New York: Random House, Inc. 1961), p. 93.

the transference relationship, or the change in the self-concept.[10]

The degree to which the encounter between the doctor and the patient may be working even without the slightest investment of any technique may be illustrated by the following experience. An American girl, a student of music, came to see me in Vienna for analysis. Since she spoke a terrible slang of which I could not understand a word, I tried to turn her over to an American physician in order to have him find out for me what had motivated her to seek my advice. She did not consult him, however, and when we happened to meet each other on the street, she explained: "See, Doctor, as soon as I had spoken to you of my problem, I felt such a relief that I didn't need help any longer." So I do not know even now for what reason she had come to me.

This was an instance of an extremely nontechnological approach. The story should be complemented, however, by another one that is an example of an extremely technological procedure. In 1941, I was called one morning by the Gestapo and ordered to come to headquarters. I went there in the expectation of being immediately taken to a concentration camp. A Gestapo man was waiting for me in one of the offices; he started involving me in a cross-examination. But soon he changed the subject and began to question me on topics such as: What is psychotherapy? What is a neurosis? How would one treat a case of phobia? Then he began to elaborate on a specific case—the case of "his friend." Meanwhile, I had guessed that it was his own case that he wished to discuss with me. I started short-term therapy in an extremely nonpersonal way; I advised him to tell "his friend" that he should do thus and so in case anxiety cropped up. This therapeutic session was not based on an I-thou relation, but rather on one of I-he. At any rate, the Gestapo man kept me for hours, and I continued treating

---

[10]Carl R. Rogers, "The Process Equation of Psychotherapy," *American Journal of Psychotherapy*, 15: 27–45 (1961).

him in this indirect manner. What effect this short-term therapy had I was, naturally, not able to discover. As for my family and myself, it was lifesaving for the moment, for we were permitted to stay in Vienna for a year before being sent to a concentration camp.

Apart from such exceptional situations, the two extremes, encounter and technique, seem to be a matter of theoretical importance only. Live practice hovers *between* the extreme poles. Neither should be looked upon contemptuously or disparagingly.

First of all, one should not make one extreme the battlefield of the other, i.e., make encounter a battlefield of technique. Technique, by its very nature, tends to reify whatever it touches. As far as the partners of a therapeutic relationship are concerned, man is seen as one thing among other things, as a *res*. To be sure, it is fashionable to blame Descartes for the dichotomy between *res extensa* and *res cogitans*. But I think he should have gone further than he did. He should have denied to man not only the attribute *extensa* but also that of *res*.

Worshiping technique at the expense of encounter involves making man not only a mere thing but also a mere means to an end. According to the second version of Kant's categorical imperative, no man should ever be taken as a mere means to an end. I doubt whether there is any realm in which the difference between indulging in, or refraining from, making man a mere means to an end is more crucial than it is in the case of politics. I dare say that the most important distinction in politics is between the sort of politician who believes that the end justifies the means and one who understands that there are means that would desecrate even the most sacred end.

Seeing in man a mere means to an end is the same as manipulating him. Referring to the issue at hand, i.e., encounter falling prey to technique, we should listen to the voice of Rudolf Dreikurs when he warns us that "the assumption of transference as the basic therapeutic agent puts the therapist in a superior position, manipulating the patient according to his training and therapeutic schemes."[11]

It is true that at the McGill Conference on Depression and Allied States, in Montreal, "a number of speakers pointed out the great danger, inherent in shock treatment and drug therapy, that the medical management may become mechanized and the patient cease to be regarded as a person." I think the danger is not so much inherent in shock treatment or drug treatment in themselves as it is in the extremely technological attitude which dominates so many therapists. I think the danger is even greater in the field of psychotherapy than in that of shock treatment or drug treatment. What matters is not the technique applied but the doctor who applies it or, more specifically, the spirit in which he applies it. And psychotherapy can be conducted in such a spirit that the patient is no more "regarded as a person" but rather his *psyche* considered merely as a set of mechanisms.

Even if the personal quality of encounter is preserved, the I-thou relation should not be regarded as a closed system. Karl Buhler, in his theory of language, distinguishes among three aspects: From the viewpoint of the one who speaks, language is expression; from that of the person to whom the speaker addresses himself, language is appeal; and from the viewpoint of the subject matter of which one speaks, language is presentation. It is the third aspect, I should say, that is overlooked whenever one forgets that the therapeutic relationship is not yet exhaustively characterized by the concept of encounter between two subjects but hinges on the object with which one subject is confronting the other. This object is usually a fact of which the patient is to become aware. In particular, he should be made conscious of the fact that there is a meaning waiting to be fulfilled by him. Thus

---

[11] Rudolf Dreikurs, "The Current Dilemma in Psychotherapy," *Journal of Existential Psychiatry*, 1: 187 (1960).

the therapeutic relationship is opened, as it were, onto a

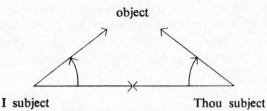

world. The world, however, is to be considered assignment and challenge.

It is a tenet of logotherapy that self-transcendence is the essence of existence. This tenet means that existence is authentic only to the extent to which it points to something that is not itself. Being human cannot be its own meaning. It has been said that man must never be taken as a means to an end. Is this to imply that he is an end in itself, that he is intended and destined to realize and actualize himself? Man, I should say, realizes and actualizes values. He finds himself only to the extent to which he loses himself in the first place, be it for the sake of something or somebody, for the sake of a cause or a fellowman, or "for God's sake." Man's struggle for his self and his identity is doomed to failure unless it is enacted as dedication and devotion to something beyond his self, to something above his self. As Jaspers puts it, "What man is, he becomes through that cause which he has made his own."

Being human fades away unless it commits itself to some freely chosen meaning. The emphasis lies on free choice. An outstanding American psychoanalyst reported, after a trip to Moscow, that behind the Iron Curtain people were less neurotic because they had more tasks to fulfill. When I was invited to read a paper before the psychiatrists of Krakow, I referred to this report, but remarked that even though the West might well confront man with fewer tasks than does the East, it leaves to him the freedom to choose among the tasks. If this freedom is denied to him, he becomes a cogwheel that has a function to carry out but no opportunity to choose it.

A psychotherapy that confronts man with meaning and purpose is likely to be criticized as demanding too much of the patient. Actually, however, people today are less endangered and threatened by too many demands than by too few. There is not only a pathology of stress, but also a pathology of the *absence* of tension. And what we have to fear in an age of existential frustration is not so much tension per se as it is the lack of tension that is created by the loss of meaning. I deem it a dangerous misconception of mental health that what man needs in the first place is homeostasis *à tout prix*. What man really needs is a sound amount of tension aroused by the challenge of a meaning he has to fulfill. This tension is inherent in being human and hence indispensable for mental well-being. What I call noö-dynamics is the dynamics in a field of tension whose poles are represented by man and the meaning that beckons him. Noödynamics orders and structures man's life like iron filings in a magnetic field. In contrast to psychodynamics, noödynamics leaves to man the freedom to choose between fulfilling or declining the meaning that awaits him.

Theodore A. Kotchen explored the relation of the concept of meaning to mental health by constructing a questionnaire and administering it to mental patients and to non-psychiatric control groups. The results gave empirical validity to a conception of mental health offered by "logotherapy, or any other variety" of existential analysis: A mind is healthy when it has achieved a sufficient store of "meaning."

In 1899, James Jackson Putnam lectured to the Massachusetts Medical Society on "Not the Disease Only, But Also the Man." This title means, in my opinion, that the doctor should treat the disease plus the patient's attitude toward it. Through the right attitude, unavoidable suffering is transmitted into a heroic and victorious achievement. That is why life does not lack a meaning until the last breath, until a man's death. Even through death, life does not lose its meaning; for this meaning does not consist in preserving anything for the future, but rather storing it in the past. Therein it is saved forever.

Edith Weisskopf-Joelson states that, by giving unavoidable suffering the status of a positive value, logotherapy "may help counteract certain unhealthy trends in the present-day culture of the United States, where the incurable sufferer is given very little opportunity to be proud of his suffering and to consider it ennobling rather than degrading." "Thus," she writes, "the burden of the unhappy is increased, since he is not only unhappy, but also ashamed of being unhappy."

"Another aspect of logotherapeutic philosophy pertains to the conception of time," Edith Weisskopf-Joelson concludes. "The past of an individual is seen, as it were, as a storehouse of everything he has brought into existence, of safely and immutably materialized possibilities, while the future consists of opportunities yet to be materialized. Thus, the past of an individual is the part of his life in which he has overcome transiency and achieved eternity. Such a positive evaluation of the past may counteract the fear of aging and death to a certain extent, and it may counterbalance the discomfort of middle-aged or old people in cultures, such as that of the United States, which stress the value of youth. Especially in the treatment of climacteric disturbances such philosophic considerations might be helpful."[12]

However, the ultimate meaning of man's life is not a matter of his intellectual cognition but rather the matter of his existential commitment. It exceeds and surpasses the intellectual capacity of a finite being such as man. Through his personal religion, man takes a stand and makes a choice. When a patient stands on the firm ground of religious belief,

---

[12]"Logotherapy and Existential Analysis," *Acta Psychotherapeutica*, 6: 193 (1958).

it is legitimate to draw upon his religious convictions; there
can be no objection to making use of the therapeutic effect of
these spiritual resources.[13]

I followed this once, for instance, when a rabbi turned to
me and told me his story. He had lost his first wife and their
six children in the concentration camp of Auschwitz where
they were gassed, and now it turned out that his second wife
was sterile. I observed that procreation is not the only
meaning in life, for if it were, life in itself would become
meaningless, and something that in itself is meaningless cannot be rendered meaningful merely by its perpetuation.
However, the rabbi evaluated his plight as an orthodox Jew.
He despaired because there was no son of his own who
would ever say *Kaddish* for him after his death. But I would
not give up. I made a last attempt to help him by inquiring
whether he did not hope to see his children again in Heaven.
My question produced an outburst of tears, and now the
true reason for his despair came to the fore: He explained
that his children, since they died as innocent martyrs,[14] were
thus found worthy of the highest place in Heaven but he, an
old sinful man, could not expect to be assigned the same
place. Once more I did not give up, but retorted, "Is it not
conceivable, Rabbi, that precisely this was the meaning of
your surviving your children; that you may be purified
through these years of suffering, so that finally you, too,
though not innocent like your children, may *become* worthy
of joining them in Heaven? Is it not written in the Psalms

---

[13]The more weakly one stands on the ground of his belief the more he
clings with both hands to the dogma which separates it from other
beliefs; on the other hand, the more firmly one stands on the ground of
his faith, the more he has both hands free to reach out to those of his
fellowmen who cannot share his belief. The first attitude entails fanaticism; the second, tolerance. Tolerance does not mean that one accepts
the belief of the other; but it does mean that one respects him as a human
being, with the right and freedom of choosing his own way of believing
and living.

[14]*L'kiddush hashem,* i.e., for the sanctification of God's name.

that God preserves all your tears?[15] So perhaps your sufferings were not in vain." For the first time in many years he found relief by seeing his suffering in the new light I had cast upon it through having him reevaluate it in his own terms.

An appropriate and adequate theory of man must follow him into the dimension of the specifically human phenomena that is the noölogical dimension of being. But it would be fragmentary if it did not recognize the essential openness of human existence to the next higher dimension. A human being, it is true, is a finite being. However, to the extent to which he understands his finiteness, he also overcomes it.

---

[15]"Thou hast kept count of my tossings; put thou my tears in thy bottle! Are they not in thy book?" (Ps. 56: 8.)

Logotherapy and the Challenge of Suffering[1]

VII

> *"Nothing in the whole world is meaningless,*
> *suffering least of all."*
> OSCAR WILDE, *The Ballad of Reading Gaol*

It has become fashionable to blame existential philosophy for overemphasizing the tragic aspects of human existence. Logotherapy, which is considered one of the schools of existential psychiatry, has become the target of the same reproaches. Logotherapy, it is true, centers on issues such as dying and suffering. This, however, must not be interpreted as evidence of a pessimistic slant and bias. What we rather have to deal with is an optimistic position; namely, the conviction that even dying and suffering are potentially meaningful. Since logotherapy, as its name indicates, focuses on meaning, it cannot avoid confronting the patient with pain, death, and guilt, or, as I call it, the tragic triad of human existence.

These three existential facts of life should be faced by the patient rather than blurred and clouded by the doctor. This is a particularly important assignment and requirement in psychotherapy today, since at present it is no longer the *instinctual aspects* of human existence which are subject to repression, but rather man's *spiritual aspirations*. And

---

[1] A major portion of this material was presented in the Peyton Lectures at the Perkins School of Theology, Southern Methodist University, Dallas, Texas, February 2–4, 1965.

neurosis is no longer a mode of escape from *sexual facts* as it was for the Victorian age. Today neurosis is an attempt to obscure *existential facts*, and an old-fashioned, one-sided psychodynamic indoctrination may well shunt aside the actual problems by providing the patient with a pan-deterministic self-image which does not allow for change and growth. We may now understand how justified Arthur Burton was in pointing out that when fear of death is indiscriminately analyzed away or reduced to castration anxiety the result is a form of denial of an existential fact.[2]

Dying and suffering are not inventions of logotherapy. They belong to the human condition. Therefore, one should not approach them as if, in a given case, he just had to deal with bad luck. Pain, death, and guilt are inescapable; the more the neurotic tries to deny them, the more he entangles himself in additional suffering.

Although the tragic triad is an undeniable fact inherent in human existence, it is rationalized away by means of technological progressivism and scientism. But even in the United States—where society is so permeated by the belief that sooner or later science will do, and will do away with man's predicament—there are rumors to the effect that man is after all a finite and mortal being who inevitably has to face dying, and even before this, suffering.

Since this paper specifically and explicitly is concerned with man's mortality and life's transitoriness, we shall begin with this facet of the tragic triad. As we teach in logotherapy, the essential transitoriness of human existence adds to life's meaningfulness. If man were immortal, he would be justified in delaying everything; there would be no need to do anything right now. Only under the urge and pressure of life's transience does it make sense to use the passing time. Actually, the only transitory aspects of life are the potentialities; as soon as we have succeeded in

---

[2]"Death as a Countertransference," *Psychoanalysis and the Psycho-analytic Review*, 49: 3 (1962–1963).

actualizing a potentiality, we have transmuted it into an actuality, and thus rescued it into the past. Once an actuality, it is one forever. Everything in the past is saved from being transitory. Therein it is irrevocably stored rather than irrecoverably lost.

This holds true irrespective of whether or not there is still anyone around who may remember, or forget, that which has been. I deem it a thoroughly subjectivistic view if one assumes that everything depends on the presence of an individual's memory in which alone there is duration. Clemens E. Benda certainly did not escape such a subjectivistic interpretation of the true ontological state of affairs when he wrote, "It is obvious that the past exists only through its impact on the imagery, which has duration."[3]

Usually, to be sure, man only considers the stubbly fields of transitoriness and overlooks the full granaries of the past, wherein he has salvaged once and for all his deeds, his joys, and also his sufferings. Nothing can be undone, and nothing can be done away with; having been is still a form of being, even its most secure form.

I think that the logotherapeutic attitude to the past implies both activism and optimism. Man is called upon to make the best use of any moment and the right choice at any time: It is assumed that he knows what to do, or whom to love, or how to suffer.

About two millenia ago, a Jewish sage, Hillel, said: "If I do not do this job—who will do it? And if I do not do this job right now—when shall I do it? But if I carry it out only for my own sake—what am I?" The first two parts of this saying suggest that each man is unique and each man's life is singular; by the same token, no man can be replaced and no man's life can be repeated. Both this very uniqueness of each human being and the singularity of his existence—and the singularity of each moment which holds a specific and

---

[3]"Existentialism in Philosophy and Science," *Journal of Existential Psychiatry*, 1: 284 (1960).

particular meaning to fulfill—add to the responsibleness of man in which logotherapy sees the essence of his existence. The third part of Hillel's dictum grapples with the fact that self-transcendence is the foremost and paramount trait and feature of human existence insofar as man's life always points to something beyond himself; it is always directed toward a meaning to fulfill (rather than a self to actualize, or one's potentialities to develop).

This means activism. As to optimism, let me remind you of the words of Lao-tse: "Having completed a task means having become eternal." I would say that this holds true not only for the completion of a task, but also for our experiences, and last but not least, for our brave sufferings as well.

What man has done cannot be undone. Whereas he is responsible for what he has done, he is not free to undo it. As a rule, being human implies being free and responsible. In the exceptional case of guilt, however, man still is responsible but no longer free. While arbitrariness is freedom without responsibleness, guilt is responsibleness without freedom—without freedom, that is, except for the freedom to choose the right attitude to guilt. Through the right attitude unchangeable suffering is transmuted into a heroic and victorious achievement. In the same fashion, a man who has failed by a deed cannot change what happened, but by repentance he can change himself. Everything depends on the right attitude in the same way and manner as in the case of his suffering. The difference lies in the fact that the right attitude is, then, a right attitude to himself.

Professor Farnsworth of Harvard University has said in an address to the American Medical Association that "medicine is now confronted with the task of enlarging its function. . . . Physicians must of necessity indulge in philosophy." Indeed, doctors today are approached by many patients who in former days would have seen a pastor, priest, or rabbi; they are confronted with philosophical problems rather than emotional conflicts. What is more, the patients often refuse to be handed over to a clergyman.

I would say that in those cases in which the doctor has to deal with an incurable disease, he should not only treat the disease but also care for the patient's attitude toward it. It may well be that the patient is thereby offered consolation. The logotherapist will gladly and readily take this risk. I am fully aware of the fact that die-hard psychoanalysts abhor the interpretation of their job in terms of consolation. A logotherapist, however, understands his task in a different way; if need be—that is to say, in a helpless case, in a hopeless situation—he does not withhold from the patient the right to be comforted. The logotherapist does not deny the patient this right; he does not dismiss his duty simply as a pastoral rather than a medical responsibility. The demand for consolation exceeds the supply furnished by pastoral care. "Preachers are no longer the pastors of the souls, but doctors have become such," said Kierkegaard. Further, coping with despair in the face of an incurable disease also constitutes a challenge to the doctor; and also to him are addressed the words, "Comfort ye, comfort ye My people" (Isa. 40: 1)

How this is enacted in actual practice may be shown by the following excerpt from the transcript of an interview with a patient, recorded during a demonstration to my students. The patient was eighty years of age and suffering from a cancer which had metastasized so that she could not be helped by surgery. She knew this, and had become increasingly depressed.

DR. FRANKL: What do you think of when you look back on your life? Has life been worth living?

PATIENT: Well, Doctor, I must say that I had a good life. Life was nice, indeed. And I must thank the Lord for what it held for me; I went to theaters, I attended concerts, and so forth. You see, Doctor, I went there with the family in whose house I have served for many decades as a maid, in Prague, at first, and afterwards in Vienna. And for the grace of all of these wonderful experiences I am grateful to the Lord.

I nevertheless felt that she was doubtful insofar as the ultimate meaning of her life as a whole was concerned. And this was the reason why I wanted to steer and pilot her through her doubts. But first I had to provoke them, and then to wrestle with them—wrestle with them as Jacob wrestled with the angel until he was blessed by him. That is how I wanted to wrestle with my patient's repressed and unconscious existential despair until the moment when she, too, finally could "bless" her life, say "yes" to her life in spite of everything. So my task consisted in having her question the meaning of her life on the conscious level rather than repressing her doubts.

DR. FRANKL: You are speaking of some wonderful experiences; but all this will have an end now, won't it?

PATIENT (*thoughtfully*): In fact, now everything ends. . . .

DR. FRANKL: Well, do you think now that all of the wonderful things of your life might be annihilated and invalidated when your end approaches? (And she knew that it did!)

PATIENT (*still more thoughtfully*): All those wonderful things. . . .

DR. FRANKL: But tell me: Do you think that anyone can undo the happiness, for example, that you have experienced? Can anyone blot it out?

PATIENT (*now facing me*): You are right, Doctor; nobody can blot it out!

DR. FRANKL: Or can anyone blot out the goodness you have met in your life?

PATIENT (*becoming increasingly emotionally involved*): Nobody can blot it out!

DR. FRANKL: What you have achieved and accomplished——

PATIENT: Nobody can blot it out!

DR. FRANKL: Or what you have bravely and honestly suffered: Can anyone remove it from the world—remove it from the past wherein you have stored it, as it were?

PATIENT (*now moved to tears*): No one can remove it! (*Pause*)

It is true, I had so much to suffer; but I also tried to be courageous and steadfast in taking life's blows. You see, Doctor, I regarded my suffering as a punishment. I believe in God.

Per se, logotherapy is a secular approach to clinical problems. However, when a patient stands on the firm ground of religious belief,[4] there can be no objection to making use of the therapeutic effect of his religious convictions and thereby drawing upon his spiritual resources. In order to do so, the logotherapist may try to put himself in the place of the patient. That is exactly what I now did.

DR. FRANKL: But cannot suffering sometimes also be a challenge? Is it not conceivable that God wanted to see how Anastasia Kotek will bear it? And perhaps He had to admit: "Yes, she did so very bravely." And now tell me: Can anyone remove such an achievement and accomplishment from the world, Frau Kotek?

PATIENT: Certainly no one can do it!

DR. FRANKL: This remains, doesn't it?

PATIENT: It does!

DR. FRANKL: By the way, you had no children, had you?

PATIENT: I had none.

DR. FRANKL: Well, do you think that life is meaningful only when one has children?

PATIENT: If they are good children, why shouldn't it be a blessing?

DR. FRANKL: Right, but you should not forget that, for instance, the greatest philosopher of all times, Immanuel Kant, had no children; but would anyone venture to doubt the extraordinary meaningfulness of his life? I rather think that if children were the only meaning of life, life would become meaningless, because to procreate something which in itself is meaningless certainly would be the most meaningless thing. What counts and matters in life is rather to achieve and accomplish something. And this is precisely what you have done. You have made the best of your suffering. You have become an

---

[4]"What is the meaning of human life, or for that matter of the life of any creature? To find a satisfying answer to this question means to be religious."—Albert Einstein

example for our patients by the way and manner in which you take your suffering upon yourself. I congratulate you on behalf of this achievement and accomplishment, and I also congratulate your roommates who have the opportunity to watch and witness such an example. (*Addressing myself now to my students*): *Ecce homo!* (*The audience now bursts into a spontaneous applause.*) This applause concerns you, Frau Kotek. (*She is weeping now.*) It concerns your life which has been a great achievement and accomplishment. You may be proud of it, Frau Kotek. And how few people may be proud of their lives. . . . I should say, your life is a monument. And no one can remove it from the world.

PATIENT (*regaining her self-control*): What you have said, Professor Frankl, is a consolation. It comforts me. Indeed, I never had an opportunity to hear anything like this. . . . (*Slowly and quietly she leaves the lecture hall.*)

Apparently, she now was reassured. A week later she died; like Job, one could say, "in a full age." During the last week of her life, however, she was no longer depressed, but on the contrary, full of faith and pride! Prior to this, she had admitted to Dr. Gerda Becker, who was in charge of her on the ward, that she felt agonized and, more specifically, ridden by the anxiety that she was useless. The interview, however, which we had had together had made her aware that her life was meaningful and that even her suffering had not been in vain. Her last words, immediately before her death, were the following: "My life is a monument. So Professor Frankl said to the whole audience, to all the students in the lecture hall. My life was not in vain. . . ."

Thus reads the report of Dr. Becker. And we may be justified in assuming that, also like Job, Frau Kotek "came to her grave like as a shock of corn cometh in in his season."

Group Psychotherapeutic Experiences
in a Concentration Camp[1]

VIII

The following exposition is supported by my own observations and experiences in the concentration camps at Auschwitz, Dachau, and Theresienstadt. However, before I take up specific experiences with psychotherapy and group psychotherapy, it seems to be advisable first to say a few words about the psychopathology of prison camp life. This may at the same time be a contribution to the knowledge of those syndromes which have been called prison psychoses, and especially of that condition which in the first world war was described as "barbed-wire sickness."

Three phases can be distinguished within the psychology of camp life: (1) the shock of entrance; (2) the typical changes in character that occur with the duration of stay; and (3) the dismissal phase.

Entrance-shock is essentially a matter of a state of panic, which is remarkable only in that it is accompanied by imminent danger of suicide. Indeed, it is only too understandable that an individual in a situation in which he is threatened with "going into the gas"—dying the death of the gas chamber—should prefer, or at least contemplate,

[1]Paper read before the Second International Congress of Psychotherapy, Leiden, The Netherlands, September 8, 1951.

"going into the wire"—committing suicide by touching the high-tension wires which fenced in the camp.

If one wanted to classify the entrance-shock phase psychiatrically, one would have to enter it among the abnormal affective reactions. Yet one must not forget that in a situation which is itself abnormal to the degree represented by a concentration camp, an "abnormal" reaction of this sort is something normal.

Very soon, however, the state of panic subsides into indifference, and herewith we come to the second phase, character changes. Along with this indifference, a marked irritation is now evidenced, so that in the end the psyche of the camp prisoner is characterized by two signs: apathy and aggression. Both ultimately correspond to and arise out of a focusing of all effort and intent upon self-preservation while everything which is associated with the preservation of the species recedes into the background. Well known indeed is the lack of sexual interest on the part of camp inmates, in which, to be sure, not only psychic but somatic factors play a role. In general, it can be said of the prisoner that he withdraws into a kind of cultural hibernation. Everything serves self-preservation.

Psychoanalysts among the inmates were accustomed, in referring to this, to speak of a regression, a retreat into more primitive forms of behavior. A different interpretation was attempted by Professor Emil Utitz, who was in one of the above-mentioned camps at the same time as I. He thought that the character changes should be understood as schizoidal.[2] Apart from any theoretic difficulties, I am of the opinion that these character changes may be more simply explained. We know that a person who gets little to eat and who can sleep very little (vermin!) is already inclined toward irritation as well as toward apathy. This was bound to become all the more noticeable in camp because of the

---

[2]Emil Utitz, *Psychologie des Lebens im Konzentrationslager Theresien-stadt* (Wien: A. Sexl, 1948).

lack of nicotine and caffein, that is, exactly those so-called poisons of civilization whose respective function it is to help suppress irritation and overcome apathy.

Emil Utitz has also attempted to interpret the inner state of the camp prisoners as, essentially, a matter of a provisional existence.[3] I, however, in opposition to that, have pointed out that the essential characteristic of this provisional existence is that this provisional state is a provisional state without end. For, indeed, the end of imprisonment could not really be envisioned. Thus the prisoner was never able to concentrate on a time in the future, a time when he would regain his freedom. In view of the essentially temporal structure which is characteristic of all human existence, it is all too easy to understand that camp life might bring about an existential loss of structure.

There is precedence for such a view. We know from the pertinent research of Lazarsfeld and Zeisel how very much a long period of unemployment influences the sense of time in human existence.[4] Something similar is also known to be true of chronic tubercular patients in sanatoria; the description in Thomas Mann's *The Magic Mountain* supports this observation.

Now he who can cling to no end point, to no time in the future, to no point of support, is in danger of allowing himself to collapse inwardly. Perhaps, instead of going into lengthy theoretical considerations and expositions, I may be permitted to show by means of a concrete example how this physical-psychic collapse, which results when the normal direction of human existence toward the future is blocked, affects the vegetative functions. At the beginning of March, 1945, a camp comrade told me that on February 2, 1945, he had had a remarkable dream. A voice which claimed to be prophetic said to him that he might ask it any question, for it

---

[3]E. Utitz, "Zur Psychologie provisorischen Daseins," *Essays in Psychology . . .* David Katz (Uppsala: Amquist and Wiksells, 1951).

[4]*Die Arbeitslosen von Marienthal* (Leipzig: Hirzel, 1933)

could tell him everything. And he asked the voice when the end of the war would come for him. The answer was: March 30, 1945.

The thirtieth of March drew near, but it did not seem at all as though the voice would be right. On March 29, my comrade became feverish and delirious. On March 30, he became unconscious. On March 31, he died; typhoid fever had carried him off. The thirtieth of March, the day on which he became unconscious, was literally for him the end of the war. We shall not err if we assume that through the disappointment which the actual course of events had prepared for him, the "biotonus" (Ewald), the immunity and power or resistance of the organism, was reduced and the infection heretofore dormant within him had all too free play.

Similar phenomena could be observed on a mass scale. In the period between Christmas, 1944, and New Year's Day, 1945, there occurred in camp a mass dying which could only be explained by the fact that the prisoners had fixed their hopes in a stereotyped manner on the catch phrase, "At Christmas we shall be home." Christmas came, and they still were not at home, but rather had to abandon the hope of getting home in the foreseeable future. This sufficed to bring about a slump in vitality which for many meant death.

In the last analysis, however, it seemed that the physical-psychic collapse was dependent upon the spiritual-moral attitude; and this attitude was a free one! And though on entering the camp everything might be taken away from the prisoner, even his glasses and his belt, this freedom remained to him; and it remained to him literally to the last moment, to the last breath. It was the freedom to bear oneself "this way or that way," and there *was* a "this or that." And again and again there were some who were able to suppress their irritation and to overcome their apathy. They were those men who walked through the camp barracks and across the mustering grounds with a good word here and a last piece of bread to spare there. They were the living witnesses to this fact: that it was in no way predetermined what the camp would make of one, whether one would become a typical "KZler" (concentration camper), or whether one would, even in this state of duress, even in this extreme borderline situation of man, remain a human being. In each case this was open to decision.

There can be no question, therefore, that a prisoner did not necessarily and automatically have to succumb to the camp atmosphere. By virtue of that which I have in another context called the "defiant power of the human spirit," he had the possibility of holding himself above the influence of his environment. If I still had any need of proof that this defiant power of the spirit is a reality, then the concentration camp was the crucial experiment. Freud asserts, "Let one attempt to expose a number of the most diverse people uniformly to hunger. With the increase of the imperative urge of hunger all individual differences will blur, and in their stead will appear the uniform expression of the one unstilled urge." But this simply was not so.

Of course those persons who had committed themselves to the fundamental possibility of preserving their humanity were rare: *"Sed omnia praeclara tam difficilia quam rara sunt"* (but everything great is just as difficult to realize as it is rare to find) reads the last sentence of the *Ethics* of Spinoza. Though a few were able to do it, they gave the others an example, and this example produced that chain reaction which was appropriate to such a model. As a complement to a famous saying of a poet, it is true that the good example productively gives birth to good.

In any case, one cannot claim that these men had undergone a regression; on the contrary they experienced a moral progression—moral, and religious. For there broke out in many a prisoner in confinement, and because of confinement, what I have designated as a subconscious or a repressed relationship to God.

Let no one judge this religiosity disparagingly, or dispose of it as "foxhole religion," as Anglo-Saxon countries term that religiosity which does not show until one is in danger. I would like to say that the religion which one does not have until things go badly is to me still preferable to that which one has only so long as things go well—I call that a "bargainer's religion."

In any event, many prisoners came forth from prison with the feeling of having learned to fear nothing except God. For them prison experience was a gain. As it was, many a neurotic person, precisely through the camp life, experienced a kind of consolation which is understandable only by analogy to a fact that is well known to master builders: A decrepit vaulting can be strengthened if one simply weights it down.

With this we are ready for the discussion of the third phase: of dismissal. The limitations of time do not allow me to go into the pertinent details, such as the singular experience of depersonalization at the time of release. Suffice it to say that dismissal means an abrupt release of pressure. Like deep-sea fish that have been unexpectedly brought to the surface of the water, so all too easily the character of the released prisoner is "deformed"—morally deformed. Whoever prefers to may in this connection speak, as I have done, of a psychic counterpart to caisson sickness, "the bends."

Let us turn now to our central theme, to psychotherapy or group psychotherapy in the concentration camp. I shall not go into such questions as that of the open or closed group (the group with which I dealt was, in any case, neither open nor closed, but rather closed-in). Neither shall I speak of that "little" or littlest psychotherapy which evolved in the form of improvisation during mustering, during marching, in the ditches, and in the barracks. Let what I can tell you, however, be said in memory of Dr. Karl Fleischmann, who died a martyr's death in the gas chamber at Auschwitz.

When I first learned to know this man, his mind was already occupied with his cherished idea, with the thought of administering mental succor to the newly arriving prisoners. The organization of this task he had assigned to me as a psychiatrist. With the all too generous amount of time at my disposal, I expanded this organization into a system of mental hygiene—which of course had to be concealed from the SS and had to be carried out clandestinely. Cutting down a comrade who had hanged himself was, for instance, strictly forbidden.

The most urgent task was to ward off entrance-shock. I succeeded in this to a certain degree with the help of a staff of psychiatrists and social workers consisting of trained personnel from all of Central Europe, who were placed at my disposal. A young rabbi was also assigned to me, Miss Jonas—to my knowledge the only, or at least the first, woman rabbi in the world (a pupil of Dr. Leo Baeck). She also met her end in Auschwitz. She was a gifted speaker, and as soon as a newly arrived transport was reported we betook ourselves—we called ourselves a shock troop—to the cold lofts or into the dark stalls of the barracks at Theresienstadt, where old and infirm figures of woe cowered on the floor, and there we improvised talks which were intended to bring these people to themselves again. I still remember how they squatted there and listened devoutly to the rabbi, among them an old woman, a hearing tube in her hand and a light on her countenance.

We had to concentrate in particular on the especially endangered ones, on epileptics, psychopaths, the "asocial," and above all the aged and infirm. In their case it was necessary to take special measures and make special arrangements. The mental vacuum of these people had to be fended off. A vacuum which is illustrated by the words of an old woman who, when asked what she did the whole time, answered, "At night I sleep, and in the daytime, I ail." To give only a single example: One of the helpers attached to me was a philologist, an Anglicist, and she was assigned to divert the intellectuals among the old people from their miserable outer and inner situation by holding conversations in a foreign language with them.

A psychotherapeutic outpatient ward was also organized. Particularly outstanding in this effort was a Berlin psychiatrist by the name of Dr. Wolf, who used the "autogenic training" of J. H. Schultz in the treatment of his patients. He also died in camp, of pulmonary tuberculosis. He recorded stenographically self-observations which he made in the terminal stages of his suffering. Unfortunately, the custodian of this record also perished. I myself repeatedly tried similar means to put myself at a distance from all the suffering that surrounded us, specifically by trying to objectify it. Thus I remember that one morning I marched out of camp, scarcely able to endure any longer the hunger, the cold, and the pain of my feet, swollen from edema, frozen and festering, and stuffed into open shoes. My situation seemed to me to be beyond comfort or hope. Then I imagined to myself that I was standing at a lectern in a large, beautiful, warm, and bright lecture hall before an interested audience. I was about to give a lecture entitled "Group Psychotherapeutic Experiences in a Concentration Camp," and I spoke precisely of all those things which I was just then going through.

Believe me, at that moment I could not hope that it would ever be granted to me one day really to deliver such a lecture.

Last but not least, we had to be concerned with the prevention of suicides. I organized a reporting service, and every expression of suicidal thoughts or actual intentions was brought to me instantly. What was to be done? We had to appeal to the will to live, to go on living, to outlive the prison. But the life-courage, or the life-weariness, turned out in every case to depend solely upon whether the person possessed faith in a *meaning* of life, of his life. A saying from

Nietzsche could have stood as a motto for the whole psychotherapeutic work in the concentration camp: "He who knows a 'why' for living, will surmount almost every 'how.'"

Under the name of logotherapy, I have tried to introduce into psychotherapy a point of view that sees in human existence not only a will to pleasure (in the sense of the Freudian "pleasure principle"), and a will to power (in the sense of the Adlerian "striving for superiority") but also what I have called the will to meaning. In the camp, psychotherapy depended on appealing precisely to this will to meaning. But in the extreme marginal state in which the human being found himself in the camp, this meaning had to be an unconditional meaning, it had to include not merely living but also suffering and dying. And perhaps the deepest experience which I myself had in the concentration camp (and forgive me if I become personal) was that, while the concern of most people was summed up by the question, "Will we survive the camp?"—for if not, then this suffering has no sense—the question which in contrast beset me was, "Has this whole suffering, this dying, a meaning?"—for if not, then ultimately there is no sense to surviving. For a life whose meaning stands or falls upon whether one survives or not, a life, that is, whose meaning depends upon such a happenstance, such a life would not really be worth living at all.

So then, it was a matter of an unconditional meaning of life. To be sure, we have to distinguish between the unconditional on the one hand and the generally valid on the other, analogous to what Jaspers has said about truth. The unconditional meaning which we had to show to people doubting it or despairing of it was in every case far from a vague and general one; it was the exact opposite, the very concrete sense of his personal existence.

I should like to clarify this with one example. One day in camp two people sat before me, both resolved to commit suicide. Both used a phrase which was a stereotype in the camp: "I have nothing more to expect of life." Now, the vital requirement was to have the two undergo a Copernican reversal such that they should no longer ask *what they could expect from life*, but were made aware of the fact that *life was awaiting something from them,*—that for each of them, indeed for all, somebody or something was waiting, whether it was a piece of work to be done or another human being.

But what if this waiting should prove to be without prospect of fulfillment? For there surely are situations in which it is certain that a man will never again return to a job or will never see a certain person again, and thus it is really true that nothing and no one is waiting for him any longer. But even then, it turned out, in the consciousness of every single being somebody was present, was invisibly there, perhaps not even living any longer but yet present and at hand, somehow "there" as the Thou of the most intimate dialogue. For many it was the first, last, and ultimate Thou: God. But whoever occupied this position, the important thing was to ask, *What does he expect of me*—that is, what kind of an attitude is required of me? So the ultimate matter was the way in which a person understood how to suffer, or knew how to die. *Savoir mourir—comprendre mourir.* This, as we have been told, is the quintessence of all philosophizing.

You will say that deliberations such as these are futile. But in the camp as we experienced it, the precept *primum vivere, deinde philosophari*—first survive, then philosophize about it—was invalidated. What was valid in the camp was rather the exact opposite of this precept, *primum philosophari, deinde mori*—first philosophize, then die. This was the one valid thing: to give an accounting to oneself on the question of ultimate meaning, and then to be able to walk forth upright and die the called-for martyr's death.

If you will, the concentration camp was nothing more than a microcosmic mirroring of the human world as a whole. And so we may be justified in applying what is to be learned from the experiences of the concentration camp to conditions in the world today. In other words, we may ask what psychotherapeutic doctrines we can derive from these experiences with regard to what I would call "the pathology of the *Zeitgeist*." This pathology, if one could describe it, is marked by provisional, fatalistic, conformist, and fanatic attitudes to life which can easily mount to the proportions of a psychic epidemic. Somatic epidemics are typical results of war; psychic epidemics are possible causes of war, and thus of new concentration camps. Therefore, let me now conclude this discussion of the application of psychotherapy to the concentration camp situation by expressing the hope that psychotherapy may also play a part in preventing the repetition of anything like a concentration camp in the future.

In Memoriam[1]

IX

In memoriam . . . in memory of . . . "What is man that you are mindful of him?" was a question which the psalmist directed to God. Let us here and now direct a similar question to ourselves and ask: What were these men, our deceased colleagues, and why do we honor their memory on this day? How they lived in your midst from 1938 to 1945, and how they lived and died in prison and in exile you already know. It is history and a history with which you are all familiar. It is my task to give testimony before you of how Viennese physicians labored and died in concentration camps; to give testimony of true physicians—who lived and died as such; of true physicians who could not see others suffer, who could not let others suffer, but who knew how to suffer themselves, who knew how to achieve the right kind of suffering—courageous suffering!

It was summer, 1942. Everywhere people, among them physicians, were being deported. One evening at the Prater Star I met a young dermatologist. We talked about being physicians in these times and about the mission of the physician under such circumstances. We spoke of Albert Schweitzer, the tropical doctor of Lambaréné, and of our

[1]Memorial speech delivered at the request of the Society of Physicians in Vienna, March 25, 1949, for the members who died in the years 1938–1945.

admiration for him. And then we agreed that we surely could not bemoan a lack of opportunity to emulate his great personal and professional dedication. We had numerous opportunities, similar to his, to give medical help under the worst possible conditions. We had no need to travel into the African jungle. As we spoke of these things we promised one another that evening that, should we have to face deportation, we would see therein a call and a challenge. A short time later, this day came for my young colleague. However, little time remained for her to use the opportunity which, because of her heroic concept of medical ethics, she saw in her deportation. A short time after her arrival in the camp, she acquired a typhoid infection. A few weeks later she was dead. Her name is Dr. Gisa Gerbel. We revere her memory. . . .

Then there was the physician for indigents of the Sixteenth District—the "Angel of Ottakring"—a true Viennese character; a man who, while in the camp, spoke longingly and ardently of celebrating his reunion in Viennese style and who, in a happy mood but with tears in his eyes, would sing the "Wine Song," "but when it will be finished. . . ." That was the "Angel of Ottakring." But who protected and befriended him like the "guardian angel" he himself was, when in Auschwitz, in front of my eyes, he was directed at the railroad station to the left side—and this meant directly into the gas chambers? That was the "Angel of Ottakring." His name is Dr. Plautus. We shall remember him. . . .

Then there was Dr. Lamberg—the son of the first directing physician of the world-famous Viennese Society for Voluntary First Aid, well known through his textbook to all students of first aid. Dr. Lamberg was a gentleman of the old world both in his appearance and in his behavior, as anyone who has ever seen him in his splendor will readily testify. But I saw him too when he lay dying in a half-underground hut in the midst of a dozen half-starved bodies packed closely together; and his last request to me was to push the dead body which was next to him and half lying on top of him, to push it aside a little. This was the previous Grand Seigneur Dr. Lamberg—one of the few camp comrades with whom a person could, even during the hardest work at the railroad tracks in a snowstorm, discuss philosophy and religion. We shall remember him. . . .

Then there was Dr. Martha Rappaport, my former assistant at the Vienna Rothschild Hospital, and also former assistant to Wagner Jauregg. With her womanly tenderness, she could not see anybody cry without being moved to tears herself. Who cried for her when she was deported? This was Dr. Rappaport. We shall remember her. . . .

Then there were, from the same hospital, a young surgeon, Dr. Paul Furst, and a general physician, Dr. Ernst Rosenberg. I was able to talk with both of them in the camp before they died there. And in their last words there was not a single word of hate, only words of longing came from their lips and words of forgiveness, because what they hated was not human beings—a person must be able to forgive humans—but what they hated and what we all hate was the system, the system which brought some men to guilt and which brought others to death.

I mention only a few names, and these not according to scientific rank. I speak of individuals, but I include all who died there. The few stand for the many, because about the many one cannot write a personal chronicle. However, they need no chronicle; they need no monument. Each deed is its own monument, and more imperishable than a monument that is merely the work of human hands. Because the deeds of a man cannot be undone, what he has done cannot be removed from the world; although past, it is not irrecoverably lost in the past, but therein is irrevocably preserved.

It is true that in those years medical ethics were desecrated by some doctors; but it is equally true that in those years some others lived up to the highest professional standards. There were physicians in the camp who experimented on those doomed to die; but there were other physicians who experimented on themselves. I remember, for instance, a psychiatrist from Berlin with whom I had quite a few nocturnal discussions about topical problems of modern psychotherapy. When he was dying he carefully set down in writing for posterity the experiences of his last hours in the form of a self-description.

In a sense, living through the concentration camp was one big experiment—a crucial experiment. Our dead colleagues passed the test with honors. They proved to us that even under the most deprived, the most humiliating conditions, man can still remain man—true man and true physician. What was honor to them who gave this proof, should be a lesson to us. It should teach us what man is, and what man can become.

What then is man? We have learned to know him, as possibly no generation before us. We have learned to know him in camps, where everything unessential had been stripped from man, where everything which a person had—money, power, fame, luck—disappeared: while only that remained which a man does not "have" but which he must "be." What remained was man himself, who in the white heat of suffering and pain was melted down to the essentials, to the human in himself.

What then is man? We ask again. He is a being who continuously decides what he is: a being who equally harbors the potential to descend to the level of an animal or to ascend to the life of a saint. Man is that being, who, after all, invented the gas chambers; but at the same time he is that being who entered into those same gas chambers with his head held high and with the "Our Father" or the Jewish prayer of the dying on his lips.

This then is man. We now have an answer to the question which we put to ourselves in the beginning: What is man that you are mindful of him? "He is a reed," said Pascal, "but a reed which thinks!" And it is this thinking, this consciousness, this responsibility that constitute the dignity of man, the dignity of each individual human being. And it is always to be ascribed to the individual person whether he preserves this dignity or tarnishes it. Whereas the first behavior is personal merit, the second constitutes personal guilt. And there is only personal guilt; collective guilt is a concept which has no meaning. Certainly there is also the personal guilt of a man who has "done nothing wrong," but who has failed to do "something right"; failed to do so because of apprehension for himself or anxiety for his family, But whoever wishes to condemn such a man as a coward must first prove that in the same situation he himself would have been a hero.

But it is better and more prudent not to sit in judgment on others. Paul Valéry has said: *"Si nous jugeons et accusons, le fonds n'est pas atteint"*—as long as we judge and accuse, we have not arrived at the fundamental truth. And so we do not only want to remember the dead, but also to forgive the living. As we extend our hand to the dead, across the graves, so we also extend our hand to the living, across all hatred. And if we say, "Honor to the dead," we want to add, "and peace to all the living, who are of good will."

Collective Neuroses of the Present Day[1]

X

The subject of my lecture is to be "the disease of our time." Now you have entrusted this task to a psychiatrist, and I am asking myself if I am therefore expected to give, as it were, the opinion of a psychiatrist on contemporary man: that my theme is to be "the neurosis of mankind."

One might well be tempted to this view on taking up a book entitled: "The Nervous Condition—The Disease of Our Time." The author's name is Weinke and the book was published in '53—not 1953, however, but 1853. . . .

The nervous condition, the neurosis, is thus not exactly a contemporary disease. Hirschmann of the Kretschmer Clinic, Tübingen University, showed statistically that neuroses have by no means increased during the last decades; all that has changed is their aspect, their symptoms. But it is surprising to find that in this context anxiety has comparatively decreased in prominence. Thus it is not altogether correct to say that anxiety constitutes the disease of our time.

Yet not only in the last decades but also in the last centuries—as far as we can ascertain—anxiety has not been on the increase. The American psychiatrist, Freyhan, asserts that earlier centuries had both more anxiety and more reason for anxiety than our own age and points to the witch trials,

[1]Lecture held at Princeton University, September 17, 1957.

the religious wars, the migration of nations, the slave trade, and the great plagues.

One of the most commonly quoted statements of Freud is that the narcissism of mankind has suffered a severe shock on three occasions: first, through the teaching of Copernicus; second, through the teaching of Darwin; and third, through that of Freud himself. We can easily accept the fact of the third shock. But of the other two we cannot understand why an explanation of the "where" (Copernicus) or the "where from" (Darwin) of humanity should have been a shock. The dignity of man does not suffer in the least from the fact that he inhabits the earth, a planet of the sun, and is not the center of the universe. Being disturbed by this fact is like being disappointed because Goethe was not born at the center of the earth or because Kant did not live on a magnetic pole. Why should the fact that man is not the center of the universe affect the worth of man? Is the achievement of Freud impaired because the greatest part of Freud's life was not spent in the center of Vienna but in the Ninth District of the city? It is obvious that anything like the dignity of man depends on grounds other than his location in the material world. In brief, we are confronted here with a confusion of different dimensions of being, with a neglect of ontological differences. Only for materialism are light-years a measure of greatness.

Thus, if—in the sense of a *quaestio juris*—the right to make worth and dignity depend on spatial catagories can be questioned, then—in the sense of a *quaestio facti*—it is doubtful whether Darwinism degraded man's self-esteem. It would seem rather to have increased it. For it seems to me that the progress-minded, progress-intoxicated generation of the Darwinian epoch did not at all feel themselves humbled, but rather seemed proud of the fact that their monkey ancestors had progressed magnificently far, so far that nothing blocked the road any longer for further development, for "superman." Indeed, man's ability to stand erect had "gone to his head."

What then did give rise to the impression that the incidence of neuroses had increased? In my opinion it is due to the growth of something that one might call the psychotherapeutic need. In actual fact, some of the people who nowadays call on the psychiatrist in former days would have seen a pastor, priest, or rabbi. But now they refuse to go to a priest, so that the doctor is forced into what I call medical ministry. It is a ministry occupied not only by the neurologist or by the psychiatrist, but by every doctor. The surgeon, for example, must perform its functions when faced with inoperable cases or with those that he must maim by amputation; likewise, the orthopedist is confronted with problems of medical ministry when he is dealing with cripples; finally, the dermatologist dealing with disfigured patients, the physician dealing with incurables, and the gynecologist dealing with steriles must participate in this ministry.

Not only the neuroses, but also the psychoses have, in the course of time, not increased but have remained surprisingly constant. Here again there have been changes of aspect, different symptoms. I should like to illustrate this point with the condition known as masked depression: Only one generation ago the mask consisted of obsessional scruples, that is to say, guilt feelings and self-reproaches. Nowadays, however, the symptomatology is dominated by hypochondriacal complaints. Well, a condition of depression is sometimes attended by delusional ideas. It is interesting to note how the contents of these delusions have changed in the course of the last few decades. One is left with the impression that the delusional ideas of our patients are shaped by the spirit of the age and change with it; that therefore the spirit of the age makes itself felt right into the depth of psychotic mental life. Thus Krantz in Mainz and Von Orelli in Switzerland were able to show that the delusional ideas of today are less dominated by a feeling of guilt—the guilt of man before God—and more by worry over the body, physical health, and working capacity than formerly. We notice time and again how the delusion of sin is replaced by fear of disease or poverty. The patient of our time is less concerned with the state of his morals than that of his finances.

Having glanced at the statistics for neuroses and psychoses, let us turn to those of suicide. There we see that the figures do change in the course of time, but not as the layman would expect. For it is a well-known empirical fact that in times of war and crises the number of suicides decreases. If you asked me for my explanation I should quote what an architect once said to me: The best way to buttress and strengthen a dilapidated structure is to increase the load it has to carry. In fact, mental and somatic strains and burdens—what in modern medicine is known as "stress"—are by no means always and necessarily pathogenic or disease producing. We know from our experience with neurotics that relief from stress is potentially at least as pathogenic as the imposition of stress. Ex-prisoners of war, former concentration camp inmates, and refugees all had to contend with great suffering, yet under the pressure of circumstances were not only forced but were also able to do their utmost, to give their best; these people were psycho-hygienically in grave danger as soon as the stress was taken from them—by sudden release. In this connection I am always reminded of the disease called "the bends," which afflicts divers who are brought up too quickly to the surface from regions of increased pressure.

Let us return to the fact that the incidence of neuroses—at least in the precise clinical sense of the word—has not increased. This means that the clinical neuroses have by no means become collective and do not threaten to engulf mankind as a whole. But we can also put it in a more cautious way: It just means that what we are justified in calling collective neuroses are not necessarily the same as neurotic conditions in the narrower clinical sense of the word!

Having made these limitations clear, let us now turn to those traits in the character of contemporary man, which may be termed neurosis-like, "similar to neuroses." Well, the "collective" neurosis of our time shows, according to my experience, four main symptoms:

1) An ephemeral attitude toward life. In the last war, man learned—by necessity—to live from one day to another; he never knew whether he would see the next dawn. Since the war, this attitude has remained with us and it appears justified by the fear of the atom bomb. People seem to be in the grip of a mid-century mood, the slogan of which is: *"Après moi la bombe atomique."* And thus they have given up the idea of planning far ahead or of organizing their lives around a definite purpose. The man of today lives provisionally, lives from one day to the other, and is not aware of all that he is missing thereby. And he is not aware of the truth of a saying of Bismarck: "In life we experience much the same thing as at the dentist; we always believe the real thing is yet to come, and meanwhile it has already happened." Let us take as our models many a person in the concentration camp. For a Rabbi Jonas, for a Dr. Fleischmann, and for a Dr. Wolf even the camp life was not provisional. They never regarded it as a mere episode. For them it was rather the confirmatory test and became the high point of their existence.

2) A further symptom is the fatalist attitude toward life. Ephemeral man says: There is no need to plan my life since the atom bomb will explode one day in any case. Fatalist man says: It is not even possible. He tends to consider himself a plaything of external circumstances or internal conditions and therefore lets himself be shifted around. But he himself does some shifting as well—he shifts the guilt onto this or that, all according to the teachings of contemporary

nihilism. Nihilism has held a distorting mirror with a distorted image in front of his eyes, according to which he seemed to be either a psychic mechanism, or simply a product of economic environment.

I call this sort of nihilism "homunculism," for man misinterprets and misunderstands himself as a product of environment, of his psycho-physical makeup. This latter view can be well supported by the popular interpretations of psychoanalysis which appear to supply plenty of arguments in favor of fatalism. A depth-psychology, which considers its main task to be that of "unmasking" comes in most handy for the neurotic's own tendency toward "devaluation." At the same time we must not neglect the fact pointed out by the well-known psychoanalyst Karl Stern when he said: "Unfortunately, the reductive philosophy is the most widely acclaimed part of psychoanalytical thought. It harmonizes so excellently with a typical petit bourgeois mediocrity, which is associated with contempt for everything spiritual."[2] Well, the contempt for everything pertaining to the spirit and religion in particular is made very easy for the contemporary average neurotic by the help of a mis-conceived psychoanalysis. With all due respect for the genius of Sigmund Freud and his pioneering achievement, we must not close our eyes to the fact that Freud himself was a child of his time and not independent of the spirit of his age. Surely, Freud's consideration of religion as an illusion or an obsessional neurosis and God as a father-image was an expression of that spirit. But even today, after some decades have passed, the danger of which Karl Stern warned us should not be underestimated. With all that, Freud himself was by no means the man to look down on everything spiritual and moral. Did he not say that man was not only often much more immoral than he believed but also much more moral than he thought himself to be? I should like to complete this formula by adding that he is often much more

---

[2] K. Stern, *Die dritte Revolution* (Salzburg: Müller, 1956), p. 101.

religious than he suspects. I should not like to exclude even Freud himself from this rule. After all, it was he who once referred to "our God Logos."

Even the psychoanalysts themselves are now feeling something which one might call—in allusion to the title of Freud's book *Civilization and Its Discontents*—Popularity and Its Discontents. The word "complex" has become a shibboleth in our days. American psychoanalysts are already complaining that the so-called free associations—after all, part of the basic technique in analysis—have for a long time no longer been really free: The patients know far too much about psychoanalysis even before they come for treatment. And even the patients' dreams can no longer be relied upon by their interpreter. They too have been given a slant, so as to be welcomed by the doctor and fit in with his type of interpretation. This, at least, is being claimed by eminent analysts. So we get a situation—as pointed out by the well-known psychoanalyst Emil Gutheil, editor of the *American Journal of Psychotherapy*—in which patients of Freudians are always dreaming of Oedipus complexes, patients of Adlerians dream of power conflicts, and patients of Jungians fill their dreams with archetypes.

3) After this short reflection on psychotherapy in general and psychoanalysis in particular, we turn again to the collective neurotic character traits in contemporary man and come to the third of the four symptoms: conformist or collectivist thinking. This shows itself when the average man in ordinary life desires to be as inconspicuous as possible, preferring to be submerged in the mass. Of course we must not overlook the essential difference between mass and community. It is this: A community needs personalities in order to be a real community and a personality again needs a community as a sphere of activity. A mass is different; it is only disturbed by individual personalities, and therefore it suppresses the freedom of the individual and levels the personality down.

4) Conformist or collectivist man denies his own personality. The neurotic who suffers from the fourth symptom, fanaticism, denies the personality of others. No one else may prevail. No opinion other than his own can expect a hearing. Yet in actual fact he has no opinion of his own, but simply expresses public opinion—which, so to speak, has him. Fanaticism politicizes humans more and more; while actually politics should rather be humanized. We must not conceal the fact that the first two symptoms, i.e., ephemeral attitude and fatalism, seem to me to be more widespread in the Western world, whereas the two latter symptoms, conformist or collectivist thinking and fanaticism, dominate the Eastern world.

How widespread are these collective neurotic traits among our contemporaries? I asked some of my collaborators to test patients who appeared mentally healthy, at least in a clinical sense, and had only been treated in my clinic for organic-neurological complaints. They were given four questions to ascertain to what extent they displayed any of the four symptoms mentioned. The first question, directed at the ephemeral attitude, was: Do you consider it worthwhile to act, since after all we shall possibly be finished off by the atom bomb one day? The second question, aimed at fatalism, was formulated like this: Do you believe that man is a product and plaything of outer and inner forces and powers? The third question, intended to unmask a tendency toward conformist or collectivist thinking, was: Do you think it is best to make oneself inconspicuous? And finally the fourth, really a trick question: Do you believe that someone who has the best intentions toward his fellowmen is justified in using any means he considers appropriate to achieve his aim? In actual fact the difference between fanatical and humanized politics is this: that the fanatic believes that the end justifies the means, whereas we know that there are means which desecrate even the most sacred ends.

Well, of all these people tested only one single person appeared to be free from all symptoms of collective neurosis; 50% displayed three, if not all four, symptoms.

I have discussed these and similar subjects in North and South America and everywhere they asked me whether I felt that this state of affairs was something restricted to Europe alone. I improvised the following answer: It may be that the Europeans are more acutely endangered by these collective neurotic traits, but the danger itself—and it is the danger of nihilism—is a global one. And in actual fact all the four symptoms can be shown to derive from fear of and flight from freedom and responsibility; yet freedom and responsibility together make man a spiritual being. And nihilism should in my opinion be defined as being weary and tired of the spirit. As this worldwide wave of nihilism rolls forward with increasing momentum, Europe constitutes, so to speak, a seismographic station, registering at an early stage the advancing spiritual earthquake. Maybe the European is more sensitive to the poisonous fumes emanating from nihilism in his direction; let us hope that he is thereby enabled to produce the antidote while there is still time.

I have just spoken about nihilism. In this connection I should like to point out that nihilism is not a philosophy which says that there is only nothing, nihil, and therefore no Being; nihilism is that attitude toward life which says that Being has no meaning. A nihilist is a man who considers Being, and above all his own existence, meaningless. But, apart from this academic and theoretical nihilism, there is also a practical, as it were, "lived" nihilism: There are people—and this is more manifest today than ever—who consider their life meaningless, who can see no meaning in their existence and therefore think it is valueless.

Deep down, in my opinion, man is neither dominated by the will to pleasure nor by the will to power, but by what I call the will to meaning: his deep-seated striving and struggling for a higher and ultimate meaning to his existence. This will to meaning can be frustrated. I call this condition existential frustration and oppose it to the sexual frustration which has so often been incriminated as an etiology of neuroses.

Every age has its neuroses, and every age needs its own psychotherapy. Existential frustration seems to me today to play at least as great a part in the formation of neuroses as formerly the sexual one did. I call such neuroses noögenic neuroses. When a neurosis is noögenic, that is, when it has its roots not in psychological complexes and traumata but in spiritual problems, moral conflicts, and existential crises, then such a spiritually rooted neurosis requires a psychotherapy focusing on the spirit; that is what I call logotherapy—in contrast to psychotherapy in the narrower sense of the word. However, even in a number of neurotic cases which are not noögenic but psychogenic logotherapy is indicated.

Adler has made us conversant with the important part played by what he called the sense of inferiority in the formation of neuroses. Well, it appears to me that today something else is playing at least as important a part, the sense of meaninglessness: not the feeling of being less valuable than others, but the feeling that life has no longer any meaning.

What threatens contemporary man is the alleged meaninglessness of his life, or as I call it, the existential vacuum within him. And when does this vacuum open up, when does this so often latent vacuum become manifest? In the state of boredom. And now we can understand the actual meaning of Schopenhauer's words when he said that mankind was apparently doomed to vacillate eternally between the two extremes of want and boredom. In actual fact, boredom is nowadays giving us—and certainly us psychiatrists—more problems to solve than want, even the so-called sexual want.

This problem of boredom is becoming increasingly topical. For the second industrial revolution, as automation is being called, will probably lead to an enormous increase in the leisure hours of the average worker. And they will not know what to do with all that free time.

But I can see further dangers arising from automation: One day man's understanding of himself might be influenced and endangered. Man might begin to misinterpret himself by analogy with the thinking and adding machine. At first he understood himself as a creature—in the image of his creator, God. Then came the machine age and he began to see himself as a creator—in the image of his creation, the machine: *l'homme machine*, as La Mettrie puts it. And now we find ourselves right inside the age of the thinking and adding machine. In 1954, a Swiss psychiatrist wrote in the Viennese Journal of Neurology: "The electronic computer differs from the human mind only in that it works comparatively without a hitch—which can unfortunately not be said about the human mind." Here lies in wait the danger of a new homunculism. The danger that man may once more misunderstand and misinterpret himself as a "nothing but." According to the three great homunculisms—biologism, psychologism, and sociologism—man was "nothing but" either an automaton of reflexes, a bundle of drives, a psychic mechanism, or simply a product of economic environment. Nothing but that was left of man, whom the psalmist had called *"paulo minor Angelis"* and had thus placed only just below the angels. The human essence had been removed. Nor should we forget that homunculism can make history—indeed, has already done so. We have only to remember how in recent history the conception of man as "nothing but" the product of heredity and environment or, as it was then termed, "Blood and Soil" pushed us all into historical disasters. In any case, I believe it to be a straight path from that homunculist image of man to the gas chambers of Auschwitz, Treblinka, and Maidenek. The corruption of man's image by automation is still a distant danger; but after all it is our task as doctors not only, whenever possible, to recognize and, where necessary, to treat diseases, including diseases of the mind and even diseases of the spirit of our age, but also to prevent them, whenever possible; and therefore we must be permitted to raise our voices in warning.

I was saying before that existential frustration, the lack of knowledge about a meaning to existence which alone can make life worth living, is capable of creating neuroses. Well, I described what I called the neurosis of unemployment. In recent years another form of existential frustration has become increasingly urgent: the psychological crisis of retirement. This will have to be dealt with by psycho-gerontology or gerontopsychiatry.

To direct one's life toward a goal is of vital importance. When the professional task is no longer there, other life tasks must be found and, therefore, sought. In my opinion, it is the first and foremost aim of psychohygiene to stimulate man's will to meaning by offering him possibilities of meaning. And these exist outside the professional sphere as well. Nothing helps man to survive[3] and keep healthy like the knowledge of a life task. Thus we understand the wisdom in the words of Harvey Cushing as quoted by Percival Bailey: "The only way to endure life is always to have a task to complete." I myself have never seen such a mountain of books waiting to be read as that on the desk of the ninety-year-old Viennese professor of psychiatry, Josef Berze, whose theory of schizophrenia many decades ago contributed so much to research in that field.

The spiritual crisis of retirement constitutes, so to speak, a permanent unemployment neurosis. But there is also a

---

[3]The American psychiatrist J. E. Nardini ("Survival Factors in American Prisoners of War of the Japanese," *The American Journal of Psychiatry*, 109: 244 [1952]) pointed out that American soldiers taken prisoner by the Japanese were more likely to survive their miserable life situation if they had a positive view of life directed toward a goal worthy of survival.

temporary, periodical one, the Sunday neurosis: a depression which afflicts people who become conscious of the lack of content in their lives—the existential vacuum—when the rush of the busy week stops on Sunday and the void within them suddenly becomes manifest.

Usually, of course, existential frustration is not manifest, but latent and masked, and we know the various masks and guises under which it appears.

In "Executive's Disease" the frustrated will to meaning is vicariously compensated by the will to power. The professional work into which the executive plunges with such maniacal zest only appears to be an end in itself: Actually it is a means to an end, that of self-stupefaction. What the old scholars used to call "horror vacui" exists not only in the realm of physics but also in that of psychology; man is afraid of his inner void, of the existential vacuum, and runs away into work or into pleasure. The place of his frustrated will to meaning is taken by the will to power, though it be just economic power, that is to say, the most primitive form of the will to power, the will to money.

Things work differently in what I call Mrs. Executive's Disease. While the executive has too much to do and therefore not enough time for a breather or a meeting with himself, the wives of many executives do not have enough to do and therefore have more time on their hands than they know what to do with. Least of all do they know what to do with themselves. They, too, seek to stupefy themselves when faced with existential frustration; only they do it by drugging themselves—even literally—with the help of alcohol. For the work mania of their husbands they substitute dipsomania: They flee from their inner void to cocktail parties, to gossipy social parties, and to bridge parties.

Their frustrated will to meaning is thus compensated not by the will to power—as is the case with their husbands—but by the will to pleasure. This pleasure can, of course, also be sexual. We often notice that existential frustration can lead to sexual compensation; that apparent sexual frustration hides a real background of existential frustration. Sexual libido only becomes rampant in the existential vacuum.

Besides work mania, dipsomania, gossip mania, and gambling mania, there is another possibility of escaping from the inner void and the existential frustration: the craze for speed. And here I want to clear up a widespread misunderstanding: The pace of our age, which is made possible, but not necessarily produced, by technical progress, is a source of disease only on the physical plane. It is known that in the last few decades far less people have perished by infectious diseases than ever before. But this "deficit of death" is richly made up for by fatal road accidents. On the psychological plane, however, the position is different: The speed of our age is by no means as productive of disease as is often assumed. On the contrary, I consider the pace, the haste of our times, to be rather an attempt— albeit an unsuccessful one—to cure ourselves of existential frustration. The less a man is able to discover a goal for his life, the more he speeds the pace of his living.

I regard the attempt to drown the existential vacuum with the noise of engines as the *vis a tergo* of motorization which is increasing so rapidly. Not only the feeling of meaninglessness, but also the feeling of inferiority in the most banal sense of the word can be compensated for by motorization. Does not the behavior of so many motorized parvenus remind us of what the animal psychologists term behavior intended to impress?

A vehicle is frequently bought in order to compensate for a feeling of inferiority: The sociologists call that prestige consumption. I know of a patient, a big industrialist, who presented the classical picture of Executive's Disease. His entire life was dominated by one single desire to the point where he overworked himself and thereby ruined his health; although he possessed a sports plane, he was not satisfied, but wished for a jet plane. Apparently his existential vacuum was so great that it could only be overcome by supersonic speed.

We have spoken of the psycho-hygienic danger to man presented in our days by "lived" nihilism and a homunculist image of man; well, psychotherapy will be able to banish this danger only if it can keep itself free from a homunculist image of man. But it will remain homunculist and nothing but a caricature of man as long as it considers him as "nothing but" a being that is "driven" or just satisfies the conflicting claims of id and superego by compromise.

Man is not "driven," man decides. Man is free. But we prefer to speak of responsibility instead of freedom. Responsibility implies something for which we are responsible—namely, the accomplishment of concrete, personal tasks and demands, the realization of that unique and individual meaning which every one of us has to fulfill. Therefore, I consider it misleading to speak of self-fulfillment and self-realization. Only in the degree to which man accomplishes certain specific tasks in the surrounding world will he fulfill himself. Thus not *per intentionem* but *per effectum*.

Similar conditions prevail with regard to the will to pleasure. It must fail, since it contradicts and even opposes itself. We can see that time and again in sexual neuroses: The more a man strives for pleasure the less pleasure he achieves. And vice versa: The harder a man tries to evade unpleasure, or suffering, the deeper he plunges himself into additional suffering.

We have seen that there exists not only a will to pleasure and a will to power but also a will to meaning. Now we see further: We have not only the possibility of giving a meaning to our life by creative acts and beyond that by the experience of Truth, Beauty, and Kindness, of Nature, Culture, and human beings in their uniqueness and individuality, and of love; we have not only the possibility of making life meaningful by creating and loving, but also by suffering—so that when we can no longer change our fate by action, what matters is the right attitude toward fate. Where we can no longer control our fate and reshape it, we must be able to accept it. For the creative shaping of our fate we need courage; for the right kind of suffering, when faced with inevitable and unchangeable fate, we need humility. Even a man who finds himself in the most dire distress —distress in which neither activity nor creativity can bring value to life nor experience give meaning to it—such a man can still give his life meaning by the way and manner in which he faces his fate, in which he takes his suffering upon himself. Precisely in this way he has been given a last chance to realize values.

Thus, life has a meaning to the last breath. The possibility of realizing what I call attitudinal values—by the very attitude with which we face our suffering—is there to the very last moment. Now we can understand the wisdom of Goethe when he said: "There is no condition which cannot be ennobled either by a deed or by suffering." But we should add that the right kind of suffering is in itself a deed, nay, the highest achievement which has been granted to man.

Yet the meaning of human existence is threatened not only by suffering but also by guilt—and death. That which causes our guilt, for which we are responsible, can no longer be changed; but the guilt itself can be redeemed and here again everything depends on the right attitude toward ourselves—upon true repentance. (I am not referring to the cases where damage caused can be undone by expiation.)

And what about death—does it not completely cancel the meaning of our life? By no means. As the end belongs to the story, so death belongs to life. If life is meaningful, then it is so whether it is long or short, whether a man can live in his children or dies childless. If the meaning of life consisted in reproduction, then every generation would find its meaning only in the next generation. Hence, the problem of meaning would be postponed from one generation to another but never solved. If the life of each generation of men has no meaning, is it not likewise meaningless to perpetuate something that has no meaning?

We have seen that life, every life, in every situation and to the last breath, has a meaning, retains a meaning. This is equally true of the life of a sick person, even the mentally sick. The so-called life not worth living does not exist. And even the manifestations of psychosis conceal a real spiritual person, unassailable by mental disease. Only the possibilities of communication with the outside world are inhibited by the disease; but the nucleus of man remains indestructible. And if this were not the case, it would be futile to be a psychiatrist.

When I was in Paris seven years ago for the first World Congress of Psychiatry, I was asked by Père Beirnaert whether I, as a psychiatrist, believed that idiots could become saints. I answered in the affirmative. But more than that, I told him that the very fact, horrible as it is, of having been born an idiot could be an occasion and a chance to prove oneself so well—by an inner attitude—that one might well be tantamount to a saint. Of course, other persons, even we psychiatrists, would hardly notice anything, since the very possibility of manifesting the self outwardly would be blocked by mental disease. Only God can know how many saints were concealed behind the miens of idiots. But then I asked Père Beirnaert whether it was not intellectualist self-conceit even to doubt this possibility. Did not doubting it mean supposing that saintliness or any moral qualifications of man were dependent on his I.Q., so that one might for instance say: Below an I.Q. of 90 there is not a chance. And another thing: Who would doubt that a child has, or rather is, a personality? Yet what else is an idiot but a man who is infantile and has thus remained a child?

There is, therefore, and I hope I have shown it, no reason to doubt the meaning of even the most miserable life. Life has an unconditional meaning and we need an unconditional *belief* in it. This is more essential than ever in a time like ours, when man is threatened by existential frustration, by frustration of the will to meaning, by the existential vacuum.

But psychotherapy can only have an unconditional belief in the meaning of life, every life, if it starts with the right kind of philosophy, if it chooses the right philosophy. Thus we understand how Waldo Frank could write in an American journal that logotherapy gave testimony to the efforts everywhere to supplant the unconscious invalid philosophical hypotheses of the Freudians and Adlerians by a conscious philosophy. Modern psychoanalysts, particularly in the United States, have already understood and agreed that a psychotherapy without a conception of the world, without a hierarchy of values, however unconscious, cannot exist. It is all the more important to make the psychoanalyst himself conscious of his often unconscious image of man. A psychoanalyst of all people should realize the dangers of leaving it unconscious. In any case, the only way for him to straighten his image of man, distorted as it was by the influences of the past century, is to realize that what he has often taken as a starting point is really a caricature of man and not a true image and that it is necessary to correct his image of man.

That is precisely what I have attempted to do with existential analysis and logotherapy: to supplement, not to supplant, the existing psychotherapy and, thereby, to make the underlying image of man into a whole, a total image of true man, an image in all its dimensions, thus doing justice to that reality which belongs only to man and is called existence.

I am quite aware of the fact that you may now reproach me for having produced a caricature of that image of man which I have contended I would correct. And perhaps there is something in it. Perhaps I have really been one-sided; perhaps I have exaggerated when I sensed the threatening danger of nihilism, of homunculism, as I called it, behind many a theory and unconscious philosophical system of modern psychotherapy; perhaps I am really hypersensitive to the slightest suggestion of nihilism. But if that is the case, please understand that I am so hypersensitive only because I have had to overcome nihilism within myself. And that is perhaps why I am so capable of smelling it out, wherever it may hide.

And if I may be allowed to tell tales out of the school of my own existential self-analysis, perhaps I can see the mote in the other's eyes so well because I have had to tear the beam out of my own.

Existential Analysis and
Dimensional Ontology[1]

XI

Existential analysis (*Existenzanalyse*) and logotherapy are really the same, insofar as both represent a certain aspect of one and the same theory.[2] However, *Existenzanalyse* should not be confused with *Daseinsanalyse,* even though both of these German terms have been translated into English as "existential analysis."[3]

Existential analysis and daseinsanalysis both strive for something like the illumination of existence (*Existenzerhellung,* Karl Jaspers). The accent of daseinsanalysis, however, is placed on the illumination of existence understood in the sense of being. Existential analysis, on the other hand, over and above all illumination of *being,* dares to make the

[1] Abridgment and revision of a paper read before the Fourth International Congress of Psychotherapy, Barcelona, Spain, September 5, 1958.

[2] Edith Weisskopf-Joelson, "Logotherapy and Existential Analysis," *Acta Psychotherapeutica,* 6: 193 (1958).

[3] Paul Polak, "Frankl's Existential Analysis," *American Journal of Psychotherapy,* 3: 517 (1949).
The term "existential analysis" as used in the present paper applies only to the theory developed by Dr. Frankl, while the term daseinsanalysis applies to the theory of Ludwig Binswanger. Quite independently of the endeavors of Binswanger which were later formulated as *Daseinsanalyse,* Dr. Frankl began to speak of *Existenzanalyse* as early as 1932 and used the term in publications beginning in 1939. [Editor's note.]

advance to an illumination of *meaning*.[4] The accent thus shifts from an illumination of ontic-ontological realities to an illumination of the possibilities of meaning. That is perhaps why existential analysis supersedes each bare analysis and is a therapy, viz., logotherapy, whereas daseinsanalysis, at least according to the definitions given by leading daseinsanalysts themselves, does not in itself represent a (psycho-) therapy in the true sense of the word. As Medard Boss writes: "Daseinsanalysis has nothing to do with psychotherapeutic practice."[5] Logos first of all signifies meaning. Thus logotherapy is a psychotherapy that is oriented toward meaning and reorients the patient toward meaning.

Ludwig Binswanger's daseinsanalysis amounts to an ontologizing of Alfred Adler's tenet of tendentious apperception. Daseinsanalysis (which is sometimes, perhaps more rightly, called onto-analysis) sets out to lay bare what it calls the a priori structure of *Daseinsgestalten*. This refers to the specific mode of being-in-the-world which corresponds to a specific subjective mode of experiencing the world. What Adler called the person's style of life, of which tendentious apperception, the subjective mode of experiencing the world, is an aspect, represents the same general idea.

I am aware that daseinsanalysts would abhor speaking of a "subjective mode of experiencing," for this would presuppose an objectively given world. Logotherapy, however, holds that no matter how subjective (or even pathologically distorted) the segment we are "cutting out" of the world (which as a whole always remains inaccessible to a finite spirit) may be, nonetheless it is cut out of the objective world. The typical daseinsanalytic terminology

---

[4]Paul Polak, "Existenz und Liebe: Ein kritischer Beitrag zur ontologischen Grundlegung der medizinischen Anthropologie durch die 'Daseinsanalyse' Binswangers und die 'Existenzanalyse' Frankls," *Jahrbuch für Psychologie und Psychotherapie*, 1: 355 (1953).

[5]"Die Bedeutung der Daseinsanalyse für die Psychologie und die Psychiatrie," *Psyche*, 6: 178 (1952).

which claims to have closed the gap between subjectivity and objectivity seems to me to be self-deceptive. Man is neither capable of bridging such a gap, nor would such an accomplishment be commendable.[6] Cognition is grounded, indispensably, on a field of polar tension between the objective and the subjective, for only on this basis is the essential dynamics of the cognitive act established. I call this dynamics "noödynamics," in contrast to all psychodynamics.

Daseinsanalysis has contributed to our understanding of psychosis. Existential analysis, on the other hand, attempts to be of service to the treatment of neurosis. In this sense, daseinsanalysis and existential analysis are not opposed to each other, they rather complement each other. To further the understanding of psychosis, daseinsanalysis focuses upon the unity of being-in-the-world (*In-der-Welt-sein*, Martin Heidegger), while existential analysis emphasizes the manifold character of body-mind-spirit within the unity of human existence. It does this in order to be able to appeal to what is called in logotherapy the defiant power of man's spirit (*Trotzmacht des Geistes*). If the spiritual person were allowed to be dissolved in a neutral noëtic-psychic-somatic existence, as occurs in daseinsanalysis, then to what could such an appeal be made? Whose defiant power could be appealed to? How could such an appeal be made when the distinction between the spiritual[7] person and the pathological process has been denied in favor of a monistic picture of man? The psychotic individual, whose unique mode of being-in-the-world daseinsanalysis sets out to clarify so successfully, is so dominated by, and imprisoned within, this existential mode that it is necessary to speak of an infiltration of psychosis into the individual's existence.

---

[6]Even the most intimate togetherness of two beings, i.e., love, does not do away with the otherness of both beings. If this were the case, the subject would immediately lose the object toward whom to transcend himself. Love—the very paradigm of human self-transcendence and coexistence—may bridge existences but cannot merge them.

[7]The use of this term by no means implies a religious connotation.

According to daseinsanalysis, there is no way for the psychotic individual to get out of his psychotic skin, his peculiar mode of being-in-the-world.

Existential analysis attempts to be not only an analysis of the concrete person, that is, an analysis in the ontic sense, but also an analysis in the ontological sense; in other words, it attempts to be an analysis and explication, an unfolding of the essence of personal existence, apart from the self-unfolding of personal existence as this happens in life and is made visible in biographies.

What does existence mean? It means a certain kind of being—the specific manner of being of which man and man alone is capable. One characteristic of human existence is its transcendence. That is to say, man transcends his environment toward the world; but more than this, he also transcends his being toward an *ought*. When he does this, he rises above the level of the somatic and the psychic and enters the realm of the genuinely human. This realm is constituted by a new dimension, the noetic, the dimension of the spirit. Neither the somatic nor the psychic alone represent the genuinely human; they represent only two sides of the human being. Thus there can be no talk of a parallelism in the sense of dualism, nor of an identity in the sense of monism. Nevertheless, in spite of all the ontological variations of the somatic, psychic, and noetic, the anthropological unity and wholeness of a human being are preserved and saved as soon as we turn from an analysis of existence to what I call dimensional ontology.[8]

Rising spiritually above one's own psychophysical condition might also be called the existential act. By this very act man opens and enters the noölogical dimension of being; nay, he even creates this dimension as a dimension of its own. But this does not in the least detract from the fact

---

[8]V. E. Frankl, "On Logotherapy and Existential Analysis," *American Journal of Psychoanalysis*, 18: 28 (1958).

that humans and animals have the biological[9] and the psychological dimensions in common. It is true that the animal-like properties in man are stamped by his humanness, but this does not mean that he stops being an animal any more than an airplane stops being an airplane when it moves on the ground in much the same way and manner as a motor car. On the other hand, the airplane will not prove to be a true airplane until it rises into the air, into the dimension of space. The same holds true for man. In a sense, he remains an animal, and yet he infinitely surpasses his animal properties. As the airplane becomes an airplane only by rising into the third dimension, so man manifests his humanness only by emerging into the noölogical dimension, or transcending himself.

As you see, I am speaking of dimensions and not, as has formally and generally been done, of layers of being. For, in my opinion, the only way to cope with the age-old psychophysical problem in man without disrupting his wholeness and unity seems to be this approach which I have termed dimensional ontology. This means that we no longer speak of the physical, psychical, and spiritual layers, because as long as we do so it would appear that the layers could be separated from one another. On the other hand, if we try to understand body, psyche, and mind as different dimensions of one and the same being, its wholeness is not in the least destroyed. Such a dimensional interpretation

---

[9]Paying due tribute to the biological foundation of human existence is as legitimate in theory as the recognition of therapeutic resources obtainable through drug treatment and shock treatment is in practice. As for the latter, it is certainly indicated in severe cases of endogenous depression. I do not think it justified to withhold from a patient suffering from endogenous depression those opportunities of relief which are offered by ECT. The problem is different in a case of psychogenic, or neurotic, depression. Then ECT or drugs may well be contraindicated. It would be a sort of pseudo-therapy which blurs the etiology in much the same way that morphine does in a case of appendicitis. But let us not forget that this also holds for psychotherapy, e.g., in those cases for which I have coined the term "noögenic."

refrains from seeing the whole phenomenon as though it were composed of many elements.

Let me demonstrate by an example. A glass on the table, if projected out of three-dimensional space into a two-dimensional plane, would appear as a circle. The same glass projected into its side view and seen in profile would appear as a rectangle. But nobody could claim that the glass is composed of a circle and a rectangle. Neither can we claim that man is composed of parts, such as a body and a soul. It is a violation of man to project him out of the realm of the genuinely human into the plane of either soma or psyche.

This image of dimensions and projections enables us to grasp the simultaneity of man's wholeness and unity on one hand and, on the other, the differences between bodily, psychic, and mental processes. Art has been defined as unity in diversity. Something analogous, I would say, holds for man inasmuch as he could be defined as diversity in unity. For, in fact, there are manifold dimensions involved in being human, and psychotherapy must follow man into all these dimensions. None of these dimensions must be neglected, neither the somatic nor the psychic nor the noetic. Psychotherapy must not disregard its own metaclinical problems, nor should it quit the firm ground of empirical facts and clinical data. If it wanders off to esoteric heights, we must call it back and bring it down to earth.

A dimensional approach offers, as far as I can see, the only chance of understanding some apparent contradictions. I just want to draw your attention again to the analogy with which we started. Although the glass is an open vessel, its outline shows a closed circle. Dimensionally viewed, however, it becomes clear that this contradiction is but an apparent one, as well as that this apparent contradiction must necessarily occur. Now, it is the same thing with man. In the frame of neurology, for example, man necessarily appears as "nothing but" a "closed" system of physiological reflexes without any place left for something like the self-transcendent quality of human existence. We must beware of the self-deception that this dimension of neurology is the only one which exists.

Wherever we open the book of reality, we find it full of contradictions; reality is portrayed differently on each page. Let me illustrate this by an optical image. Here are a

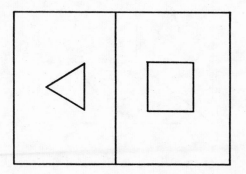

rectangle and a triangle set side by side. Even when we turn the page so that the two figures are superimposed, they

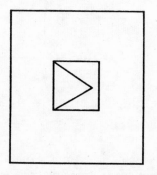

remain incongruous. Only when we include the next higher dimension and set the page with the triangle upright so that it is perpendicular to the page with the rectangle, do the contradictions resolve themselves. For we see that these two

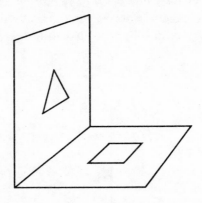

figures represent two different planes of the projection of a pyramid.

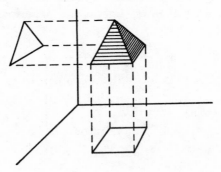

To a certain extent, it is in the nature of science to undertake a projection. In principle, science must methodically disregard the full dimensionality of reality and be based upon the indispensable fiction of a unidimensional world. Science must even treat man in this way; it must project him out of the noölogical dimension. If, for example, I examine a patient neurologically because he is suspected of having a brain tumor, then I must, of course, act "as if" he existed only in this dimension. But when I put my reflex hammer aside, I broaden my view again, and can again become aware of the human quality of the patient.

In like fashion, it may be legitimate to project man out of the noölogical dimension, not into the dimension of the biological (as in the case of the neurological examination), but into the psychological dimension. This happens, for example, within the framework of psychodynamic investigation. Yet, if this does not occur with a full consciousness that a specific methodological approach has been chosen, then it can completely lead us astray. Above all, we must bear in mind all that we have thereby filtered out; for, in an exclusively psychodynamic approach, certain human phenomena will entirely escape us. We need to think here only of things like meaning and value; they must disappear from our field of vision as soon as we consider instincts and dynamics as the only valid criteria, and indeed they must for the simple reason that values do not drive—they pull. A great difference exists between driving and pulling, which we must recognize whenever we seek, in the sense of a phenomenological analysis, an access to the total, unabridged reality of being human. In an exclusively psychodynamic approach, the genuinely human is necessarily portrayed in distortion.

Freud was enough of a genius as to be aware that his system was bound to a certain dimension of human existence and, for instance, in a letter he addressed to Ludwig Binswanger, he expressed this awareness and confessed that he had "always confined" himself "to the ground floor and basement of the edifice." He fell prey to reductionism only after expressing his belief that he had "already found a place for religion, by putting it under the category of the neurosis of mankind."[10]

We think of logotherapy as a supplement rather than a substitute for psychotherapy in the narrow sense of the word. But in addition, logotherapy might also make a contribution toward the completion of psychotherapy's picture of man, toward a picture of man in all his dimensions, toward a picture that also includes the genuinely human, that is, the noölogical dimension.

If psychotherapy is to remain therapy and not become a symptom within the pathology of the time (*Zeitgeist*), then it needs a correct picture of man; it needs this at least as much as it needs an exact technique.

[10]Ludwig Binswanger, *Sigmund Freud: Reminiscences of a Friendship* (New York: Grune & Stratton, Inc., 1957), pp. 96, 99.

Paradoxical Intention:
A Logotherapeutic Technique[1]

XII

Since the psychotherapeutic process consists of a continuous chain of improvisations, the extent to which psychotherapy can be taught and learned has frequently been questioned. In addition, one must bear in mind that the infinite diversity of patients precludes the possibility of extrapolating from one patient to another. Thus, the psychotherapist is always faced with the seemingly impossible twofold task of considering the uniqueness of each person, as well as the uniqueness of the life situation with which each person has to cope. Nevertheless, it is precisely this *individualization* and *improvisation* which must be taught and must be learned.

The choice of an appropriate treatment method to be applied in any concrete case depends not only upon the *individuality* of the patient involved but also upon the *personality* of the therapist. The difficulty of the problem lies in the fact that the last two factors must be considered as "unknowns," at least initially. To illustrate this point, I frequently tell my students that the choice of the therapeutic method to be used in a specific situation may be compared to the following algebraic equation: $\psi = x + y,$

---

[1] Read before the American Association for the Advancement of Psychotherapy, New York, February 26, 1960.

wherein ψ is the therapeutic method, x represents the individuality of the patient, and y stands for the physician involved.[2]

This equation highlights the fact that the crucial agency in psychotherapy is not so much the method, but rather the relationship between the patient and his doctor or, to use a currently popular expression, the "encounter" between the therapist and his patient. This relationship between two persons seems to be the most significant aspect of the psychotherapeutic process, a more important factor than any method or technique. However, we should not be disdainful of technique, for in therapy a certain degree of detachment on the part of the therapist is indispensable. In fact, on occasion the human element must be disregarded in order to expedite the treatment.

The therapeutic relationship develops in a polar field of tension in which the poles are represented by the extremes of *human closeness* on the one hand and *scientific detachment* on the other. Therefore, the therapist must beware lest he be beguiled into falling prey to the extreme of considering only one of these. This means that the therapist must neither be guided by mere sympathy, by his desire to help his patient, nor conversely repress his human interest in the other human being by dealing with him merely in terms of technique. The therapist must beware of interpreting his own role as that of a technician, of a *médicin technicien*. This would amount to reducing the patient (in the words of the famous French materialist La Mettrie) to *l'homme machine*.

The question of whether logotherapy includes what might justifiably be spoken of as a therapeutic technique has also been posed. In spite of the fact that this inquiry is frequently accompanied by a measure of doubt, logotherapy

---

[2]No method can claim to be the best. As long as the absolute truth is not accessible to us, we must be content with relative truths which correct each other. What is demanded of us is the courage to be one-sided and to be aware of it.

does utilize a special psychotherapeutic procedure. This method was first set forth by the author in 1946, in *The Doctor and the Soul*,[3] and in a more detailed manner in 1956.[4]

In order to understand fully what takes place when this technique is utilized, we shall use as a starting point a phenomenon which is known to every clinically trained psychiatrist, anticipatory anxiety. It is commonly observed that such anxiety often produces precisely that situation feared by the patient. The erythrophobic individual, for example, who is afraid of blushing when he enters a room and faces a group of people, will actually blush at precisely that moment.

In case histories which display anticipatory anxiety, the fear of some pathologic event (which, ironically, precipitates it), one may frequently observe an analogous phenomenon. This is the compulsion to self-observation. For instance, in cases of insomnia, the patients often report in the anamnesis that they become especially aware of the problem of falling asleep when they go to bed. Of course, this very attention inhibits the sleeping process.

In addition to the fact that excessive *attention* proves to be an intrinsically pathogenic factor with regard to the etiology of neuroses, we observe that in many neurotic patients excessive *intention* may also be pathogenic. Many sexual neuroses, at least according to the findings and teachings of logotherapy, may be traced back to the forced intention of attaining the goal of sexual intercourse—be it the male seeking to demonstrate his potency or the female her ability to experience orgasm. The author has discussed this subject at length in various papers, pointing out that as a rule the patient seeks pleasure intentionally (one might say

[3]V. E. Frankl, *Aerztliche Seelsorge* (Wien: Deuticke, 1946). American edition: *The Doctor and the Soul, An Introduction to Logotherapy* (New York: Alfred A. Knopf, Inc., 1955).
[4]V. E. Frankl, *Theorie und Therapie der Neurosen, Einführung in Logotherapie und Existenzanalyse* (Wien: Urban & Schwarzenberg, 1956).

that he takes the "pleasure principle" literally). However, pleasure belongs to that category of events which cannot be brought about by direct intention but, on the contrary, is a mere side effect or by-product. Therefore, the more one strives for pleasure, the less one is able to attain it. Thus we see an interesting parallel in that anticipatory anxiety brings about precisely what the patient fears, while excessive intention, as well as excessive self-observation with regard to one's own functioning, makes this functioning impossible.

It is upon this twofold fact that logotherapy bases the technique known as *paradoxical intention*. For instance, when a phobic patient is afraid that something will happen to him, the logotherapist encourages him to intend or wish for, even if only for a second, precisely what he fears.

The following clinical report will indicate what I mean:

A young physician came to our clinic because of a severe hidrophobia. He had been troubled by disturbances of the autonomic nervous system for a long time. One day he happened to meet his chief on the street, and as the young man extended his hand in greeting, he noticed that he was perspiring more than usual. The next time he was in a similar situation he expected to perspire again, and this anticipatory anxiety precipitated excessive sweating. It was a vicious circle; hyperhidrosis provoked hidrophobia and hidrophobia, in turn, produced hyperhidrosis. We advised our patient, in the event that his anticipatory anxiety should recur, to resolve deliberately to show the people whom he confronted at the time just how much he could really sweat. A week later he returned to report that whenever he met anyone who triggered his anticipatory anxiety, he said to himself, "I only sweated out a liter before, but now I'm going to pour out at least ten liters!" What was the result of this paradoxical resolution? After suffering from his phobia for four years, he was quickly able, after only one session, to free himself of it for good by this new procedure.

The reader will note that this treatment consists not only in a reversal of the patient's attitude toward his phobia —inasmuch as the usual "avoidance" response is replaced by an intentional effort—but also that it is carried out in as humorous a setting as possible. This brings about a change of attitude toward the symptom which enables the patient to place himself at a distance from the symptom, to detach himself from his neurosis. This procedure is based on the fact that, according to logotherapeutic teaching, the pathogenesis in phobias and obsessive-compulsive neuroses is partially due to the increase of anxieties and compulsions caused by the endeavor to avoid or fight them. A phobic person usually tries to avoid the situation in which his anxiety arises, while the obsessive-compulsive tries to suppress, and thus to fight, his threatening ideas. In either case the result is a strengthening of the symptom. Conversely, if we succeed in bringing the patient to the point where he ceases to flee from or to fight his symptoms, but on the contrary, even exaggerates them, then we may observe that the symptoms diminish and that the patient is no longer haunted by them.

Such a procedure must make use of the unique potentiality for self-detachment inherent in a sense of humor. Along with Heidegger's assertion that "sorrowful concern" (*Sorge*) is the essential feature permeating human existence, and Binswanger's subsequent substitution of "loving togetherness" (*liebendes Miteinandersein*) as the chief human characteristic, I would venture to say that humor also deserves to be mentioned among the basic human capacities.[5] No animal is able to laugh.

As a matter of fact, when paradoxical intention is used, the purpose, to put it simply, is to enable the patient to develop a sense of detachment toward his neurosis by laughing at it. A statement somewhat consistent with this is found in Gordon Allport's book, *The Individual and His Religion*: "The neurotic who learns to laugh at himself may

---

[5]In addition to being a constituent element in man's existence, humor may well be regarded as an attribute of deity. (Cf. Pss. 2: 4, 37: 13, and 59: 8.)

be on the way to self-management, perhaps to cure."[6]
Paradoxical intention is the clinical application of Allport's
statement.

A few more case reports may serve to develop and clarify
this method further:

I once received a letter from a young medical student who had
in the past listened to my clinical lectures on logotherapy. She
reminded me of a demonstration of paradoxical intention that
she had attended and continued: "I tried to apply the method
which you had used in the classroom demonstration to myself.
I, too, suffered continually from the fear that, while dissecting
at the Institute of Anatomy, I would begin to tremble when the
anatomy instructor entered the room. Soon this fear actually did
cause a tremor. Then, remembering what you had told us in
the lecture that dealt with this very situation, I said to myself
whenever the instructor entered the dissecting room, 'Oh, here is
the instructor! Now I'll show him what a good trembler I am—
I'll really show him how to tremble!' But whenever I deliberately
tried to tremble, I was unable to do so!"

Unwittingly and unwillingly, paradoxical intention has
certainly been used all along. One of my American students
who had to take an exam I was giving and in this setting
explain paradoxical intention resorted to the following
autobiographical account:

"My stomach used to growl in the company of others. The
more I tried to keep it from happening, the more it growled.
Soon I started to take it for granted that it would be with me
the rest of my life. I began to live with it—I laughed with others
about it. Soon it disappeared."

Once I encountered the most severe case of stuttering that
I have seen in my many years of practice: I met a man who
had stuttered severely all his life—except once. This
happened when he was twelve years old and had hooked a
ride on a street car. When he was caught by the conductor,

---

[6]New York: The Macmillan Company, 1956.

he thought that the only way to escape would be to evoke his sympathy, and so he tried to demonstrate that he was just a "poor, stuttering boy." But when he tried to stutter, he was utterly unable to do it! Without meaning to, he had practiced paradoxical intention, though not for therapeutic purposes.

Another instance of paradoxical intention with regard to stuttering was reported to me by the chief of the psychiatric department of the University of Mainz in West Germany. When he was in junior high school his class was to present a play. One of the characters was a stutterer, and so they gave this role to a student who actually stuttered. Soon, however, he had to give up the role because it turned out that when standing on the stage he was completely unable to stutter. He had to be replaced by another boy.

Another case which was treated by one of my assistants, Dr. Kurt Kocourek, concerned a woman, Mary B., who had been undergoing various treatment methods for eleven years, yet her complaints, rather than being alleviated, had increased. She suffered from attacks of palpitation accompanied by marked anxiety and anticipatory fears of a sudden collapse. After the first attack she began to fear that it would recur, and consequently, it did. The patient reported that whenever she had this fear, it was followed by palpitations. Her chief concern was, however, that she might collapse in the street. Dr. Kocourek advised her to tell herself at such a moment: "My heart shall beat still faster! I will collapse right here on the sidewalk!" Furthermore, the patient was advised to seek out deliberately places which she had experienced as disagreeable, or even dangerous, instead of avoiding them. Two weeks later, the patient reported: "I am quite well now and feel scarcely any palpitations. The fear has completely disappeared." Some weeks after her discharge, she reported: "Occasionally mild palpitations occur, but when they do, I say to myself, 'My heart should beat even faster,' and at that moment the palpitations cease."

Paradoxical intention may even be used therapeutically in cases which have an underlying somatic basis:

The patient was suffering from a coronary infarct. Subsequently, he developed anxiety as a psychic response to his somatic illness, and this anxiety became so intense that it became his main complaint. He began to withdraw from his professional and social contacts; eventually, he could not bear to leave the hospital where he had been a patient for six months and where a heart specialist was at hand. Finally, the patient was transferred to our hospital and logotherapeutic treatment was begun by Dr. Gerda Becker. The following is a brief summary of tape-recorded comments of the patient:

"I felt very anxious and the pain in my heart region began to trouble me again. Then I asked the nurse to call the doctor. She stopped in for a moment and told me to try to make my heart beat faster and to *increase* the pain and fear until she could return a little later. I tried this and when she came back after about a quarter of an hour, I had to confess to her that, to my great surprise, my endeavors had been in vain—I could increase neither the pain nor the palpitations but, as a matter of fact, both had disappeared! . . . Encouraged by this turn of events, I left the hospital for an hour or so and went for a walk through the streets—something that I had not attempted for more than six months. Upon entering a store I felt a slight palpitation, but as the doctor had suggested, I immediately started saying to myself, 'Try to feel even more anxiety!' Again it was in vain, I simply could not do it! I returned to the clinic happy over my achievement of strolling around alone." We invited the patient to visit us six months later, and he reported that he was free of any complaints and had, meanwhile, resumed his professional work.

Now let us turn to the following case:

Mrs. H. R. had been suffering for fourteen years when she came to the hospital. She was severely handicapped by a counting compulsion as well as the compulsion to check whether or not her dresser drawers were in order and securely locked. She did this by continually checking the contents of the drawers, closing them by a sharp rapping of her knuckles, and finally by attempting to turn the key in the lock several times. Eventually this condition became so chronic that her knuckles were often bruised and bleeding, and the keys and locks on the bureau were ruined.

On the day of her admission, Dr. Eva Niebauer demonstrated to the patient how to practice paradoxical intention. She was shown how to throw things carelessly into her dresser and closet, to try to create as much disorder as possible. She was to say to herself, "These drawers should be as messy as possible!" The result was that two days after admission her counting compulsion disappeared, and after the fourth day, she felt no need to recheck her dresser. She even forgot to lock it— something that she had not failed to do for decades! Sixteen days after hospitalization she felt free of any complaints or symptoms, was very proud of her achievement, and was able to do her daily chores without compulsive repetition. She admitted that obsessive-compulsive ideas occasionally recurred but reported that she was able to ignore them or to make light of them. Thus she overcame her compulsion not by frantically fighting it (which only strengthens it) but, on the contrary, by "making a joke of it"—in other words, by applying paradoxical intention.

A remarkable fact about this case is that after her symptoms had cleared up, the patient spontaneously, during a psychotherapeutic interview, revived some significant memories. She remembered that when she was five years old, her brother had destroyed a favorite doll. Thereafter she began locking her toys in her dresser drawer. When she was sixteen, she caught her sister in the act of putting on some of the patient's best party clothes without her permission. From that time on she always carefully locked up her clothes. Thus, even if we take it for granted that her compulsions were rooted in these traumatic experiences, it is, nevertheless, the radical *change of attitude* toward her symptoms which was therapeutically effective.

Bringing such psychic traumata to consciousness cannot,

at any rate, *in itself* be the appropriate treatment, inasmuch as a method which does not include such a procedure proved to be so efficient. This brings to mind a statement made by Edith Weisskopf-Joelson in her article "Some Comments on a Viennese School of Psychiatry": "Although traditional psychotherapy has insisted that therapeutic practices have to be based on findings in etiology, it is possible that certain factors might cause neuroses during early childhood and that entirely different factors might relieve neuroses during adulthood."[7] The traumata merely provide the contents of the respective obsessions, compulsions, and phobias. Even psychoanalysts are more and more inclined to assume that traumata in themselves do not directly cause neuroses. In some cases, I would dare to say that even the opposite is true: The trauma does not cause the neurosis, but rather, the neurosis makes the trauma reappear. One illustration may serve to clarify this point. A reef that appears at low tide is not the cause of the low tide: rather it is the low tide that causes the reef to appear. Be that as it may, the therapy that we use must be independent of the validity of the etiologic assumptions of any particular neurotic symptoms. Thus Weisskopf-Joelson's comment is pertinent. At any rate, it is interesting to note that more or less "free associations" leading back to the traumatic experiences which produced certain habits and symptoms may occur *after* therapy has brought relief.

Thus we see that paradoxical intention works even in cases in which either the actual *somatic* basis (the patient with the coronary infarct) or the presumed *psychic* cause (the case of Mrs. H. R.) were not touched upon. Paradoxical intention is effective irrespective of the underlying etiologic basis: in other words, it is an intrinsically nonspecific method. According to the author's opinion, based upon clinical experience, in every severe case involving phobic symptoms one has to reckon with an

---

[7]*The Journal of Abnormal and Social Psychology*, 51: 701 (1955).

autonomic-endocrine or an anankastic substructure. This does not entail a fatalistic viewpoint, however, for a full-fledged neurosis is nothing but a superstructure built upon these constitutional elements; it may well be that it can be psychotherapeutically alleviated without necessarily removing, or even taking into account, the underlying basis. Such a therapy is palliative rather than causal. This is not to say that it is a symptomatic therapy, however, for the logotherapist, when applying paradoxical intention, is concerned not so much with the symptom in itself but with the patient's *attitude* toward his neurosis and its symptomatic manifestations. It is the very act of changing this attitude that is involved whenever an improvement is obtained.

This nonspecificity helps to clarify why paradoxical intention is sometimes effective in severe cases. I wish to emphasize "sometimes"; for I do not wish to convey the impression that beneficial results are *always* obtained, nor that paradoxical intention is a universal panacea or a miracle method. On the other hand, I feel obliged to present the range of its applicability and the degree of its effectiveness accurately. I should like to add parenthetically that the percentage of cures or cases improved to a degree that has made further treatment unnecessary is somewhat higher (75.7%) than the figures reported in the literature.[8]

Paradoxical intention is also applicable in cases more complex than those involving monosymptomatic neurosis. The following will demonstrate that even instances of severe obsessive-compulsive character neurosis (in German clinical terminology referred to as anankastic character structure) may be appropriately and beneficially treated by means of paradoxical intention.

The patient was a sixty-five-year-old woman who had suf-

[8]K. Kocourek, E. Niebauer, and P. Polak, "Ergebnisse der klinischen Anwendung der Logotherapie," in *Handbuch der Neurosenlehre und Psychotherapie*, ed. V. E. Frankl, V. E. von Gebsattel, and J. H. Schultz, Vol. III (München and Berlin: Urban und Schwarzenberg, 1959).

fered for sixty years from a washing compulsion of such severity
that she was admitted to our clinic for a period of observation
in order that I might certify her for a lobotomy (which I expected to be the only available procedure for bringing relief in
this severe case).[9] Her symptoms began when she was four years
of age. When she was prevented from indulging her washing
compulsion, she would even lick her hands. Later on she was
continually afraid of being infected by people with skin diseases.
She would never touch a doorknob. She also insisted that her
husband stick to a very complicated prophylactic ritual. For a
long time the patient had been unable to do any housework, and
finally she remained in bed all day. Nevertheless, even there she
persisted in scrubbing things with a cloth for hours, up to three
hundred times or more, and having her husband repeatedly
rinse out the cloth. "Life was hell for me," she confessed.

In the hope of avoiding brain surgery, my assistant, Dr. Eva
Niebauer, started logotherapeutic treatment by means of paradoxical intention. The result was that nine days after admission
the patient began to help in the ward by mending the stockings
of her fellow patients, assisting the nurses by cleaning the instrument tables and washing syringes, and finally even emptying
pails of bloody and putrid waste materials! Thirteen days after
admission she went home for a few hours, and upon her return
to the hospital she triumphantly reported having eaten a roll
with soiled hands. Two months later she was able to lead a normal life.

It would not be accurate to say that she is completely symptom
free, for frequently obsessive-compulsive ideas come to her mind.
However, she has been able to get relief by ceasing to fight her
symptoms (fighting only serves to reinforce them) and, instead,
by being ironical about them—in short, by applying paradoxical
intention. She is even able to joke about her pathologic thoughts.
This patient still kept in contact with the outpatient clinic, for
she continued to need supportive logotherapy. The improvement
in her condition persisted, however, and thus the lobotomy,
which previously had seemed unavoidable, became unnecessary.

---

[9] In this connection I should like to stress my conviction that in some
cases this operation is the only way to help. I have ventured to give such
indications in a few cases and have in no instance regretted my decision.

The author has included a number of cases that were treated by his collaborators rather than by himself. This is not accidental. It serves to indicate that it is the method that works and not the personality of the creator of the method (though, as I pointed out previously, the personal factor must never be neglected).

The reader has undoubtedly noticed, with respect to the above-mentioned case reports, that paradoxical intention is particularly useful as short-term therapy, especially in phobic cases[10] with an underlying anticipatory anxiety mechanism. The following is a remarkable instance of such short-term therapy that was successful in spite of long-standing pathologic manifestations. It is taken from a tape-recorded report of the patient, Mrs. Rosa L.

"Once I had forgotten to lock the door, and when I returned home it was open. That frightened me very much. After that, whenever I left the house, I couldn't get rid of the feeling that the door was still open. I would go back again and again to check. This went on for twenty years. I knew that the obsession was silly, for every time I went back the door would be locked, but I couldn't seem to keep from obeying the impulse. Life became unbearable. Since my interview with Dr. Becker, however, things have changed completely. Whenever I have the compulsion to check whether or not the door is locked, I say to myself: 'What if the door *is* open! Let them steal everything in the whole apartment!' and at that moment I am able to ignore the impulse and go calmly on my way."

Three months later we invited her back to report on her condition. She said: "I feel wonderful; not the slightest obsession. I can't even imagine how I could have had all those thoughts in the past years. *For twenty long years* I was tormented by them, but now they're gone and I'm very happy."

---

[10]At least in some instances, paradoxical intention seems to be effective in cases of psychosis as well; for example, a patient at our hospital reported to one of the doctors at the first interview that she had read about paradoxical intention and had successfully applied it with reference to the "voices" she was hearing. She had taken her acoustic hallucinations for a neurosis!

One should be careful to avoid the impression, held in many psychotherapeutic circles, that short-term therapy necessarily brings short-lived results. The following excerpts from another tape recording will illustrate this point:

"There was practically not one minute during the day when I was free of the thought that I might break a store window. But Dr. Frankl told me to go right up to the window with the intention of smashing it. When I did this, the fear disappeared completely, and I knew that I wouldn't go through with it. It all seems like a dream now; the fears and impulses to do these things have all vanished."

The noteworthy thing about this report is that it was given twenty years after the treatment!

In connection with short-term therapy, I should like to quote Gutheil's statement regarding "the more common illusions of Freudian orthodoxy, such as that the length of therapy is synonymous with the depth of therapy; that the depth of therapy depends on the frequency of interviews; that the results of therapy are proportionate to the length and depth of treatment; that the durability of results corresponds to the length of therapy."[11] Such a warning may point up the fact that paradoxical intention is not as superficial as it may first appear to be. Something is certainly happening at a deeper level whenever it is applied. Just as a phobic symptom originates beneath the surface of consciousness, so paradoxical intention also appears to affect the deeper level. The humoristic formulations of its method are based on a restoration of basic trust in Being (*Urvertrauen zum Dasein*).[12] What transpires is essentially

[11]E. A. Gutheil, discussion of "Emergency Methods of Psychotherapy," by Joost A. M. Meerloo in "Proceedings of the Association for the Advancement of Psychotherapy," *American Journal of Psychotherapy*, 10: 134 (1956).

[12]V. E. Frankl, *Das Menschenbild der Seelenheilkunde, Drei Vorlesungen zur Kritik des dynamischen Psychologismus.* (Stuttgart: Hippokrates-Verlag, 1959), p. 41.

more than a change of behavior patterns; rather, it is an existential reorientation (*existentielle Umstellung*).

It is in this respect that paradoxical intention represents a truly "logo"-therapeutic procedure in the truest sense of the word.[13] Jorge Marcelo David, a logotherapist from Argentina, has pointed out that its use is based on what is called in logotherapeutic terms psychonoëtic antagonism (or, sometimes, *Die Trotzmacht des Geistes*), which refers to the specifically human capacity to detach oneself, not only from the world but also from oneself. Paradoxical intention mobilizes this basic human potentiality for the therapeutic purpose of combating neuroses.

Of course one is bound to find individual differences in the degree to which this ability can be applied. It cannot be used indiscriminately, and the therapist must be aware of its limitation with regard to certain patients and situations.[14] It would undoubtedly be desirable to establish criteria for evaluating the extent to which a specific patient is likely to mobilize his own psychonoëtic antagonism. At any rate, such testing procedures have yet to be devised. The author himself insists that this ability is present in every human being, since it is an essential feature of being human.

With paradoxical intention one enters into the noëtic dimension as the characteristic and constitutive dimension of human existence. Seen from the point of view of logotherapeutic teachings, this dimension, the realm of the spiritual, covers more than merely rational or intellectual processes, although these are certainly included. Because of this inclusion, one can appreciate the statement that Gutheil made in his last paper, "Problems of Therapy in Obsessive-Compulsive Neurosis," namely, that "new therapeutic means must be introduced. . . . Appeal to reason, fruitless

---

[13]Edith Weisskopf-Joelson, "Logotherapy and Existential Analysis," *Acta Psychotherapeutica*, 6: 193 (1958).

[14]V. E. Frankl, in *Critical Incidents in Psychotherapy*, ed. S. W. Standal and R. J. Corsini (Englewood Cliffs, N. J., Prentice-Hall, Inc. 1959).

though it may be in other cases, holds promise in cases of obsessive-compulsive neurosis in which rationalization and intellectualization play so great a part."[15]

This, in turn, leads to another question; namely, whether or not paradoxical intention belongs to one of the persuasive methods, such as that of Paul Dubois, for example. As a matter of fact, since it is not suggested that the patient simply suppress his fears (by the rational conviction that they are groundless), but rather, that he overcome them by exaggerating them, paradoxical intention is the exact opposite of persuasion. The essential dissimilarity of paradoxical intention and suggestive techniques has been brought to our attention by Polak.[16]

As mentioned before, paradoxical intention can also be applied to cases of sleep disturbance. The fear of sleeplessness increases sleep disturbance because anticipatory anxiety completes and perpetuates the vicious circle. In addition, it results in a forced intention to sleep which makes it impossible for the patient to do so. Dubois, the famous French psychiatrist, once compared sleep with a dove which has landed near one's hand and stays there as long as one does not pay any attention to it; if one attempts to grab it, it quickly flies away. But how can one remove the anticipatory anxiety which is the pathologic basis of forced intention? In order to take the wind out of the sails of this specific fearful expectation, we advise the patient not to try to force sleep, since the necessary amount of sleep will be automatically secured by the organism. Therefore, he can safely try to do just the opposite, to stay awake as long as possible. In other words, the forced intention to fall asleep, arising from the anticipatory anxiety of not being able to fall asleep, should be replaced by the paradoxical intention of not falling asleep

[15] *American Journal of Psychotherapy*, 13: 793 (1959).

[16] Paul Polak, *Frankls Existenzanalyse in ihrer Bedeutung für Anthropologie und Psychotherapie* (Innsbruck: Tyrolia-Verlag, 1949).

at all! (Which in turn will be followed very rapidly by sleep.)[17]

In recent years the use of paradoxical intention has been increasingly reported in the literature. Authors from various countries, as well as those collaborating in the work of the Department of Neurology of the Poliklinik of Vienna, have published the results of the clinical application of this technique. In addition to David (Buenos Aires), mention may be made of the assistants of Prof. Kretschmer (Psychiatric University-Clinic of Tübingen), Langen and Volhard, and Prill (Gynecologic University-Clinic of Würzburg), and Rehder (Hamburg). Prof. Bazzi (University of Rome) has even worked out special indicators to enable the psychiatrist to distinguish those cases in which paradoxical intention should be applied and those in which the autogenous training method of Schultz is indicated.[18] At the International Congress for Psychotherapy held in Barcelona in 1958, Ledermann (London) declared: "The results [of logotherapy] are not to be denied. I have found the method helpful in cases of obsessional neurosis." Frick (Bolzano, Italy) goes still further when he states that there are cases of severe obsessive-compulsive neurosis in which a logotherapeutic procedure is the "only therapeutic way." He also refers to some of his cases in which electro-shock treatment had proved in vain, whereas logotherapy alone served in the sense of an ultima ratio. Prof. Lopez-Ibor (University of Madrid) makes a similar statement.

Among my co-workers, in addition to my associates

---

[17]It is noteworthy that this procedure, in cases of insomnia, has subsequently been worked out independently by two other workers in the field. One advises his patients to keep their eyes open as long as possible, while the other recommends to doctors who work with hospitalized patients that they let the patients punch a time clock every quarter hour. He reports that after very few fifteen-minute intervals they succumb to increasing fatigue and sleepiness.

[18]T. Bazzi, Considérations sur les limitations et les contraindications de la logothérapie. (Paper read before the Fourth International Congress of Psychotherapy, Barcelona, Spain, 1958).

Kocourek and Niebauer, who have published papers about paradoxical intention, there was a psychoanalyst whose training and orientation was strictly Freudian. For a year he treated nearly all of the cases of sexual disturbance in the outpatient ward of our hospital and, inasmuch as short-term therapy was indicated, used logotherapeutic procedures exclusively. His experience is summarized in a paper which we collaborated on, and which he read at a German Congress of Sexology.

I have previously stated that a compulsion to self-observation accompanies anticipatory anxiety, and in the etiology of a neurosis one often finds an excess of attention as well as intention. This is especially true in insomnia, in which the forced intention to sleep is accompanied by the forced attention to observe whether the intention is becoming effective or not. This attention thus joins in perpetuating the waking state.

In references to this phenomenon, logotherapy includes a therapeutic device known as "de-reflection." Just as paradoxical intention is designed to counteract anticipatory anxiety, de-reflection is intended to counteract the compulsive inclination to self-observation. In other words, what has to be achieved in such cases is more than trying to *ridicule* the trouble by using paradoxical intention and its humorous formulation; one should also be able to *ignore* the trouble to some degree. Such ignoring, or de-reflection, however, can only be attained to the degree to which the patient's awareness is directed toward positive aspects. De-reflection, in itself, contains both a negative and a positive aspect. The patient must be de-reflected *from* his anticipatory anxiety *to* something else. This conviction is supported by Allport who said: "As the focus of striving shifts from the conflict to selfless goals, the life as a whole becomes sounder even though the neurosis may never completely disappear."[19] Such goals may be discovered by a certain

[19] G. W. Allport, *The Individual and His Religion*, p. 95.

kind of analytic procedure which we call *Existenzanalyse*.[20] In this way the patient may discover the concrete meaning of his personal existence.[21]

Let us, in conclusion, review[22] the indications of paradoxical intention from the perspective of the four characteristic patterns of response toward neurotic problems presented by logotherapy:

1. *Wrong Passivity.* This refers to the behavioral pattern which may be observed in cases of anxiety neurosis or phobic conditions, or both. It is the withdrawal from those situations in which the patient, because of his anticipatory anxiety, expects his fears to recur. What we have to deal with in this case is the "flight from fear"—most commonly, fear of collapsing on the street or having a heart attack.

2. *Wrong Activity.* This behavioral pattern is characteristic, in the first place, of obsessive-compulsive neurosis. The individual, rather than trying to avoid conflict situations, *fights* against his obsessive ideas and neurotic compulsions and thus reinforces them. This struggle is motivated by two basic fears: (a) that the obsessive ideas indicate an imminent, or actual, psychotic condition, and (b) that the compulsions will someday result in a homicidal or suicidal attempt. Another aspect of "wrong activity" may be observed in sexual neurosis—namely, a struggle *for* something rather than *against* something, a striving for orgasm and potency. The underlying motivation is usually as follows: The patient feels that competent sexual

---

[20] V. E. Frankl, "Zur Grundlegung einer Existenzanalyse," *Schweizerische medizinische Wochenschrift*, 69: 707 (1939).

K. Dienelt, *Die Existenzanalyse V. E. Frankls und ihre Bedeutung für die Erziehung* (Wien: Österreichischer Bundesverlag, 1955).

Paul Polak, "Frankl's Existential Analysis," *American Journal of Psychotherapy*, 3: 517 (1949).

[21] V. E. Frankl, "Logos and Existence in Psychotherapy," *American Journal of Psychotherapy*, 7: 8 (1953).

[22] V. E. Frankl, "Logotherapy and Existential Analysis, A Review," *American Journal of Psychotherapy*, 20: 252 (1966).

performance is "demanded" of him either by the partner, by the situation, or by himself, in the event that he may have, so to speak, "scheduled" it for that moment. Due to this very "pursuit of happiness," the sexually neurotic individual founders just as the obsessive-compulsive neurotic does due to responses that are inappropriate to the situation; pressure precipitates counterpressure.

In contrast to these negative, neurotic, "wrong" behavioral patterns, there are two positive, normal ones:

3. *Right Passivity.* This is the case when the patient, by means of paradoxical intention, ridicules his symptoms rather than trying either to run away from them (phobias) or to fight them (obsessive compulsions).

4. *Right Activity.* Through de-reflection, the patient is enabled to ignore his neurosis by focusing his attention away from himself. He is directed to a life full of potential meanings and values that have a specific appeal to his personal potentialities.

In addition to this personal aspect, a social factor is involved as well. More and more we meet individuals who are suffering from what logotherapy calls man's "existential vacuum." Such patients complain that they feel a total and ultimate meaninglessness in their lives. They display an inner void or emptiness in which neurotic symptoms may abound. Filling this vacuum may thus assist the patient in overcoming his neurosis by helping him become aware of the full spectrum of his concrete and personal meaning and value possibilities or, in other words, by confronting him with the "logos" of his existence.

SUMMARY

In the frame of logotherapy or existential analysis (*Existenzanalyse*), a specific technique has been developed to handle obsessive, compulsive, and phobic conditions. This procedure, called paradoxical intention, is based on the fact that a certain amount of pathogenesis in phobias and obsessive-compulsive neuroses is due to the increase of anxieties and compulsions caused by the endeavor to avoid or fight them. Paradoxical intention consists in a reversal of the patient's attitude toward his symptom and enables him to detach himself from his neurosis. This technique mobilizes what is called in logotherapy the psychonoëtic antagonism, i.e., the specifically human capacity for self-detachment. Paradoxical intention lends itself particularly to short-term therapy, especially in cases with an underlying anticipatory anxiety mechanism.

Psychotherapy, Art, and Religion[1]

XIII

It is the task of logotherapy to bring to light the spiritual struggle of the individual; therefore, we must ask ourselves what this struggle is all about. What in this struggle makes the neurotic patient seek assistance in psychotherapy? The following case history shows how the answer to this question emerged during a logotherapeutic treatment.

Two important points must be kept in mind throughout this study. First, if an artist should become psychotic and nevertheless continue his artistic production, he does so in spite of his psychosis, never because of it. A mental disease in itself is never productive, a sickness as such never creative. Only the spirit of man can be creative, never a sickness of that spirit. And yet, confronted with the terrible fate of mental disease, the human spirit can attain the ultimate in creative ability. Similarly, the reverse holds true. Just as we cannot credit the disease as such with creative ability, we must not use the fact of mental disease as an argument against the artistic value of a piece of art. It is never within the competence of the psychiatrist to judge what has value and what has not, what is true and what is false, whether the world view of Nietzsche is true or whether the poems of Hoelderlin are beautiful.

The patient, whose medical record and treatment is

---

[1]Translated by Judith and Joseph Fabry.

presented here, was struggling for two things: her work and God. We must note that the religious problem was not apparent in the beginning of the treatment but spontaneously broke through in its course. This provides additional proof of the validity of a statement I made elsewhere: The physician has neither the moral duty nor the right to interfere with the world view of a patient (since any such interference would be a dictate by virtue of the doctor's authority). It further proves that psychotherapy, handled correctly, will release a patient's religiosity, even if that religiosity was dormant and its release was not at all intended by the therapist.

Our case deals with a middle-aged woman, an artist by profession. The complaints which originally prompted her to seek medical help concerned long-standing "lack of contact with life." "Somehow everything is a fraud," the patient declared. "I urgently need someone to help me out of this vicious circle," she wrote in a self-evaluation. "I'm choking on a great silence. The disorder of my soul keeps growing. The moment comes when one realizes that life has no content, everything has become meaningless, one cannot find a way out of the ruins. But I want to find new meaning for my life."

To all outward appearances the patient seemed perfectly well adjusted to her life, even socially; but she herself sensed how superficial were all her social, artistic, and erotic successes. She commented, "Right now I can exist only by keeping going at a rapid pace. Invitations, concerts, men, books, everything. . . . Whenever this succession of impressions slows down or stops, I face an abyss of emptiness and despair. The theater is just another escape. My painting (the only activity I really am interested in) scares me stiff—like any other deep experience! As soon as I want something very much, it goes wrong. Whatever I love I destroy—every time. I no longer dare love anything. The next time this destruction takes place I'll really hang myself."

The treatment of such a neurosis must start by drawing the attention of the patient to the typical neurotic fatalism: In a generally oriented discussion, she was helped to understand this fatalism, and how far she was free from her past and its influences, not only "free from" the old inhibitions but also "free to" find her special, personal meaning of life in all its uniqueness, and to find her "personal style" in all of her artistic expressions.

When asked about her artistic principles she answered: "I have none, except perhaps one: absolute honesty!" And then: "I paint because I feel driven to it, because I *must* paint. Occasionally, I even feel obsessed by it." Another time: "I don't quite know why I'm painting—all I know is that I have to—that's why I do it." Behind these explanations of the patient lay no playful flirting with the drive that forced her to create: She was not "in love" with this phenomenon which seemed to be close to a disease; she herself said: "I am *afraid* of this obsession." But the fact remained: "It's not a matter of why and what for—only of thirst and inhibitions." To a certain degree she was aware of the "activity" of her unconscious, of this creating out of her own unconscious. She declared, "I don't know anything but to keep working, trying, discarding, and trying again. I don't know anything about the choice of colors, for instance, except that it doesn't depend on the painter's mood. The choice is made in much deeper regions!"

Then followed complaints which later were to lead onto the path to a therapeutic result: "I often dream finished pictures which satisfy me in my dream but which I never am able to reproduce when I'm awake." Here was a lead the therapist could follow. Another time the patient said with passion: "I want to find the picture to which I can say 'yes' with all my heart. I have to escape the force of habit, stop this continuous copying of myself. I have to bring up to consciousness those form creations that dwell within me." One day she asked spontaneously: "I would like to know if one can be creative under hypnosis; if I could then, for instance, free my own experiences and shape them into works of art." She declared herself interested in bringing past impressions up to her conscious. Her artistic conscience, her self-control, even the distrust of her own artistic ability were so sharpened that she went on to ask: "I would like to know how far the surrealists are cheating. Their so-called automatic drawings are no different from the conscious ones."

The patient spoke of dreaming of color compositions which she was unable to reconstruct when awake. At this point it became necessary to relate to her unconscious dream life; thus a modified form of the systematic relaxing exercises ("autogenic training") developed by J. H. Schultz, was used. The patient described what she experienced immediately afterwards: "A feeling of great clarity. One is less conscious of oneself—but all objects are much more distinct. A feeling of freshness, as though a veil had been removed from my eyes. This is quite new. Now I am lying on the couch. Armchair, paper basket, the shadow of the desk —everything is sharp. . . . I am drawing. . . ." These were the notes the patient had put down later.

The next night she had color-form dreams. "My right hand reaches out for a pencil," she wrote. "Something in me tells me to start drawing. This woke me up several times. Finally I tried to calm myself. Slept very quietly then, till nine o'clock."

Following the Schultz formula for making resolutions, and also using posthypnotic commands, the patient started to paint the next afternoon. She reported: "Sketch for a landscape. . . . After a half hour of painting I become suddenly aware that I had been working automatically. A definite feeling of compulsion. . . . I notice that I am painting something quite different from what I thought I wanted to. A feeling of powerlessness. . . . I fight this compulsion—don't want to succumb to it. The last phase:

Some automatic painting alternating with a remnant of critical appraisal and conscious painting, and back again to automatic painting."

Then the notation: "Eyes closed, pencil in hand, I am waiting for pictures. A pink square, white half-moon crescent, dark violet oval, and suddenly the image of a female profile: a powerful light-dark. And—I paint—half-conscious. I see clearly outlined color forms which my hand then traces. I feel that I see them on the canvas, but am not quite sure. In my previous paintings I couldn't say either at what exact moment I had put my visions on the canvas. But now there is a definite difference to my conscious painting. The images are much sharper, and occasionally I work under compulsion. But today I don't fight the compulsion. I am very willing and let myself be led; sometimes I observe the picture with critical eyes, and am happy. When I placed the picture in a smaller frame by trimming top and bottom, I suddenly felt free, light, and clear."

The next day: "I like this picture! I can see two new beginnings in the painting. First, the composition, and second, the handling of my image. The color composition is like the one I wanted for the first 'automatic' picture, but which I couldn't carry out. The picture today is very harmonious." Then: "An art historian, a specialist in modern art, saw the picture today. He said. 'This picture is balanced; in its color composition it is perfect; it is harmonious—different from your usual work!'"

Then a relapse. Her notes said: "I'm no good; I paint as badly as all the others. I don't know what to do: How can I tear the personal images out of my soul? Relaxing exercises at Dr. F. Immediate relief from tension—practically floating. . . . I see scraps of pictures. Oh, to surrender to the colors rising in me, to paint. . . . I shall paint! I am painting—I can smell the colors, I can't wait to go home and work. I want to leave and start painting. I run home. More scraps of pictures; I start sketching—can't do it; no inspiration—the colors are intriguing but they don't relate in space. It gets dark. I have to stop; things to do in the kitchen. As soon as I am in the kitchen, I am able to see! The rolling pin next to the bowl: an exciting relationship between curves and straight lines—an interlacing of lines for which I have been looking for days! Why can't I do it? Because I *want* to, probably." Next day: "I've been exercising regularly by myself. But I just can't paint. I feel inhibited, empty, cold." But then again: "Today Dr. F. once more recommended exercising by myself. I am two bodies; I am separated from my weight; I feel it below and float up to the ceiling. . . .

"Tomorrow I will be able to see with an artist's eyes —tomorrow I will experience new relationships between colors and forms—and the obstacle will be gone." Then: "Slept well. . . . Practiced in the morning. The same resolution as yesterday. Suddenly: Pictures! Afterwards refreshed and optimistic. In the morning, bad news from America, and suddenly everything collapses. I have lost all support. I am all alone, everything is meaningless. What shall I hold on to? Friends are falling away. And, I can't pray. Lie down and die. . . . God will understand. But I mustn't. Strange: Just today I see like an artist. I work a little. I draw. But time and again this inner collapse. It is unbearable. . . . Somehow, I want to carry on my humanness with dignity. Surrender to God, completely, deeply. . . . But I can't do it. It's no good. Everything is lost! Another exercise to relax? But I can't make the switch. However, I do calm down."

So the crisis continued. The next day: "Exercise. Finally, after half an hour, a light trance. My resolution is formulated: Everything is unimportant; what is important is painting—and God. I will be able to pray; I will be able to paint; I am alone, with God and my painting. . . . Mornings and evenings the same exercises." And a day later: "Exercise. Trance comes quickly. Warm, blue air flows through me—my right underarm presses its weight on the

mattress. . . . Resolution: The images I experienced are to
become free again; those long-forgotten images of rare
beauty. I see them again—my most personal impressions.
And this time so clear that I can put them into form. Drew
all afternoon; seeing as an artist. Many ideas, but in such
rapid succession that I could not get them down. Very
optimistic; joyfully excited. Hardly slept." Then, the next
day: "Images rising up in me continuously. But I have to
receive guests, answer the phone—a lot of bustle. But in
between, I painted the landscapes, my very best! At a mad
speed, 'they painted themselves.' Wildly happy. As soon as I
close my eyes one image chases another; memories and
newly emerging pictures of things just seen. Also picture
compositions—very sophisticated color harmonies. Everything moves so fast that I can hardly hold it. To relax me,
an exercise before going to bed. The next day the images
continue. I am very happy! God's grace. . . . Life is beautiful.
Images move by like a reel of film, and I do sleep
wonderfully. In the morning I feel refreshed, healthy, full of
pep. Today I exercised. Immediate feeling of floating. A
kind of transfiguration: I am light. . . . Wonderful to be
nothing but light! It is so wonderful that in today's exercise
I plan nothing. Don't know how long it lasted—anyway,
worked better afterwards. Picture not quite finished—I have
time. I feel very calm, very happy. . . ."

After months in which the patient was definitely
productive and during which she needed only few
consultations with the therapist, she reported: "N. N. [a
famous art critic] looked at the ten pictures and picked one
of them as the best I've ever done. He spoke of a very
personal vision and said: 'These pictures are true art; much
more forceful and personal than your prewar pictures; they
have depth—which the others did not have. Everything is
independent, genuine, and honest; just here and there a
naturalistic remnant.' While during the first weeks of
therapy there were quite a few 'explosions' and regular work

was not possible, I am now able to work on a regular schedule; I again have those clear and steady days of work as before the war, and even without a trance. Work habits are established, and I can say, with clear conscience, that the treatment may be considered completed and successful. Just now when I am facing serious external difficulties, I see how successful was the therapy. I am neither in despair, nor disgusted, nor full of anxiety, nor do I clamor for sympathy; even though I am alone, and know that no one will help me. . . . But I take it as a test and will make the best of it. God watches me—although to say that is probably presumptuous. I am greatly enriched. Once I began to understand, the treatment removed one obstacle after the other, and things were set free. The therapy gave me the best thing one could hope to receive."

Despite an almost pathological degree of self-criticism, the patient was satisfied with her recent work. She felt capable again. Occasionally she did relaxation exercises by herself; when asked about her resolutions she offered this formula: "That everything be released—that my most personal color and form experiences become conscious—and that I be able to put them on canvas."

Now that her ability to work had been restored, a second problem—so far latent in the patient—came to the surface. From this point on, logotherapy had to go beyond the stage it had reached so far; while up to this point the therapy had been something like a midwife to the artist, it now had to become the midwife to the patient's spirit. For it now became the task of logotherapy to clarify, or perhaps to assist, our patient's struggle with the religious problems which had developed quite spontaneously during this period. One might formulate the situation of the psychotherapy at this moment as follows: Of the well-known Benedictine motto, *ora et labora,* the second part had been realized, but what remained to be done was to realize the first.

The patient's notes during that period contained this passage: "Today at dawn, after a deep sleep, I'm suddenly fully awake. The first thought: God flings me to my knees. Once again I experience the loss of my husband and realize how terribly I failed. I knew it then, too, somehow, hazily; but only now I can repent. Today God awoke me. In the morning I went to the Minorite Church. . . . I won't tell what happened during this hour—except that it suddenly occurred to me that four years ago (after the news of my husband's death in the war) I also went to this church. That time I prayed ardently for death. Today I want to live! There is so much to atone for."

Many weeks later the patient made the following entry in her diary: "I try in vain to come to grips with the hidden guilt which I have dimly felt for years but which I cannot clearly face. For, in all this time I haven't permitted myself any faith (faith, especially in God, is no virtue but bliss, grace). What was I doing? Why did I punish myself? I must find out." Thus, the patient assumed that she herself had blocked the path to her faith. On the doctor's advice she then started exercises in which the resolution was formulated as follows: Tonight I will dream what my guilt is. Her report, however, indicated that she was not successful. It is noteworthy, though, that at the same time, on the same piece of paper, she asked the doctor to interpret an old dream—from the days of war—which "still arouses me very much." May we recall here Freud's well-known and important advice to psychologically evaluate childhood memories regardless of whether they are true memories of something that really happened or only attitudes projected into the past from the unconscious—false memories. In this case, it mattered little that the dream did not come as the desired answer to her question to her unconscious. The analytical significance lies in the fact that this old dream was presented to the therapist now, for the first time, in connection with the question the patient was wrestling with.

The contents of the dream: The patient, through a corridor window, watches the door to her apartment and sees a young woman enter. She realizes immediately that this is herself. "The first *I* is looking at the second *I*," she described the situation. "Number two unlocks the door and enters the big room, then turns left—now the walls become transparent—into the little room (now my studio) and walks to the corner with the stove. There a German soldier lies on some straw. The second *I* bends over him and murders him. Then I wake up." We will not go wrong if we see in this past dream the anticipated answer to a question posed much later. We may assume that the patient—by bringing up her dream at just that time—answered her question for the doctor and for herself.

The constant artistic struggle continued, without letup, in self-examination and self-criticism. But again and again the released creative power broke through and "forced" the patient to work, regardless of her self-criticism. She reported: "A still life is ready. Either very bad or pretty good—can't say; I began painting without thinking. Finally I had to notice—the idea is my own. I go on with the Schultz exercises. They work all right, up to the feeling of warmth. But most important: I can pray again! For weeks already. The praying breaks forth all the time—almost against my will. Sometimes it's hard for me to get back to my painting."

These notes seem to prove a genuine, intrinsic struggle for an honest religious effort: "Again and again God becomes inaccessible, intangible. . . . Only in prayer does God come closer. I have to try again and again—to create my God. This seems to be part of being human, but even this was probably the way God wanted to make us. Often I would much rather pray than paint; painting is so much more difficult. But that would be sinful, in any case." Then: "I find God only in joy. But then, I feel ecstasy. I'm still not quite ready to suffer. But each day I learn a little, to sacrifice my Isaac. . . . God wants something of me, I don't exactly know what; it's up to me to find out. Sometimes I could shout, out of joy—life is beautiful, beautiful, beautiful!"

The patient proves as skeptical toward her own painting, as she does toward her religiosity. "Some things I find rather suspicious. For instance, that I come to you with these problems. Women love to adorn themselves with God. I might as well run to a priest." Or: "It's puzzling that I find my way to God just now. . . . I don't care to become the bride of Christ! I don't seek any deals with God! I desire God without eroticism and without hope for justice." Or, another time: "I don't want to love God just because N. N. doesn't care for me. If that's the way my prayers go, I'd rather open up a brothel! Men are here for loving; God I want for—can't express it in words. This much I can see: I should have learned how to suffer properly. I am again suffering the wrong way; but without grace I probably can't suffer meaningfully."

To free the patient of her inhibitions, she was asked if she remembered any frightening religious experiences in her childhood. She related: She was brought up a Catholic, in a lukewarm sort of way. At the age of 14 or 15 she experienced a religious crisis. "Why should the flesh be called sinful? I couldn't understand this. I converted to Protestantism; this signified for me most of all an enjoyable kick in the pants to authority. I don't know when I prayed the last time; the first time I prayed again in a dream, and here I experienced (I purposely say 'experienced') for the first time an image of God: Infinitely bright and incredible, not at all human. . . . No sense in asking God for a favor. The only thing worthy of God: to love God for His own sake."

"Recently, in the middle of the night, for the first time I prayed consciously. It came unexpectedly, not sought for. This certainly was the first real prayer in my life. A prayer which is already fulfillment and not just begging for something."

The patient herself guessed it: She didn't have the courage to believe. She was directed, in an "exercise," to resolve the following: "I will dream tonight about what it is that ties me up in such knots." The next day she reports the following dream: "I desperately try to construct 'the picture.' I don't paint it—I live it!" The interpretation is clear: "The picture" is her entire life which she wants to reconstruct. In the imagery of the dream, life itself has become the picture. Further: "I see a carriage leaving." Upon questioning she indicated that it was horse-drawn, of the kind people had often traveled in when she was a child. To the left of the picture, she recalled, was a strange form "which I desperately want to be whole, but which keeps breaking into pieces. To the right I see a wedge going from top to bottom through the entire picture." In answer to the question, What in your life do you feel disturbed its totality? she promptly responded: the death of her husband. (We see how the circle completes itself. Her feeling that her life was destroyed points in the same direction as the guilt feeling which disturbed her religious faith.) Even before the doctor helped her interpret this dream she had another—we might say, therapeutic—dream supplementing the diagnostic one. She remembered only one thing about this second dream. A feeling of great joy and a voice saying, "Let it sleep—let it sleep—the old pain!"

But the crisis had not yet been conquered. Another ad hoc exercise was necessary, with the resolution: "Tonight I will dream why I feel hostile toward Christianity—what it was that scared me away. And then I will wake up immediately and write it down."

Here is the patient's dream: She is in Waldegg where she had spent her childhood, and she is waiting for a train to Vienna. (By this, the patient recapitulates in her dream the path from her past to the present: She now lives in Vienna.)

Dr. K. N. lives there, and she wants to see him. (Dr. K. N. is a well-known psychotherapist, a friend of the family. This part of the dream means: Psychotherapy is needed.) She doesn't know where the doctor lives. She asks a woman and is told: "Near the church." (The patient is aware that her cure can be completed only in the realm of the religious.) In her dream, the patient knows she will find the church. (She is optimistic about finding her way back to her religious beliefs.) But everything looks different. (Finding the way back to faith is not easy and simple for the adult who has gone through the hells of life and doubt.) Which street to take, she wonders in her dream. (The patient is unsure of which way to choose to recover her faith.) She keeps wandering a long time; she has doubts. . . . (In her dream, the doubts are about the correct way to Dr. K. N.; in reality they are her doubts about God.) Suddenly, a little girl stands before her and gives directions. (During the dream analysis the patient volunteers the information that the little girl was herself in her childhood. She is asked whether she is familiar with the Bible verse, "You must become as a little child," and she affirms it.) The little girl in her dream tells her: "To the church? You have gone in the wrong direction. You must go back." (Again the theme: Before finding the church—salvation, cure—the patient must find her way back to the naïve faith of her childhood.) In her dream, she is thirsty. (During the interpretation the patient confirms that she is well acquainted with the Bible verse, "As the deer longs for water, so my soul longs after Thee. . . ." The child draws clear water from a spring, but the pitcher from which the patient is to drink is dirty. (She is familiar with the passage of my book *The Doctor and the Soul* in which the sexual unfaithfulness of the wife is contrasted to that of the husband, and which uses as a simile a spring and a pitcher.) In the dream, the patient wants to buy a pitcher—hers is broken. (She has repeatedly complained that since her husband is gone she cannot love anyone, but that on the other hand she is in need of someone.) Now, in her dream, she goes back. (This refers to the logotherapeutic treatment.) Suddenly the road is blocked by poplar trees lying across the street. (Difficulties and relapses that have occurred during the treatment.) But then the path is open again, and in the distance stands the church—a beautiful milky-white cathedral like the one in Caen. Then the patient woke up. In subsequent discussions she told of her car trip through Normandy. She had been looking forward to seeing the cathedral of Caen which she knew only from photographs. But she had arrived in Caen at night and during a heavy fog, and never had actually seen the cathedral. The appearance of the never-seen but admired cathedral in her dream signified the transformation which occurred in the patient during her analysis: a transformation of her religious experience from a God hidden by fog and darkness to a revealed God.

A little later another dream: "My face is turned toward the light. Behind me, a deep abyss into darkness. An ice-cold wind blows up from there. And yet I am not afraid, for I belong to God. A wonderful feeling of joy, humility, love, shelteredness. I expect I will have to suffer much, but God is with me. A religious surrender as I have never experienced it before; a definite, secure, and evident oneness with God. Doubts are impossible in this state! To be in God. . . ." And the dream goes on: "A woman tells me: 'You're very dirty—no wonder, after such a long trip.' And I say: 'Yes, and I've also had an operation.' " (The operation would seem to refer to the damage to the totality of her life, mentioned before.) "I feel tired. I'll go home and take a bath." (Again the theme of being dirty.) "Then follow adventures, obstacles which are overcome. I dream an entire novel. But finally I get to my apartment. And, very happily, I furnish it all anew." This dream, a few weeks after the last one quoted, expressed this experience: to be home again and to become clean again.

Following this dream theme, but without conscious connection, the patient wrote in her notes: "I must start from scratch, for I don't know a single prayer. I have forgotten all the rites, have no church to lean on. . . . But to believe in God holds an obligation."

Finally: "I am saved, like in a fairy tale. The treatment gave me back my ability to paint. And I can pray again! Pray more deeply and fervently than ever. This is grace. Am I worthy of it?"

We noted the emerging relationship between an anticipatory dream and life's experiences; now we also see how the theme of the last dream finds fulfillment in her waking life: The patient still struggled for the ultimate purity of her experience: "Am I not making it too easy for myself? Dare I believe? I'm really not worthy to have found meaning." But on the same page of her notes she wrote: "The bliss I feel in my dream I now strongly experience in my waking state, for several days already. Now it has happened. . . . Rest in God—now everything has meaning!"

Thus, the treatment—to quote the words of the patient —had really "brought out of her all that there was to bring out." Soon she learned to find and go her way independently. This was expressed in still another dream: "It's night. I hand a note to a man; an address is written on it. I have to follow him—this is our agreement. At first I'm panting, but then it becomes easy. Finally the man disappears. (This meant, of course, the end of the therapy.) At first I am afraid, but then I become very quiet and think: Why am I getting excited? I know the address. I can find the way alone through the darkness."

But the patient still was not satisfied with this progress nor with herself: "During the past months I had the strongest desire to enter a convent, not actually, but to be alone, to paint, to take things as they come. I now see that this is impossible and that I couldn't do it." "Why can't I surrender?" she complained. Then giving the answer herself:

"I long for it, and fear it at the same time." She even suspects her religious experience of being false, not quite genuine enough: "How to distinguish between the true and the false? Is my God just a symptom of age? Did I invent him, so as not to have to search for Him? I do not doubt God's existence, but all the more I question my faith. I flee from God into an intimate God-relationship.

"God is here. I know this. God is behind a paper-thin wall which I cannot penetrate. I try again and again, make a real effort, but I can get through the wall only in my dreams. As soon as I'm awake I can't." Here is one of her dreams: "Remains of a Gothic cathedral on a mountain top. Very lovely columns. . . . I sink on the rocky ground, and it becomes soft and warm. . . . I pray. . . . Everything sinks away; . . . only the columns to God remain. I think: God will be here right away. . . . A painful break and awakening."

One day the patient decided that she was cured. "Or is it hysteria, this deep, quiet closeness to God, this un-conditioned accepting and, at the same time, this cool and considered doing of what needs to be done? Not my merit—I'm not taking credit, but I'm surprised and grateful. What really happened to me this night I don't really know. I believe, though, something very wonderful. It is still with me but I cannot quite express it yet."

These conditions recurred. "It's like a painful attack. I feel I'll die, right then and there, but it doesn't frighten me; on the contrary, it would be beautiful. Extremely strong, unspeakably beautiful experiences. . . . Long hours of a state of Light, like being absorbed by God . . . united with God. Being at-one with all things and with God. Everything I see, I am; everything I touch, I am. . . . On the same wave-length with all lines and colors. . . . Contact with things. . . . Through me all earthly existence flows toward God; I am now a piece of conducting wire." Something appears to her like a "piece of God, as though it had become transparent." She speaks of a Presence and says of herself: "I'm in touch. . . ." Yet, she is "shying away from greater clarity." "That is the beginning of insanity. . . . So what? If this is insanity, then I want it always, . . . then truth lies in insanity, and I prefer this to sanity."

Then a crisis: "I feel blunt, empty." After all those great experiences the emptiness is all the more agonizing. Once, she herself interpreted this as self-punishment—she did not "deserve this happiness." Her experience is so fulfilling that her life seems fulfilled: "The feeling becomes stronger that my life is already over, that I can hardly go further, that the only thing missing is death. Everything bores me and I desire only one thing (a repetition of those ecstasies) and the heck with all else. I am addicted. I am pitiful and small before grace, and I think day and night about how to become worthy; but this may be foolish pride. I'm greatly afraid of emptiness, even though I now know that I must accept everything completely and unconditionally—even emptiness."

Finally the joyful experiencing and active living achieved victory: "This is my first springtime in God. Up to now I was deaf and blind." Now "all things are illuminated by God," and the patient was able to "experience God. It is as if another sense had been added to the five: experiencing God, like hearing or seeing. There is no name for it. It was the therapy that led me to God. There is no longer an abyss, this being-in-God carries me and I cannot fall. Life again is wonderful, rich, and full of possibilities. When related to God, everything is bearable and filled with meaning. I think I know what I have to do: bring my daily life in order for the love of God."

An Experimental Study in Existentialism: The Psychometric Approach to Frankl's Concept of Noögenic Neurosis[1]

JAMES C. CRUMBAUGH
and LEONARD T. MAHOLICK
The Bradley Center, Inc., Columbus, Georgia

XIV

Frankl's method of psychotherapeusis, *logotherapy,* is an application of the principles of existential philosophy to clinical practice. His basic contention is that a new type of neurosis is increasingly seen in the clinics today in contrast to the hysterias and other classical patterns, and that this new syndrome—which he terms noögenic neurosis, and which supposedly constitutes about 55% of the typical present-day case load—arises largely as a response to a complete emptiness of purpose in life. The chief dynamic is "existential frustration" created by a vacuum of perceived meaning in personal existence and manifested by the symptom of boredom. According to Frankl, the essence of human motivation is the "will to meaning"

[1] An abridged version of this paper was delivered before the Section on Methodology and Social Psychology of The Southern Society for Philosophy and Psychology, at the annual meeting in Miami, April 12, 1963. We are indebted to J. L. Chambers, Ph.D., Research Director of the Mix Memorial Fund of Americus, Georgia, for a critical reading of this paper and valuable pertinent comments.

183

(*Der Wille zum Sinn*); when meaning is not found, the individual becomes "existentially frustrated." This may or may not lead to psychopathology, depending upon other dynamic factors, but he feels that the incidence of clinical cases thus rooted is of major significance.[2]

The fact that existentialism accepts intuitive as well as rational and empirical knowledge in arriving at values and meanings has been anathema to American behavioral scientists, who have tended to write it off as a conglomeration of widely divergent speculations with little thread of consistency or operational sense. If, however, one may, by approaching mental illness from this frame of reference, specify a symptomatic condition which is measurable by an instrument constructed from this orientation, but which is not identical with any condition measured from the usual orientations, then there is evidence that we are in truth dealing with a new and different syndrome. Frankl has specified such a condition, but has made only rather informal and loosely quantitative attempts to measure it (as will be shown later).

Kotchen has published a quantitative attack upon the relation of mental illness to existential concepts.[3] He analyzed the literature for the traits pertinent to mental

---

[2] *Noögenic neurosis* should not be identified with *existential vacuum*. The former, according to Frankl, is an illness, while the latter is a human condition. In those cases which show pathology (by which Frankl means "symptoms"), the term *noögenic neurosis* applies, while cases lacking symptoms of pathology are victims of *existential vacuum* and/or frustration of the *will to meaning*. His insistence upon drawing a distinction here is due in large measure to his claim that treatment of neuroses (whether they be somatogenic, psychogenic, or noögenic) should be limited to M.D.'s, while treatment of existential vacuum should be open to psychologists, social workers, educators, and pastoral counselors as well. Apart from this policy, however, Frankl would certainly agree with the broader use of his concept of noögenic neurosis as implied in the present paper, which he has read and approved with the exception of the above point.

[3] T. A. Kotchen, "Existential Mental Health: An Empirical Approach," *Journal of Individual Psychology*, 16: 174 (1960).

health as conceived by the existential writers, found seven characteristics of the kind of life meaning which is supposed to be present in good mental health (such as uniqueness, responsibility, etc.), and then constructed an attitude scale with items representing each of these seven categories. He predicted that the level of mental health operationally defined by the nature of each of five population samples of 30 cases each, from locked-ward patients in a mental hospital to Harvard Summer School students, would agree with the scoring level on the questionnaire. The prediction was affirmed at a generally satisfactory level of statistical significance. His scale, however, had some open-end items which could be quantified only by a rating code, and three items applied only to hospital patients and had to be omitted from the scoring. Further, his samples were composed entirely of males, and this is an area in which there may well be sex differences, as will be seen later.

The purpose of the present study is to carry further the quantification of the existential concept of "purpose" or "meaning in life," in particular to measure the condition of existential frustration described by Frankl, with a view to determining whether his noögenic neurosis exists apart from the usual neuroses as dynamically conceived. We may rationally define the phrase, "purpose in life" as the ontological significance of life from the point of view of the experiencing individual. Operationally we may say that it is that which is measured by our instrument,[4] and this is the frame of reference adopted herein. The task then becomes one of showing that the instrument measures something which is (a) what Frankl is referring to by the phrase in question, (b) different from the usual pathology, and (c) identifiable as a distinguishing characteristic of pathological groups in contrast to "normal" populations.

---

[4] R. L. Ebel, "Must All Tests Be Valid?" *American Psychologist*, 10: 640 (1961).

Subjects

A total of 225 subjects comprised five subpopulations as follows: Group I, 30 "high purpose" nonpatients, composed of six Junior League females and 24 Harvard summer school graduate students (14 males and 16 females).[5] Group II, 75 undergraduate college students, nonpatients (44 males and 31 females).[6] Group III, outpatients of various cooperating psychiatrists in private practice in Georgia,[7] a total of 49 (25 male and 24 female) cases of mixed diagnoses. Group IV, outpatients of the Bradley Center, Inc. (a privately endowed nonprofit outpatient psychiatric clinic), a total of 50 (22 male and 28 female) cases of mixed diagnoses. Group V, hospitalized patients, all alcoholics, a total of 21 (14 males and 7 females). Ages ranged from 17 to over 50, all groups except the undergraduate college students being pretty well mixed, but with averages near 30.

Materials

1. *The "Purpose in Life" Test (PIL).* An attitude scale was specially designed to evoke responses believed related to the degree to which the individual experienced "purpose in life." The a priori basis of the items was a background in the literature of existentialism, particularly in *logotherapy,* and a "guess" as to what type of material would discriminate patients from nonpatients. The structure of all items followed the pattern of a seven-point scale as follows:

---

[5]Our gratitude is due Dr. Viktor Frankl for permission to administer our scale to his Harvard seminar, summer 1961, as well as for his cooperation in administering our pilot version of the PIL to his Vienna classes, and for his great encouragement throughout this study.

[6]We are also grateful for the cooperation of Mr. Ed Shivers who arranged for the administration of the PIL, A-V-L, and Frankl Questionnaire to students at MacAlester College.

[7]We wish to express appreciation to the following Georgia psychiatrists who kindly gathered data upon their own patients: Alfred Agren, M.D.; R. E. Felder, M.D.; Sidney Isenberg, M.D.; Harry R. Lipton, M.D.; Joseph Skobba, M.D.; Carl A. Whitaker, M.D.

1. I am usually:

1	2	3	4	5	6	7
completely bored			(neutral)			exuberant, enthusiastic

A pilot study was performed using 25 such items; on the basis of the results half were discarded and new items substituted. Twenty-two then stood up in item analysis, and these were utilized in the present study.

The scale was designed on the unorthodox principle that, while theoretically a subject cannot accurately describe his real attitudes and these must be arrived at indirectly, in practice—and particularly in this attitude area—he can and will give a pretty reliable approximation of his true feelings from conscious consideration. This is also the theory upon which Kotchen proceeded. If this assumption be wrong, it would show up both in low reliability and in low validity as measured against an operational criterion of either mental health or "life purpose."

The PIL was so designed that each item becomes a scale within the scale. This is similar to the Likert technique except that the quantitative extremes of each item were in the present case set by qualitative phrases which seemed a priori to be identified with quantitative extremes of attitude. It was felt that if these choices were wrong, low item validity would eliminate them, whereas if they were right, the scale would be less monotonous and would stimulate more meaningful responses. The score was simply the sum of individual ratings assigned to each of the items. The direction of magnitude was randomized for the items, in order that position preferences and the "halo" effect might be minimized.

2. *The Frankl Questionnaire.* To demonstrate his thesis, Frankl utilized a rather informal series of questions which he evaluated clinically, apparently depending heavily upon Item 3 to determine the percentage of "existentially frustrated" individuals. For the present study Frankl

translated his questionnaire into English and the present experimenters quantified it by assigning a value of "1" to item choices which seemed to represent the least degree of purpose or meaning in life, a value of "2" to intermediate responses, and "3" to responses which appeared to involve the greatest degree of purpose. For example, Item 3 ("Do you feel that your life is without purpose?") was scored as follows: 1 = frequently (*häufig*); 2 = seldom (*selten*); 3 = never (*niemals*). Six of the 13 items (Nos. 1, 3, 7, 8, 10, 11) could be similarly quantified, and a total score was obtained from the sum of these six.

3. *The Allport-Vernon-Lindzey Scale of Values* (*A-V-L*). This best-known measure of values was administered and scored according to the published instructions. Scores were then computed as deviations from the published sex norms, and the deviations were then coded for IBM processing.

4. *The Minnesota Multiphasic Personality Inventory.* Administered and scored according to published instructions. Only the "T" scores were recorded.

PROCEDURE

The Purpose in Life Test was administered to all five groups of subjects. The Frankl Questionnaire and the Allport-Vernon-Lindzey Scale of Values were given only to Groups II, III, and V, while the MMPI was administered only to Group IV (being part of the regular intake battery at the Bradley Center). Because of the extensive tests already required of the latter it was not possible to add the Frankl or A-V-L scales, and pressure of time also prevented their administration to Group I. All of these measures are virtually self-administering, and both patients and nonpatients experienced no difficulty in following the printed directions. Each Bradley Center patient (Group IV) was further evaluated by the therapist's ratings, after the first therapeutic session, of each PIL item as he thought the patient should have rated himself if he were accurate in judgment.

RESULTS

1. *The Purpose in Life Test.* There is significant discrimination between patients and nonpatients, and a progressive decline in mean scores from Group I through Group V, both for the total scores and for most of the individual items (Table 1). An item analysis (Pearson r's between the total score and the score on each item, N = 225) revealed a correlation range of from $-.06$ (Item 19) to .82 (Item 9), 17 items being above .50 and 20 above .40. The reliability of the PIL revised total score, determined by the odd-even method (Pearson r, N = 225) is .81, Spearman-Brown corrected to .90.

The most appropriate norms (means, rounded to the nearest whole number) for the PIL (based on the "revised" total score, N = 47 female nonpatients, 58 male nonpatients, 59 female patients, 61 male patients) are: Nonpatients, 119; patients, 99; females, 111; males, 107. Patients are more variable than nonpatients. Being a patient drops the scores of males more than those of females: The norm for female nonpatients is 121, for female patients, 102; while that for male nonpatients is 118, for male patients, 97. The sex difference, while not significant, is suggestive. Females are more variable than males (except in Group V, alcoholics), and the instrument proved to predict more efficiently for males.

The following cutting scores halfway between patient and nonpatient norms for each sex were employed: For females, 111.5; for males, 107.5. At these cutting points the predictive power of the PIL revised total score was: For females, 65.4% correct classifications (of which 34.6% were patients and 30.8% were nonpatients); for males, 75.4% correct classifications (of which 35.6% were patients and 39.8% were nonpatients).

A partial "concurrent" validation of the PIL revised total score against one type of criterion, the ratings assigned by patients' therapists of each PIL item as the therapists

Table 1 Results of the Purpose in Life Test (PIL). Scores Are Sum of Ratings for All 22 Items.

Total Score	Nonpatients				Patients						Diff. in M between patients & nonpatients
	Group I		Group II		Group III		Group IV		Group V		
	M	SD	M	SD	M	SD	M	SD	M	SD	
Males	122.86	10.04	116.14	13.17	98.24	20.06	100.45	17.41	87.50	17.63	21.19**
Females	126.50	12.90	117.84	15.04	105.50	24.02	101.96	18.67	93.72	13.40	18.37**
Both	124.78	11.80	116.84	14.00	101.80	22.38	101.30	18.14	89.57	16.60	19.66**

**Difference significant at $p = .01$.

thought the patients should have rated themselves in order to be accurate, yielded an *r* of .27 (Pearson product-moment, N = 39). The PIL scores were not related to the subject's age, but it should be noted that the extremes of age are not covered in the population samples. In particular, a significant relationship at the upper level may have been missed.

2. *The Frankl Questionnaire.* The total score norms are 15.7 for nonpatients and 13.7 for patients, with an overall range of 8 to 19. The predictive power of the total score (using a cutting score of 14.5, halfway between patient and nonpatient norms) was 66.9% correct classifications (of which 26.5% were patients and 40.4% nonpatients). This total score correlated .68 (Pearson product-moment, N = 136) with the total score of the PIL.

3. *The A-V-L.* Of the six value scales, none discriminated adequately between patients and nonpatients, although the social scale gave a difference at the 5% level of confidence. There was little relationship between any of the A-V-L scales and the PIL.

4. *The MMPI.* Since data were available only on Group IV, no comparison of patients and nonpatients could be made, but the published norms are well known. Of all the scales, only the K (Validity) and D (Depression) scores showed any substantial relationship to the PIL (respectively .39 and −.30, Pearson product-moment, N = 45). Since the K scale is a measure of defensiveness, the indication is that subjects who have a high degree of "purpose in life" tend to have adequate defenses; they also tend to be less depressed than others.

DISCUSSION

The Purpose in Life Test distinguished significantly between patient and nonpatient populations (Table 1) and also showed—in most of its items individually as well as in the total score—a consistent progression of scoring from the

nonpatient group that was considered most highly motivated (Group I) to the most seriously ill patient group
(Group V). This is consistent with predictions from the
orientation of *construct validity*.[8]

The much greater variability of patients (Table 1)
suggests that some patients become such because of loss of
"purpose in life" while others break down because of dynamic factors as conventionally conceived. Possession of a
substantial degree of "purpose" seems to be one of the usual
properties of normal function, but there may or may not be
a lack of it in the abnormal personality. All of this is consistent with Frankl's belief that a new type of neurosis is present in the clinics alongside the conventional forms.

The study of *concurrent validity* in correlating the PIL
scores with therapists' ratings of "purposefulness" in
patients yielded only very modest success. This was at least
partially due to making the ratings after the first therapy
session, which proved too soon for the therapist to know the
patient's dynamics well. To have made them after a number
of sessions, however, would have confounded the effects of
therapy (if any) with the increased knowledge of the
patient. Further, the obtained relationship is probably
somewhat lower than the true value because of restriction of
the range of variability through use of only patients in the
sample, but it was not possible to secure such ratings upon
the nonpatients.

The high relationship between the PIL and the Frankl
Questionnaire indicates that the PIL gets at essentially the
same functions which Frankl describes as "existential
frustration" (since his questionnaire may be presumed to
represent his effort to define operationally what he is talking
about). This, he holds, is the basic ingredient of noögenic
neurosis.

The low relationships between the PIL and the A-V-L

[8]L. J. Cronbach and P. E. Meehl, "Construct Validity in Psychological
Tests," *Psychological Bulletin*, 52: 281 (1955).

scales suggest that "purpose or meaning in life" is not just another name for values in the usual sense. Frankl insists that it represents a basic human motivating force best described as spiritual.[9]

The low relationships between the PIL and the MMPI scales indicate that the PIL's significant discrimination between normal and pathological populations is not just another measure of the usual forms of pathology. Once again Frankl's hypothesis of a new type of neurosis is supported. Because of restriction of the range of variability by the use of only patients (Group IV) in the sample, the true relationships may be somewhat greater, but only for the K and D scales could they be large enough to indicate appreciably overlapping measures. And some overlap would be predicted, since Frankl postulates that noögenic factors may cause a breakdown of defenses and thus affect the patient's other dynamic mechanisms. The tendency of highly depressed patients to show a loss of life purpose and meaning is clearly observable in the clinic.

This raises the question of whether the PIL is an indirect measure of depression. The limited though significant correlation with the D scale suggests that the test is not primarily this, and it is probable that the causes of both depression and lack of life meaning and purpose are complex and variable. It is likely that lack of meaning can be both a cause and an effect of depression, and that both lack of purpose and depression can result from other causes. Depression, for example, could be due to an abundance of meaning but a deficiency in techniques of acquiring meaningful ends, while lack of meaning and purpose may be present in a rhathymic (far from depressed) personality who drifts aimlessly because of a lack of organization in life experience. From the orientation of psychopathology as behavior disorder, herein adopted, that which

---

[9]V. E. Frankl, "The Will to Meaning," *Journal of Pastoral Care*, 12: 28 (1958).

makes a trait a reflection of pathology is its incapacitating effect upon the individual's ability to adjust efficiently to life problems. Lack of purpose or meaning implies a failure to perceive an integrated pattern of goals and values in life, with a consequent dissipation of energies which can be only debilitating. Existence may become boring and not worth the struggle to overcome obstacles. Needs still operate within, and the individual may be highly frustrated, but he has no organized frame of reference from which to perceive meaning in the elements of experience, and consequently he can plan no active attack upon the causes of frustration. So he drifts along in constant search of new diversion to ease tensions he is often unaware of having. Depression, often interpreted dynamically as a hostile aggression against real or imagined causes of frustrations, similarly represents an ineffectual means of dealing with the situation. Lack of purpose is probably a more generic term than depression, for the latter represents a relatively specific and inadequate technique of adjustment to conflict. Loss of meaning and purpose may follow failure of any adjustment technique.

Some variables which it was impossible to control in the available samples of patients and nonpatients require discussion. The question arises whether the differential in PIL scores between population samples is a reflection of educational levels rather than psychopathology, since the nonpatient samples were college students while the patients were of mixed educational level. Exact educational status was available only for our own patients (Group IV), but they seemed typical of *private* psychiatric outpatients: Two-thirds attended college; 18% held a Master's degree or higher; the mean is one year of college. Although this still leaves a little educational balance in favor of the non-patients samples, the correlation between the PIL and educational level for Group IV is only .19 (Pearson

[10]H. R. Snavely, An unpublished special course project, Carleton College, 1962.

product-moment, N = 49). Further, Snavely[10] found that freshmen score significantly *higher* than seniors on the PIL. Thus it would seem unlikely that the patient-nonpatient differences could be attributed to education.

It may be suspected that such other variables as intelligence and socioeconomic class correlate with the PIL scores and are significantly different from patient to nonpatient samples. There is, of course, some relationship between education, intelligence, and socioeconomic class; and it would seem probable that the latter two variables follow education fairly closely in the present samples. It seems very possible that the extremes of intelligence do correlate with the presence of purpose and meaning in life, since there is a known tendency for people of genius level to achieve much (and logically, therefore, to have found much meaning and purpose), while it is difficult to see how the mentally retarded can integrate their lives very well around purposeful goals. The present samples of both patients and nonpatients were, however, composed primarily of subjects of higher than average education with few at either extreme, and the known substantial relationship between education and intelligence suggests that the latter was not appreciably different, at least between Groups II (nonpatient college students) and III (private outpatients) where the PIL differences are greatest. Therefore it seems unlikely that the differences between patients and nonpatients are due primarily to these variables.

One might ask whether the PIL responses of Frankl's Harvard class were influenced by his teaching. These students were all professional people functioning at high level (ministers, teachers, social-service workers, and the like), and it is probable that they already had highly purposive orientations to life. His instruction likely did not change this much, because it was slanted entirely to the theoretical side and not toward helping lost students find themselves. Further, it is improbable that such basic attitudes toward life would be changed by anything in the few weeks devoted to the course, though a response set could have been established toward "purposive" goals. But the Junior Leaguers who form part of Group I score similarly, and the group level probably reflects genuine purposiveness.

There is a question of the possible influence of social desirability upon the PIL answers. The moderate relationship between the K scale of the MMPI and the PIL scores could be interpreted as indicating the subject's defensive effort to make himself look purposive. As previously noted, it seems likely that individuals of genuinely high level of purpose would have strong defenses which would be reflected in the K scale. It also could be true, however, that highly defensive individuals exercise their defenses in responding to the PIL items. It is obvious that the instrument could not be used in a competitive situation, since, like other "self" tests, it could be either willfully or through unconscious motivation distorted in the direction of desirable or purposive responses. But the findings in relation to most such measures have been that there is relatively little willful distortion in most noncompetitive situations. Unconscious distortion would probably reflect the presence of at least some degree of emotional disturbance and should be present more often in patients than in nonpatients. This would partially account for the greater patient variability which has been found, and suggests that the patient-nonpatient differences have been somewhat affected by spuriously high or purposive scores among the patients. But this is on the side of "safety" in that instead of spurious differences between these populations being created by this effect, the obtained differences are reduced, which encourages the belief that the significances can be depended upon.

SUMMARY

The question of the existence of Frankl's noögenic neurosis—breakdown due to "existential frustration" or a lack of perceived meaning or "purpose" in life—was attacked psychometrically, through an attitude scale designed to measure the degree of awareness of such meaning among different populations. The concept of "purpose in life" was operationally defined as what the instrument measures; thus the problem became the threefold one of showing that its scores represent (a) what Frankl is describing, (b) something different from the usual neuroses, and (c) a characteristic of psychopathological as distinguished from "normal" groups.

The results of 225 subjects,[11] comprising two nonpatient and three patient samples, consistently support the noögenic hypothesis: (a) The relationship between the scale and a questionnaire designed by Frankl to describe the factors involved in his concepts was high; (b) the relationship of the scale to an established measure of traditionally conceived psychopathology, the MMPI, was low; and (c) the scale significantly distinguished patient from nonpatient populations, showing a predicted progressive drop in scores to match the level of pathology assumed by the nature of the group.

Further study of noögenic neurosis by the Purpose in Life Test and other methods is needed in order to answer a number of questions which present data treat only partially, to define the dynamic properties which would make possible diagnostic isolation of this syndrome, and to determine the variables which affect it. The work reported herein is considered primarily heuristic and exploratory rather than definitive.

---

[11]By this time, the test has been administered to 1,200 subjects, with the same results. See J. C. Crumbaugh, "Experimental Studies in Existentialism: II. The Purpose in Life Test As a Measure of Frankl's Noögenic Neurosis" (delivered before Sec. 24 of Amer. Psychol. Assn. Annual Meeting in New York City, Sept., 1966), *Newsletter for Research in Psychology* (Veterans Administration Center, Hampton, Virginia), 1966, VIII (14), 45 (Summary). [Editor's note.]

The Treatment of the Phobic and the Obsessive-Compulsive Patient Using Paradoxical Intention Sec. Viktor E. Frankl

HANS O. GERZ, M.D.[1]

XV

The treatment of phobic and obsessive-compulsive patients has always been a most difficult task, even for the experienced psychiatrist. The psychoanalytic theory and "depth psychology" of these neurotic conditions is very interesting, but all too often is of little help to the patient. Many times I have attempted (as have many other psychiatrists) to treat these patients with psychoanalytically oriented psychotherapy, without much success. We have tried to apply psychoanalytic concepts and theories and have spent years analyzing the patients' unconscious conflicts such as their Oedipus complexes and the like. When such a patient does not improve, then the frustrated psychiatrist, who tried so hard to "work with the patient through the underlying psychodynamics," many times tends to label the patient's resistance as responsible for the persistence of the neurotic symptoms; or, as has happened in some of the cases I am about to report, the psychiatrist labels the patient "schizophrenic" and, with that, eases his own anxiety about

[1]Dr. Gerz is associated with the Connecticut Valley Hospital, Middletown, Connecticut. Excerpts of this paper were discussed by Frankl at the Symposium on Logotherapy at the International Congress for Psychotherapy, Vienna, August, 1961.

not making the patient better and places the responsibility for the failure of therapy entirely on the patient.

Before I report on 7 cases out of the 24 I have been able to treat successfully with Paradoxical Intention in the past four years, I should like to refer to this technique of logotherapy as it was outlined by Frankl[2] himself and recently presented by him in an American journal.[3]

A characteristic phenomenon in the phobic neurosis is anticipatory anxiety—the fear of various symptoms such as passing out, blushing, becoming panicky when riding in cars, buses, subways, crossing bridges; the fear of heights, heart palpitation, etc. Such anticipatory anxiety frequently will cause the symptoms to actually materialize. The more the patient fears the occurrence of the symptom and the more he tries to avoid it, the more liable it is to occur. For example, the patient who has a fear of blushing will actually do so as soon as he is afraid that this might happen to him and as soon as he tries hard not to blush. How would it be, then, Frankl thought, if instead of trying *not* to blush, the patient would *try to blush;* or if, instead of trying not to pass out, or not to get panicky, etc., he would try to do that which he is so afraid of? Since we have no voluntary control over our autonomic nervous system, naturally the patient will not be able to blush as soon as he tries to do so, and it is precisely this phenomenon which is used in the technique of Paradoxical Intention. Furthermore, by intentionally trying to produce the neurotic symptoms, the patient not only is unable to do so, but also changes his attitude toward his neurosis. Whereas the patient had previously been afraid to blush, or to pass out, in using Paradoxical Intention he will be striving to accomplish this. As soon as he changes his attitude from being afraid of a symptom to liking it, he will find himself in

[2] *Aerztliche Seelsorge* (Wien: Deuticke, 1946), English edition, *The Doctor and the Soul* (New York: Alfred A. Knopf, Inc., 1959).
[3] V. E. Frankl, "Paradoxical Intention: A Logotherapeutic Technique" *American Journal of Psychotherapy*, 14: 520 (1960).

a funny situation indeed. He will feel humorous about his symptoms and start laughing at them, and with that he will put distance between himself and his neurosis. The removal of the fear will strangle the neurotic symptoms; subsequently the patient will find out that, paradoxically, the more he tries to produce his symptoms, the more he finds himself completely unable to do so.

My utilization of this technique is described and illustrated in the following case histories:

Case #1: W. S., aged 35, married, father of three children, was referred to me by his family physician because the patient was afraid he would die of a heart attack, particularly in relation to sexual intercourse. The patient had received a complete physical checkup, including electrocardiogram, and was found to be in excellent physical health. When I saw the patient for the first time, he was anxious, tense, fearful, and somewhat depressed. He reported that he has always been a "worrier and the nervous type" but "had never had anything like this." In the patient's anamnesis, it is important to note that his sister died of rheumatic heart disease at the age of 24, and his mother died of heart disease complicated by pneumonia at the age of 50. The patient related that one night after having had sexual intercourse, he went to the bathroom to wash himself and bent over the bathtub. He suddenly felt "a sharp pain like you pull something inside my chest where the heart is." In that moment, the patient became extremely fearful and panicky, and his latent anticipatory anxiety, which he had because of his family history, became actualized. He feared he would "die from a heart attack at any moment." He went to bed and broke out in a sweat. ("I laid awake and could not sleep. I figured this is the end.") After some time, he finally fell asleep from sheer exhaustion. From that time on, he developed the phobia that he would die of a heart attack, particularly after intercourse, and he developed a phobia of not being able to go to sleep. ("It is a horror to go to bed.") The anticipatory anxiety, in turn, made him more fearful and caused heart palpitations and a need to constantly check his pulse. The patient was completely preoccupied with his fear of sudden death and also developed some superimposed depression. After a few days, he consulted his family physician, who told him that physically he was well. This, however, gave the patient little reassurance, and after he had seen his doctor several times, the patient was referred to me. He admitted that because of his family history he had anxiety about dying of a heart attack. On the particular evening that his phobia began, he must have strained a muscle in the anterior chest wall as he was bending over the bathtub, and it was precisely this pain which triggered off his phobic neurosis. The pain brought on anticipatory anxiety; and in turn, through the autonomic nervous system, caused profuse sweating and heart palpitations. This led to more anticipatory anxiety and into a vicious cycle and feedback mechanism. In the course of logotherapy it was explained to him that anticipatory anxiety produces exactly that situation of which the patient is so afraid. As he anticipates that his heart will beat fast, this anxiety in itself will make his heart do so. Since, as mentioned above, we have no voluntary control over our autonomic functions, one will see that if the patient tries "real hard" to make his heart beat fast, he will find himself absolutely unable to do so. Therefore, when I asked the patient in my office to "try as hard as possible" to make his heart beat fast and die of a heart attack "right on the spot," he laughed and replied, "Doc, I'm trying hard, but I can't do it." Following Frankl's technique I instructed him to "go ahead and try to die from a heart attack" each time his anticipatory anxiety troubled him. As the patient started laughing about his neurotic symptoms, humor helped him to put distance between himself and his neurosis. The patient left the office relieved after having been instructed to "die at least three times a day of a heart attack"; and "instead of trying hard to go to sleep, try hard to remain awake." He had succeeded in using Paradoxical Intention effectively. He was seen a total of three times and reported to me four weeks later that he felt well. This was one and a half years ago. I am quite certain that with psychoanalysis, one could make quite a case out of this patient. Instead of "defocusing"[4] his attention from his symptoms, as logotherapy would indicate should be done, one could push him further into his neurosis, particularly once one became involved in underlying dynamics and so caused an iatrogenic neurosis.

[4]See Chapter XII, p. 160.

In looking back one might ask, "What actually made this patient better?" In that moment when he started laughing at his symptoms and when he became willing to produce them (paradoxically) intentionally, he changed his attitude toward his symptoms. Whereas, before treatment, the patient was afraid of dying of a heart attack, and was afraid of not being able to sleep, he now "tried" to die of a heart attack and "loved" to remain awake. With this change in attitude, he "took the wind out of the sails" of his neurosis (to quote Frankl) and in so doing, he himself interrupted the vicious cycle and strangled the feedback mechanism.

It is important to note that I place great emphasis on the fact that the *patient* is the one who changes his attitude toward his fear and, therefore, *cures himself.* This focuses the responsibility on the patient and prevents his becoming dependent on the doctor. Making the patient responsible is in line with logotherapeutic principles.[5] Paradoxical Intention consists of a reversal of the patient's attitude toward his symptoms to enable him to detach himself from the neurosis.[6]

I have found that this logotherapeutic technique can also be fully successful in chronic cases of phobic neurosis. The following clinical report will demonstrate this:

Case #2: A. V., aged 45, married mother of one 16-year-old son, has a 24-year history of a grave phobic neurosis consisting of severe claustrophobia such as fear of riding in cars. She had fear of heights, of riding in elevators, of crossing bridges, of collapsing, of leaving the house (when forced to do so, she would "hang on to trees, bushes, anything"). She also had a fear of open spaces, being alone, and becoming paralyzed. She was treated for her phobic neurosis over the past 24 years by various psychiatrists and received, repeatedly, long-term psychoanalytically oriented psychotherapy. In addition, the patient was

[5]V. E. Frankl, *Man's Search for Meaning: An Introduction to Logotherapy* (New York: Washington Square Press, Inc., 1963).

[6]V. E. Frankl, "The Spiritual Dimension in Existential Analysis and Logotherapy," *Journal of Individual Psychology,* 15: 157 (1959).

hospitalized several times, received several series of electroconvulsive treatments (ECT), and finally lobotomy was suggested. During the four years before I saw her, she had been hospitalized continuously in a disturbed ward in a state hospital. There she received ECT and intensive drug therapy with barbiturates, phenothiazines, monoamine oxidase inhibitors, and amphetamine compounds—all to no avail. She had become so paralyzed by her numerous phobias that she was unable to leave a certain part of the ward which surrounded her bed. She was constantly in acute distress in spite of receiving large doses of tranquilizers. Her tension was so great that her muscles hurt intensely. She tried constantly "not to collapse," "not to get nervous," and "not become panicky." Diagnoses of her illness, made by private psychiatrists, ranged from psychoneurosis to schizophrenic reaction, schizo-affective type. Diagnosis at the hospital, just a few months before I treated her, was schizophrenic reaction, pseudoneurotic type, with phobic anxiety and depressive manifestations. While in the hospital, she had been treated for a year and a half with "intensive analytically oriented psychotherapy" by an experienced clinical psychologist.

On March 1, 1959, all medication was discontinued and I began treatment with Paradoxical Intention. The technique was fully explained to her and we worked together, symptom by sympton and fear by fear. We started off first with removing the smaller fears, such as the one of not being able to sleep. The patient was removed from the disturbed ward and was instructed to "try to pass out and become as panicky as possible." At first, she said angrily, "I don't have to be afraid! I am afraid! This is ridiculous. You are making me worse!" After a few weeks of struggle, the patient was able to remain on a ward located on the third floor and "unsuccessfully" tried hard to pass out and become paralyzed. Both the patient and I one day went to the elevator to ride to the fifth floor. The patient was instructed to walk into the elevator and ride up with the strong intention of passing out and showing me "how wonderfully she can become panicky and paralyzed." While on the elevator, I commanded her to pass out, but at this she laughed and replied: "I am trying so hard— I can't do it. I don't know what is the matter with me—I can't be afraid any more. I guess I'm trying hard enough to be afraid." Upon reaching the fifth floor, the patient was proud and overjoyed as well. This seemed to be the turning point in the treatment. From then on, she used Paradoxical Intention any time she needed it. For the first time in many years, the patient walked outside alone around the hospital without fear, but "constantly trying hard to become panicky and paralyzed." After five months of this therapy, she was symptom free. She returned home for a weekend visit and enjoyed her stay there without any phobias for the first time in 24 years. When she returned to the hospital from this trip, she was contented and stated that there was only one fear left, namely that of crossing bridges. The same day we went together in my car and crossed a bridge. While crossing, I ordered her to pass out and become panicky, but she only laughed and said, "I can't! I can't!" Shortly thereafter, she was released from the hospital. Since then she has seen me every two to three months for a checkup "because of gratefulness." It is important for me to emphasize that quite purposefully I did not familiarize myself with her past history, nor with the underlying psychodynamics.

Two months ago she wanted a special appointment. When I saw her, she was quite tense, expressing anticipatory anxiety about getting sick again. Her husband had been out of work for several months and also had been suffering from a neurological disorder which was in the process of clearing. At the same time the patient was menstruating. This pressure caused her to become anxious and she was just beginning to slide back into the vicious cycle of her previous illness. In one session, however, she was able to understand what had happened and to avoid a reestablishment of the destructive pattern of her phobias. This patient has been out of the hospital and living a full and happy life with her family for two and a half years. Recovery was brought about with no attempt on my part to "understand" the patient's symptoms in terms of psychoanalytic theory and "depth psychology."

The question might well be asked: What really goes on in the sessions? Therapy is begun with taking the case history, recording symptomatology, etc., explaining to the patient the basic principles of Paradoxical Intention, and discussing case histories of my own and some of the typical cases reported by Frankl, Niebauer, and Kocourek.[7] This usually takes between one and a half and two hours. This will do two things for the patient: He will learn to understand what we are trying to do; and he will gain confidence that this therapy is effective. I have, for instance, found it very valuable to have a patient who has been cured with this type of treatment meet with the one who is starting in therapy, both in hospital and private practice. This can be done very well individually, and also is valuable in the group psychotherapy setting. I do not deny that this sort of thing has suggestive value, but may I ask, what doctor or psychiatrist can treat his patients without this factor? As far as the technique itself is concerned, it must not be confused with suggestion. In fact, Paradoxical Intention represents just the opposite. It does not tell the patient as Coué did, "everything will get better and better," but it instructs the patient to *try intentionally to get worse*. The logotherapist asks the patient himself to wish that the feared thing will happen to him. Frankl says very specifically that "Paradoxical Intention is most genuine logotherapy. The patient shall objectivize his neurosis by distancing himself from his symptoms. The spiritual in man shall detach itself from the psychic within him, and the patient shall call on the '*Trotzmacht des Geistes*,' man's spiritual capacity to resist, and by his inner freedom choose a specific attitude in any given situation."[8]

When I feel that the patient thoroughly understands the mechanism involved in the technique, we apply and practice it together in my office. For instance, the patient who is afraid he might lose consciousness is asked to get up and try to "pass out." To evoke humor in the patient I always exaggerate by saying, for example, "Come on; let's have it;

---

[7]V. E. Frankl, *Theorie und Therapie der Neurosen—Einfuebrung in Logotherapie und Existenzanalyse* (Wien: Urban und Schwarzenberg, 1956).

[8]V. E. Frankl, Seminar on Logotherapy conducted at Harvard Summer School, 1961.

let's pass out all over the place. Show me what a wonderful 'passer-out' you are." And, when the patient tries to pass out and finds he cannot, he starts to laugh. Then I tell him, "If you cannot pass out here on purpose, intentionally, then you cannot pass out any other place if you try." So together we practice Paradoxical Intention in the office over and over again; but also, if necessary, in the patient's home or wherever his neurotic symptoms appear. Once the patient has successfully used Paradoxical Intention on one of his phobias, he enthusiastically applies the technique to his other symptoms. The number of therapy sessions depends largely on how long the patient has been sick. When the illness is acute, and duration has been of only a few weeks or months, most patients respond to this therapy within about four to 12 sessions. Those who have been sick for several years, even as long as 20 years or more (in my experience I had six such cases, although more have been reported in the literature), need six to 12 months of biweekly sessions to bring about recovery. It is necessary during the course of treatment to repeatedly teach and encourage the patient to use the technique according to his specific symptoms. Since the nervous system in itself is well known for its repetitious qualities, and since our feelings are carried and expressed through nerve tissue, namely, the autonomic nervous system, a once-established neurotic feeling pattern will tend to repeat itself and become a sort of reflex, even when the causes of the neurotic symptoms have been resolved and removed. Because of this repetitious quality of the nervous system, it is also absolutely essential in therapy to repeat the application of Paradoxical Intention over and over.

Initially, patients show very good response to Paradoxical Intention, but during the course of therapy, particularly in chronic cases, patients will repeatedly suffer little setbacks. This is caused by the fact that as soon as patients *try to get better*, they enter the vicious cycle again, striving for health and providing the neurosis with new fuel. In other words, they "forget" to apply Paradoxical Intention and become worse by Coué's method of suggestion. This failure of the patient to continue to practice the technique is precisely because of repetitive neurotic behavior patterns. ("I have tried to fight my neurosis for so many years the wrong way. It is hard to re-learn.") But there is another element involved here: The therapist demands from the patient tremendous courage, namely, to do the things he so much fears. For instance, the patient who has the fear of blushing when in a group, is asked to do just that. Here, we appeal to the personal pride of the patient and his inner freedom in his spiritual dimension. And thus we practice logotherapy in its true meaning. For all these reasons the therapist must never tire of encouraging the patient to continue to use Paradoxical Intention over and over—just as his neurosis produces the symptoms over and over. Then, finally, the neurotic symptoms will "become discouraged" and disappear. Only too often "they try to come back," but then Paradoxical Intention strangles them. "When they saw that they could not get anywhere with me any more, they gave up completely."

Case #3: D. F., aged 41, married father of two teenage girls, was referred to me for the treatment of delirium tremens. Once his toxic psychosis had cleared, we tried in psychotherapy to understand some of the causes of his excessive drinking. He could not be considered a true alcoholic, but he had used alcohol excessively in order to relieve on the one hand what is called in logotherapy "existential vacuum" or "existential frustration,"[9] and on the other hand, to overcome his phobic-neurotic symptoms such as the trembling of his hand when writing in front of people. In his job as an engineer, his phobic condition interfered greatly with his ability to perform detailed mechanical work in front of others. For a long time he had not been able to sign checks in the presence of others, and had been greatly

---

[9]V. E. Frankl in *Handbuch der Neurosenlehre und Psychotherapie*, ed. V. E. Frankl, V. E. von Gebsattel, and J. H. Schultz, Vol. III (München and Berlin: Urban und Schwarzenberg, 1959).

anxiety ridden to the point of becoming panicky when he had to give a report in business meetings. On social occasions he had found himself unable to lift a cup or a glass without fear of trembling and spilling the contents. Lighting someone's cigarette was an act to be avoided at all costs. These neurotic symptoms were partially responsible for his symptomatic abuse of alcohol. Again, Paradoxical Intention was fully explained to the patient and he was instructed to "jump right into" the phobic situations, rather than avoid them as he had been doing. He was asked to seek every possible opportunity to demonstrate before groups "what a wonderful shaker" he was. He was to show others "how nervous he could get and how he could spill his coffee all over the place." Having suffered so long from these crippling neurotic symptoms, he gladly followed my advice. After three sessions, he reported to me: "I cannot shake, I cannot tremble. I cannot get panicky any more. No matter how hard I try." Characteristically, we again see in this case how the patient has utilized his inner freedom to change his attitude toward his neurotic symptoms and by taking a humorous attitude toward them, put distance between himself and his symptoms, *thus ridding himself* of the symptoms. Subsequently, as we were able to help the patient in the course of logotherapy to find a new meaning to his existence, he recovered from his noögenic neurosis.

The following case is presented in full detail because of the dramatic and immediate response to Paradoxical Intention of a patient with an acute phobic reaction:

Case #4: A. S., aged 30, mother of four children, was referred to me by her family physician because of the following symptoms: severe panic and anxiety, fear of heart attack, of smothering and strangling. "I cannot swallow. My throat is paralyzed. I have a pressure in my head. I am scared of dying of a heart attack." She complained of dizziness, headaches, and feelings "like taking off or floating." Also of tingling around her mouth, numbness, heart pounding, and that "the strangest feelings come over me." While in my office during her first visit, she was so overwhelmed by her fear of sudden death, that she grabbed my hands, trembled all over, and exclaimed, "Doctor, I must stay with you! I cannot leave your office! With you I am safe. Check my pulse. Listen to my heart." In fact, the patient absolutely refused to leave my office. In this situation, it would not have helped to explain Paradoxical Intention because her anxiety was so intense that she was not able to listen. Her husband was called into the office and I instructed them to "go downtown and pick out a nice coffin" for the patient. I asked the husband how much he wanted to spend on the coffin, and turning to the shocked patient, I said, "What color silk would you like to have in the coffin—pink or green?" The husband sensed my intentions. I continued, saying to the patient, "Go ahead and try as hard as you can to die instantly from a heart attack," which elicited a smile from her and the remark, "Doctor, you are teasing." Then, along with her husband and myself, she was able to join in the laughter. More time was spent explaining to the patient and to her husband the technique of Paradoxical Intention. Gradually, she showed signs of relief and comprehension. When the session was terminated, the patient arose, saying, "Doctor, I feel so much better." And, as she left the office, she was instructed not to forget to "die at least three times a day of a heart attack."

In subsequent logotherapeutic sessions she told me how it all started: About a year before, the patient had been shopping in a supermarket where, for no apparent reason, she suddenly got a "wobbly feeling" in her knees and became afraid of passing out. At that point, she ran out of the market and tried to forget the incident. On her next trip to the market she was "hoping this would not happen again." Actually, she was already experiencing anticipatory anxiety. When she went again to the supermarket, she "tried hard not to pass out," only to become more fearful and panicky. From then on she avoided all supermarkets, stores, etc., and reached the point where she was unable to leave her house at all. She demanded that her husband remain with her constantly so that he could call the doctor "in case." Mrs. S. responded promptly to Paradoxical Intention. I must mention that what Frankl has described as "somatogenic neurosis" or, more specifically, a "tetanoid pseudoneurosis" was ruled out by laboratory tests. The numbness and tingling around her mouth and in her hands was, of course, due to hyperventilation, and the physiological mechanism of this phenomenon was explained to her. The cause of the neurosis, as brought out in psychotherapy, was an acute conflict in the marital situation. This conflict was straightened out, and the patient has remained symptom free.

Again, I would like to emphasize that the application of Paradoxical Intention does not exclude the understanding and solving of the patient's neurotic conflict; indeed, this is done or attempted in each case as far as this is possible or is considered necessary.

One can expect that psychoanalysts will claim this type of nonanalytic treatment is "only" symptomatic, and nothing but suggestion, that these patients must develop other symptoms or relapse. Not only Frankl but also a great number of other leading psychiatrists have been able to prove that this is not the case. Wolpe[10] in a recent report states that "a survey of follow-up studies comprising 249 patients whose neurotic symptoms have improved markedly after psychotherapy of various kinds other than psychoanalysis shows only 4 relapses (1.6%)." He concludes, "This evidence contradicts the psychoanalytic expectation of inferior durability of recoveries obtained without psychoanalysis and does away with the chief reason for regarding analysis as a treatment of choice for neurotic suffering." If one needs, however, to apply psychoanalytic theory to explain why Paradoxical Intention is successful, one could—again only in theory—assume that if phobias can be understood as displaced hostile impulses, the therapist in telling the patient to proceed to do just that which he fears gives the patient permission to symbolically act out his hostile impulse.

One often hears the argument that it is "suggestion" that makes these patients better. Some of my colleagues have attributed the results to my "authoritarian" approach. Frankl

---

[10]T. Wolpe, "The Prognosis in Unpsychoanalyzed Recovery from Neurosis," *The American Journal of Psychiatry*, 118: 35 (1961) and *Psychotherapy by Reciprocal Inhibition* (Stanford, Calif.: Stanford University Press, 1958).

has been accused of having made Paradoxical Intention successful because he is the great authority, the professor, the Director of the Neurological Poliklinik of the University of Vienna, and helps his patients with "massive authoritative suggestion." The fact is, however, that many other European psychiatrists as well as a few in this country have been using Frankl's technique successfully. Cases have been reported as remaining symptom-free even for decades.

As to the treatment of the obsessive-compulsive patient, we have to consider a major difference: where the phobic patient *avoids* the fearful situation, the obsessive-compulsive patient will do just the opposite, namely, *fight it*.[11] And, the more he fights his symptoms, the more he will increase the symptomatology. Therefore, in these cases the basis of therapy is, in logotherapeutic terminology, to defocus the patient from his symptoms and help him to change his attitude toward his specific symptomatology. Since most obsessive-compulsive patients are known to be perfectionists, the basic underlying theme must be—"Heck, who wants to be perfect! I don't give a damn!" The case history of the following patient who had both phobic and obsessive-compulsive features will illustrate this concept:

Case #5: P. K., aged 38, married, father of two teenage children, has been suffering from a multitude of symptoms involving anxiety, panic states, phobias, obsessions, and compulsions, accompanied by depressive features for more than 21 years. He became sick two years before his marriage when he began to have obsessive doubts and fears about the correctness of his actions, and when married, ruminated over whether or not he loved his wife. As a child he had had fears of being alone and of going to the movies alone. He suffered from guilt feelings about masturbation after his mother told him that his brother's admission to a mental hospital was due to "self-abuse." The patient recalled that a friend had told him a girl suffered a nervous breakdown after riding a horse for the sexual sensation.

---

[11]See Chapter XII, p. 161.

Almost immediately the patient became plagued with a sexual sensation while walking. He developed the fear that he might become a homosexual, and he became increasingly fearful lest he "disgrace" himself by "grabbing a male's genital." A diagnosis had been made of schizophrenia. Mr. K. was treated over the years with psychoanalytically oriented psychotherapy. He also received from various psychiatrists both intensive drug therapy and ECT. None of these treatments brought him measurable relief. When Mr. K. first came to me, he was in a tense and agitated state, and quite tearfully related that for many years he suffered various neurotic symptoms. "For more than 20 years I have gone through a life of Hell! I keep it all a secret, but my wife knows. I am only relieved when I am asleep!" The patient went on to say that his greatest fear was that he might, when sitting in a barber's chair, or driving a car, or sitting at a counter, "grab somebody's penis." He feared that this act would result in loss of his job and in public disgrace. He feared that he might even confess to a sex crime which he had not committed. Further, he complained of inability to concentrate, of restlessness, and of fear that his heart might stop beating. He also feared he might scream out loud. He would hold his hands tightly to his body in order not to lose control and not "disgrace" himself. Jealousy of his wife was his most recently developed obsession. He constantly wondered whether or not he loved his wife, would disgrace himself, or become insane. He felt compelled to look at certain objects, places, etc. He had never been able to go on vacations with his family because of his severe neurosis. To my knowledge, at no time did he show overt psychotic symptoms.

Mr. K. was seen over a period of six months in biweekly logotherapeutic sessions. As in previous cases, symptom after symptom was removed. His obsessive doubts about his love for his wife disappeared once he adopted the attitude of: "Who wants to love his wife?" When he was instructed to seek every possible opportunity on the streets, restaurants, in the car, at work, to grab a man's penis (the therapist's included), Mr. K. started to laugh at his obsessions and they completely disappeared. One of the highlights during treatment was when he went for the first time in his life on a plane to Florida for a vacation. When he returned, the patient reported that he had tried very hard to be as panicky as possible on the plane and to go around "grabbing everybody"; instead, he experienced no anxiety and enjoyed the trip and the vacation. He still comes to see me once a month and is presently enjoying a normal and full life with his family and is completely asymptomatic.

Paradoxical Intention somehow seems to be a natural or physiological type of treatment for phobic conditions. This may be illustrated by the report of the successful self-treatment of a case of phobic neurosis by a friend of mine.

Mrs. L. K., aged 38, married, suffered from a fear of dying of a heart attack because of attacks of tachycardia and severe palpitations. Her husband, a physician, had assured her many times that there was nothing wrong with her heart. During World War II, while in the British Army in Africa, she had experienced for the first time an acute anxiety state during a period of extremely hot weather. She got herself into a vicious cycle— "each time when the palpitations and fear came, I laid down on the couch avoiding the slightest physical activity, but I would become even more scared and my heart would beat faster." After she had suffered from this almost intolerable condition for several years, she decided one day "not to give a damn any more. I went into the yard and started digging," saying meanwhile to herself, "performing hard work is either going to kill me or not, but I am going to find out." After she had worked for some time, she noticed that both her fear and the palpitations disappeared and she thought, "if this hard labor didn't kill me, nothing will." Thereafter when the palpitations and anticipatory anxiety occurred, she would "go ahead and work hard." Soon after learning how to "treat" herself, she became completely symptom free and has not had an attack for more than eight years.

It is interesting to note that this woman, since there was no psychiatrist available, had instinctively used Paradoxical Intention successfully.

It can be assumed that not only patients but psychiatrists have unconsciously used Paradoxical Intention, utilizing the philosophy that patients will never overcome their fears until they meet them.

Toll[12] reports she has been using Frankl's method of Paradoxical Intention and logotherapy successfully for over six years. She also found patients in group psychotherapy will spontaneously—without knowledge of Frankl's technique—use Paradoxical Intention and even recommend it to members of the group who suffer from phobic and obsessive-compulsive conditions. Frankl's own group psychotherapeutic experiences are referred to in two of his papers.[13]

Reviewing the literature, however, one finds it was Frankl who not only specifically systematized the technique but was able to explain the basic psycho-mechanisms involved which make the technique so successful.[14]

The following two case histories further illustrate the rather dramatic and lasting remissions achieved with this treatment:

Case #6: A. A., 31-year-old married female, suffered for nine years from a phobic neurosis with fear of insomnia, claustrophobia, "psychotophobia."[15] She complained of inability to remain in church, or at work, or to remain alone at home, and forced her husband to be with her constantly. She became "afraid of everything," developed a fear of crowds, of water, and finally confined herself completely to her home. She had been treated off and on in state hospitals and also in the outpatient clinic of the psychiatric department of a large university's medical school. During the course of treatment she received psychoanalytically oriented psychotherapy, ECT, and large amounts of various tranquilizers. Psychological testing indicated that "individual psychotherapy would probably be extremely difficult;

[12]N. Toll. Personal communication.

[13]See Chapter II, p. 26, and Chapter VIII, p. 95.

[14]V. E. Frankl, *Die Psychotherapie in der Praxis, Eine kasuistische Einfuehrung fuer Aerzte* (Wien: Deuticke, enlarged edition, 1961), and *Aerztliche Seelsorge* (Wien: Deuticke, enlarged edition, 1966).

[15]See Chapter XII, p. 161.

supportive therapy might be sufficiently effective to allow her to maintain a superficial and marginal adjustment when she leaves the hospital." A psychoanalytically oriented psychiatrist stated in the record: "No love expressions were either witnessed by patient between her parents, nor experienced from either of them. . . . Sexual guilt and poorly resolved Oedipal situation have played a role in bringing her phobias about. The prognosis, with long-lasting, 'expert' psychotherapy (by this one can assume he means therapy by a trained psychoanalyst) should not be too bad, though doubtful as to complete cure."

This patient was treated successfully within six weeks by one of my assistants—after I had taught him Frankl's technique. It must be noted that this young doctor possesses neither a dynamic nor an authoritarian personality. The patient has remained completely symptom free since her release from the hospital more than three years ago.

Case #7: S. H., 31-year-old female, suffered from a phobic neurosis with the same symptomatology as that in Case #6 above, for more than 12 years. Many hospitalizations in state institutions as well as in private sanitariums, together with all types of therapy, were completely unsuccessful. In 1954, lobotomy was performed and the patient's condition remained unimproved. A psychoanalytically oriented colleague traced her phobias back to "latent, but very powerful fellatio drives directed toward her father at a young age, but repressed because it was intolerable. . . hearing this 'interpretation' the patient became very angry. . . ."

Under treatment with Paradoxical Intention, she recovered within six weeks. She has remained symptom free since her discharge from the hospital three and a half years ago.

Cases #8–#24: These cases which were successfully treated with Paradoxical Intention are equally impressive, but because of limited space cannot be reported here.

EPICRISIS

Even though I have been using logotherapy, and in these cases specifically Paradoxical Intention, only for the past four years and on only 24 patients, it is my opinion that Paradoxical Intention is a rather specific and effective treatment for phobic and obsessive-compulsive conditions.

The obsessive-compulsive neurosis is usually more severe and incapacitating, and the results of treatment with Paradoxical Intention are not so impressive as in cases of phobia. However, the patient suffering from obsessive-compulsive neurosis can, with this technique, recover or at least be greatly relieved. I have at times found it very helpful to support logotherapy with small doses of Librium and Tofrānil combined, particularly in the early phase of treatment. Most of these patients suffer from some superimposed depression which is relieved by Tofrānil. The marked anxiety associated with the neurotic disorder is considerably reduced with the use of Librium.

Antidepressant and antianxiety medication makes it easier for the patient to have the courage to apply Paradoxical Intention. As soon as the treatment shows results, medication is discontinued, and the patient, having become convinced that "it works," continues quite readily to use the technique of Paradoxical Intention.

In the course of logotherapy, the therapist does not merely attempt to remove symptoms, but patient and therapist together try to understand the patient in terms of his history and life situation with its present conflicts and the factors involved which might have brought about the neurosis. Paradoxical Intention does not attempt to do away with helping the patient to understand himself better or to solve his problems; on the contrary, it encourages just this. But the patient's understanding of his symptoms in terms of dynamics alone does *not* usually remove his symptoms. In particular, it was always differentiated whether the patient suffered from a somatogenic, psychogenic, or noögenic neurosis (to use this differentiation introduced by Frankl). The latter indicates an existential frustration or existential vacuum.

The psychoanalytically oriented doctor may object to the belief that the removal of symptoms does not mean that new symptoms must replace them, and to the writer's strong rejection of the theory that only deep analysis can relieve symptoms and show lasting results. Had psychoanalytic therapy been so effective, Paradoxical Intention need never have been developed.

In many cases the realization by the patient of his underlying conflict, dating years back, and the solution of this conflict (either by psychotherapeutic process or perhaps the removal of the conflict by healing experiences in later life) does not seem to remove the patient's symptoms. Hence, the many unsuccessful psychoanalytic therapies with persistence of symptoms. Logotherapy is usually short-term therapy applicable in the treatment of a large number of patients, in contrast to psychoanalytic therapy extending over many years and benefiting only a limited number of patients.

Interestingly enough, for years the two trained Freudian analysts on the staff at Frankl's Clinic in Vienna have not been using psychoanalysis in treatment of phobic and obsessive-compulsive patients, but have used Paradoxical Intention with successful results.

As to the follow-up of these neurotic patients, it is thought that although symptoms have been removed and old neurotic patterns changed by a complete reversal of the patient's attitude toward his symptoms, neurotic habits and patterns which are being expressed through the autonomic nervous system tend to resume former patterns and "jump back into the old groove." It is the task of the logotherapist, once the patient tends to fall back into the vicious cycle, to help him to apply Paradoxical Intention again. Once the patient has succeeded he must only be reminded that he can do it over and over.

It is interesting to hear the patients' comments, once they have recovered, regarding what they believe was instrumental in their recovery. Here I would like to quote and summarize what one of my patients (Case #5) said: "If I had to sum up what got me well, I would say (*1*) the confidence that this therapy works after you have presented some case histories to me and after I talked to one of your patients whom you cured having been worse than me; (*2*) your teaching me to apply Paradoxical Intention in the various situations; (*3*) accepting my neurosis (I am a nervous type) instead of fighting it; (*4*) my change in attitude toward my symptoms. This way I could take them out of my body and set them aside and laugh at them. Humor has helped me a great deal; (*5*) your changing my wife's attitude." [I asked her to join me in encouraging her husband to practice Paradoxical Intention and she took a humorous attitude toward his symptoms, instead of anxiously watching him to see if he became worse.] (*6*) You made me do things and you let me talk about my symptoms. My previous psychiatrists would get angry when I talked about them. They always wanted me to talk about the past; (*7*) the things I was so worried about and ashamed of, what I had thought was so awful, you broke them down to natural things; (*8*) I never left your office confused after a session because you did not 'interpret' my symptoms and give me new things to worry about. I left many sessions happy and relieved. (*9*) I developed dependability on myself with Paradoxical Intention. I cured myself and I learned to use Paradoxical Intention any time I need it. I carry it always with me. I developed no dependency on you as I did on other doctors. If you called me to change an appointment, I would not 'die'; (*10*) my willingness to be sick and dedicate my suffering to God relieved me tremendously." (Nietzsche: "He who has a *why* to live (or suffer) for can bear with almost any *how*.")

Comments such as those above are frequently made by patients who have been under psychoanalytic therapy for years, and they certainly show that Paradoxical Intention is logotherapy in the true sense.

This writer's four years' experience with this specific technique and the logotherapeutic approach will not convince all readers of the success of this therapy and its lasting results. This only time and further follow-up studies can do.[16] Nevertheless, credit must be given Frankl who reports that cases treated by him more than 20 years ago have remained symptom free.

It is good to see that Frankl's logotherapy and existential analysis[17] which have such a tremendous impact on present-day psychiatry in Europe, have finally found their way to this country where Freudian psychoanalytic theories have prevailed longer than in other countries and have all too often been accepted as the gospel and as the only acceptable technique.

It is understandable that the psychiatrist with many years of psychoanalytic training might tend to be prejudiced and to reject Frankl's technique without having tried it. We must be open-minded with regard to any new theory and approach it with an academic spirit. Logotherapy and Paradoxical Intention do not attempt to do away with conventional psychotherapy, but merely to supplement and broaden the psychotherapeutic resources of the psychiatrist.

---

[16]The author reports that of 51 patients treated during a six-year period by the logotherapeutic technique of paradoxical intention, almost 90% recovered or made considerable improvement. See H. O. Gerz, "Experience with the Logotherapeutic Technique of Paradoxical Intention in the Treatment of Phobic and Obsessive-Compulsive Patients," *The American Journal of Psychiatry*, 123:548 (1966). [Editor's Note.]

[17]P. Polak, "Frankl's Existential Analysis," *American Journal of Psychotherapy*, 3:517 (1949).

SUMMARY

Twenty-four phobic and obsessive-compulsive patients, who had been suffering from their illnesses over a period ranging from two weeks to more than 24 years, were successfully treated with Frankl's logotherapeutic technique of Paradoxical Intention. It was concluded that this psychotherapeutic method is an effective nonanalytic therapy for phobic and obsessive-compulsive patients.

Bibliography

1. BOOKS

FABRY, JOSEPH B. *The Pursuit of Meaning: Logotherapy Applied to Life.* Preface by Viktor E. Frankl. Boston: Beacon Press, 1968.

FRANKL, VIKTOR E. *Man's Search for Meaning. An Introduction to Logotherapy.* Preface by Gordon W. Allport. Boston: Beacon Press, 1962. Paperback edition, New York: Washington Square Press, 1963.

————. *The Doctor and the Soul. From Psychotherapy to Logotherapy* (second, expanded edition). New York: Alfred A. Knopf, Inc., 1965.

————. *The Will to Meaning: Foundations and Applications of Logotherapy* (The Dallas Lectures). New York: NAL-World, 1969.

LESLIE, ROBERT C. *Jesus and Logotherapy. The Ministry of Jesus as Interpreted Through the Psychotherapy of Viktor Frankl.* New York and Nashville: Abingdon Press, 1965.

TWEEDIE, DONALD F. *Logotherapy and the Christian Faith. An Evaluation of Frankl's Existential Approach to Psychotherapy.* Preface by Viktor E. Frankl. Grand Rapids, Mich.: Baker Book House, 1961.

————. *The Christian and the Couch. An Introduction to Christian Logotherapy.* Grand Rapids, Mich.: Baker Book House, 1963.

UNGERSMA, AARON J. *The Search for Meaning. A New Approach in Psychotherapy and Pastoral Psychology.* Philadelphia: Westminster Press, 1961. Paperback edition, Foreword by Viktor E. Frankl, 1968.

223

2. CHAPTERS IN BOOKS

ARNOLD, MAGDA B., AND JOHN A. GASSON. "Logotherapy and Existential Analysis," in *The Human Person.* New York: Ronald Press, 1954.

FRANKL, VIKTOR E. contributions to *Critical Incidents in Psychotherapy,* ed. S. W. Standal and R. J. Corsini. Englewood Cliffs, N.J.: Prentice-Hall, 1959.

————. "Logotherapy and the Collective Neuroses," in *Progress in Psychotherapy,* ed. J. H. Masserman and J. L. Moreno, New York: Grune & Stratton, 1959.

————. "From Psychotherapy to Logotherapy," in *Readings in Psychology,* ed. Annette Walters. Westminster, Md.: Newman Press, 1963.

————. "The Philosophical Foundations of Logotherapy," in *Phenomenology: Pure and Applied,* ed. Erwin W. Straus. Pittsburgh: Duquesne University Press, 1964.

————. "Fragments from the Logotherapeutic Treatment of Four Cases. With an Introduction and Epilogue by G. Kaczanowski," in *Modern Psychotherapeutic Practice. Innovations in Technique,* ed. Arthur Burton. Palo Alto, Calif. Science and Behavior Books, 1965.

————. "The Significance of Meaning for Health," in *Religion and Medicine: Essays on Meaning, Values and Health,* ed., David Belgum. Ames, Iowa: The Iowa State University Press, 1967.

————. "Comment on Vatican II's Pastoral Constitution on the Church in the Modern World," in *World.* Chicago: Catholic Action Federations, 1967.

————. "Paradoxical Intention: A Logotherapeutic Technique," in *Active Psychotherapy,* ed. Harold Greenwald. New York: Atherton Press, 1967.

FRIEDMAN, MAURICE. "Viktor Frankl," in *The Worlds of Existentialism.* New York: Random House, 1964.

PATTERSON, C. H. "Frankl's Logotherapy," in *Theories of Counseling and Psychotherapy.* New York: Harper & Row, 1966.

STRUNK, ORLO. "Religious Maturity and Viktor E. Frankl," in *Mature Religion.* New York and Nashville: Abingdon Press, 1965.

VANDERVELDT, JAMES H., AND ROBERT P. ODENWALD. "Existential Analysis," in *Psychiatry and Catholicism.* New York: McGraw-Hill, 1952.

ZAVALLONI, ROBERTO. "Human Freedom and Logotherapy," in *Self-Determination.* Chicago: Forum Books, 1962.

3. *ARTICLES AND MISCELLANEOUS*

ANSBACHER, ROWENA R. "The Third Viennese School of Psychotherapy," *Journal of Individual Psychology,* Vol. 15 (1959), 236–37.

BIRNBAUM, FERDINAND. "Frankl's Existential Psychology from the Viewpoint of Individual Psychology," *Journal of Individual Psychology,* Vol. 17 (1961), 162–66.

CRUMBAUGH, JAMES C. "The Application of Logotherapy," *Journal of Existentialism,* Vol. 5 (1965) 403–12.

––––––. "Experimental Studies in Existentialism: II. The Purpose of Life Test as a Measure of Frankl's Noögenic Neurosis" (delivered before Sec. 24 of Amer. Psychol. Assn. Annual Meeting in New York City, Sept. 1966), *Newsletter for Research in Psychotherapy,* Veterans Administration Center, Hampton, Virginia, 1966, VIII (4), 45 (Summary).

CRUMBAUGH, JAMES C., AND LEONARD T. MAHOLICK. "The Case for Frankl's 'Will to Meaning,' " *Journal of Existential Psychiatry,* Vol. 4 (1963), 43–48.

––––––. "An Experimental Study in Existentialism: The Psychometric Approach to Frankl's Concept of Noögenic Neurosis," *Journal of Clinical Psychology,* Vol. 20 (1964), 200–207.

DUNCAN, FRANKLIN D. "Logotherapy and the Pastoral Care of Physically Disabled Persons." Master thesis submitted to the Southern Baptist Theological Seminary.

FABRY, JOSEPH. "A Most Ingenious Paradox." *The Register-Leader of the Unitarian Universalist Association,* Vol. 149 (June 1967), 7–8.

–––––– and Max Knight (pseud. Peter Fabrizius): "Viktor Frankl's Logotherapy." *Delphian Quarterly,* XLVII, No. 3 (1964), 27–30.

––––––. "The Use of Humor in Therapy." *Delphian Quarterly,* XLVIII, No. 3 (1965), 22–36.

FRANKL, VIKTOR E. "Logos and Existence in Psychotherapy," *American Journal of Psychotherapy,* Vol. 7 (1953), 8–15.

––––––. "Group Psychotherapeutic Experiences in a Concentration Camp" (paper read before the Second International Congress of Psychotherapy, Leiden, The Netherlands, Sept. 8, 1951), *Group Psychotherapy,* Vol. 7 (1954), 81–90.

––––––. "The Concept of Man in Psychotherapy" (paper read before the Royal Society of Medicine, Section of Psychiatry, London, England, June 15, 1954), *Pastoral Psychology,* Vol. 6 (1955), 16–26.

_____. "From Psychotherapy to Logotherapy," *Pastoral Psychology,* Vol. 7 (1956), 56–60.

_____. "On Logotherapy and Existential Analysis" (paper read before the Association for the Advancement of Psychoanalysis, New York, Apr. 17, 1957), *American Journal of Psychoanalysis,* Vol. 18 (1958), 28–37.

_____. Guest Editorial, *Academy Reporter,* III, No. 5 (May 1958), 1–4.

_____. "The Will to Meaning," *Journal of Pastoral Care,* Vol. 12 (1958), 82–88.

_____. "The Search for Meaning," *Saturday Review,* Sept. 13, 1958.

_____. "The Spiritual Dimension in Existential Analysis and Logotherapy" (paper read before the Fourth International Congress of Psychotherapy, Barcelona, Sept. 5, 1958), *Journal of Individual Psychology,* Vol. 15 (1959), 157–65.

_____. "Beyond Self-Actualization and Self-Expression" (paper read before the Conference on Existential Psychotherapy, Chicago, Dec. 13, 1959), *Journal of Existential Psychiatry,* Vol. 1 (1960), 5–20.

_____. "Paradoxical Intention: A Logotherapeutic Technique" (paper read before the American Association for the Advancement of Psychotherapy, New York, Feb. 26, 1960), *American Journal of Psychotherapy,* Vol. 14 (1960), 520–35.

_____. "Logotherapy and the Challenge of Suffering" (paper read before the American Conference on Existential Psychotherapy, New York, Feb. 27, 1960), *Review of Existential Psychology and Psychiatry,* Vol. 1 (1961), 3–7.

_____. "Religion and Existential Psychotherapy," *Gordon Review,* Vol. 6 (1961), 2–10.

_____. "Dynamics, Existence and Values," *Journal of Existential Psychiatry,* Vol. 2 (1961), 5–16.

_____. "Psychotherapy and Philosophy," *Philosophy Today,* Vol. 5 (1961), 59–64.

_____. "Basic Concepts of Logotherapy," *Journal of Existential Psychiatry,* Vol. 3 (1962), 111–18.

_____. "Psychiatry and Man's Quest for Meaning," *Journal of Religion and Health,* Vol. 1 (1962), 93–103.

_____. "Logotherapy and the Challenge of Suffering," *Pastoral Psychology,* Vol. 13 (1962), 25–28.

_____. "The Will to Meaning," *Living Church,* Vol. 144 (June 24, 1962), 8–14.

_____. "Angel as Much as Beast: Man Transcends Himself," *Unitarian Universalist Register-Leader,* Vol. 144 (Feb. 1963), 8–9.

_____. "Existential Dynamics and Neurotic Escapism" (paper read before the Conference on Existential Psychiatry, Toronto, May 6, 1962), *Journal of Existential Psychiatry,* Vol. 4 (1963), 27–42.

_____. "Existential Escapism," *Motive.* Vol. 24 (Jan.-Feb. 1964), 11–14.

_____. "The Will to Meaning" (a section of a paper read before the Conference on Phenomenology, Lexington, Kentucky, Apr. 4, 1963), *Christian Century,* Vol. 71 (April 22, 1964), 515–17.

_____. "In Steady Search for Meaning," *Liberal Dimension,* Vol. 2, No. 2 (1964), 3–8.

_____. "The Concept of Man in Logotherapy" (175th Anniversary Lecture, Georgetown University, Washington, D.C., Feb. 27, 1964) *Journal of Existentialism,* Vol. 6 (1965), 53–58.

_____. "Logotherapy and Existential Analysis: A Review" (opening paper, Symposium on Logotherapy, Sixth International Congress of Psychotherapy, London, England, Aug. 26, 1964), *American Journal of Psychotherapy,* Vol. 20 (1966), 252–60.

_____. "Self-Transcendence as a Human Phenomenon," *Journal of Humanistic Psychology* (Fall 1966), 97–106.

_____. "What Is Meant by Meaning?" *Journal of Existentialism,* Vol. 7, No. 25 (Fall 1966), 21–28.

_____. "Time and Responsibility." *Existential Psychiatry,* I (1966), 361–6.

_____. "Logotherapy and Existentialism." *Psychotherapy: Theory, Research and Practice,* IV, No. 3 (August 1967), 138–42.

_____. "What Is a Man?" *Life Association News,* LXII, No. 9 (September 1967), 151–57.

GERZ, HANS O. "The Treatment of the Phobic and the Obsessive-Compulsive Patient Using Paradoxical Intention sec. Viktor E. Frankl," *Journal of Neuropsychiatry,* Vol. 3, No. 6 (July-Aug. 1962), 375–87.

_____. "Experience with the Logotherapeutic Technique of Paradoxical Intention in the Treatment of Phobic and Obsessive-Compulsive Patients" (paper read at the Symposium of Logotherapy at the Sixth International Congress of Psychotherapy, London, England, August 1964), *The American Journal of Psychiatry,* Vol. 123, No. 5 (Nov. 1966), 548–53.

_____. "Reply." *American Journal of Psychiatry,* CXXIII, No. 10 (April 1967), 1306.

GROLLMAN, EARL A. "Viktor E. Frankl: A Bridge Between Psychiatry and Religion," *Conservative Judaism,* Vol. 19, No. 1 (Fall 1964), 19–23.

————. "The Logotherapy of Viktor Frankl," *Judaism,* Vol. 14 (1965), 22–38.

HALL, MARY HARRINGTON. "A Conversation with Viktor Frankl of Vienna," Psychology Today, Vol. 1, No. 9 (February 1968), 56–63.

HARRINGTON, DONALD SZANTHO. "The View from the Existential Vacuum," *Academy Reporter,* Vol. 9, No. 9 (Dec. 1964), 1–4.

HAWORTH, D. SWAN. "Viktor Frankl," *Judaism,* Vol. 14 (1965), 351–52.

JOHNSON, PAUL E. "Logotherapy: A Corrective for Determinism," *Christian Advocate,* Vol. 5 (Nov. 23, 1961), 12–13.

JONES, ELBERT WHALEY: "Nietzsche and Existential-Analysis." A dissertation in the Department of Philosophy submitted to the faculty of the Graduate School of Arts and Science in partial fulfillment of the requirements for the degree of Master of Arts at New York University 1967.

KACZANOWSKI, GODFRYD. "Frankl's Logotherapy," *The American Journal of Psychiatry,* Vol. 117 (1960), 563.

————. "Logotherapy—A New Psychotherapeutic Tool." *Psychosomatics,* Vol. 8 (May-June 1967), 158–161.

LESLIE, ROBERT C. "Viktor E. Frankl's New Concept of Man," *Motive,* Vol. 22 (1962), 16–19.

MAHOLICK, LEONARD T. "...to Comfort Always," *Journal of the Medical Association of Georgia,* Vol. 50 (1961), 559–60.

MASLOW, A. H. "Comments on Dr. Frankl's Paper," *Journal of Humanistic Psychology,* VI (1966), 107–12.

"Meaning in Life," *Time* Magazine (February 2, 1968), 38–40.

MÜLLER-HEGEMANN, D. "Methodological Approaches in Psychotherapy: Current Concepts in East Germany," *American Journal of Psychotherapy,* Vol. 17 (1963), 554–68.

"Originator of Logotherapy Discusses Its Basic Premises," *Roche Report: Frontiers of Clinical Psychiatry,* Vol. 5, No. 1 (January 1, 1968), 5–6.

PERVIN, LAWRENCE A. "Existentialism, Psychology, and Psychotherapy," *American Psychologist,* Vol. 15 (1960), 305–309.

POLAK, PAUL. "Frankl's Existential Analysis," *American Journal of Psychotherapy,* Vol. 3 (1949), 517–22.

ROWLAND, STANLEY J., JR. "Viktor Frankl and the Will to Meaning," *Christian Century,* Vol. 79 (June 6, 1962), 722–24.

SCHACHTER, STANLEY J. "Bettelheim and Frankl: Contradicting Views of the Holocaust," *Reconstructionist,* Vol. 26, No. 20 (Feb. 10, 1961). 6–11.

"That Nothing Feeling," *Time* Magazine (June 1, 1962), p. 48.

"The Doctor and the Soul. Dr. Viktor Frankl," *Harvard Medical Bulletin*, Vol. 36, No. 1 (Fall 1961), 8.

"The Father of Logotherapy," *Existential Psychiatry*, Vol. 1 (1967), 439.

"Viktor Frankl," *The Colby Alumnus*, Vol. 51 (Spring 1962), 5.

VICTOR, RALPH G., and CAROLYN M. KRUG, "'Paradoxical Intention' in the Treatment of Compulsive Gambling," *American Journal of Psychotherapy*, Vol. XXI, No. 4 (October 1967), 808–14.

WAUGH, ROBERT J. L. "Paradoxical Intention," *American Journal of Psychiatry*, Vol. 123, No. 10 (April 1967), 1305–6.

WEISS, M. DAVID. "Frankl's Approach to the Mentally Ill," *Association of Mental Hospital Chaplains' Newsletter* (Fall 1962), 39–42.

WEISSKOPF-JOELSON, EDITH. "Some Comments on a Viennese School of Psychiatry," *Journal of Abnormal and Social Psychology*, Vol. 51 (1955), 701–703.

————. "Logotherapy and Existential Analysis," *Acta Psychotherapeutica*, Vol. 6 (1958), 193–204.

————. "Paranoia and the Will-to-Meaning." *Existential Psychiatry*, I (1966), 316–20.

WIRTH, ARTHUR G. "A Search for Meaning," *Improving College and University Teaching*, 1961. 155–59.

4. FILMS, RECORDS, AND TAPES

FRANKL, VIKTOR E. "Logotherapy," a film produced by the Department of Psychiatry, Neurology, and Behavioral Sciences, University of Oklahoma Medical School.

————. Three Lectures on Logotherapy, given at the Brandeis Institute, Brandeis, California. Long-playing records.

————. "Man in Search of Meaning: Two Dialogues," tape produced by Sound Seminars, Recorded Lectures for Colleges and Universities, 50 East Hollister, Cincinnati, Ohio.

FRANKL, VIKTOR E. and HUSTON SMITH. "Value Dimensions in Teaching," a color television film produced by Hollywood Animators, Inc., for the California Junior College Association. Rental or purchase through Dr. Rex Wignall, Director, Chaffey College, Alta Loma, California.

ABOUT THE AUTHOR

Viktor E. Frankl is Professor of Neurology and Psychiatry at the University of Vienna Medical School, President of the Austrian Medical Society of Psychotherapy, and Head of the Neurological Department of the Poliklinik Hospital of Vienna, and has been visiting professor at the Harvard University summer school and the Southern Methodist University summer session.

Born in 1905, Dr. Frankl received the degrees of Doctor of Medicine and Doctor of Philosophy from the University of Vienna. During World War II he spent three years at Auschwitz, Dachau, and other concentration camps.

The leading figure in what has come to be called the Third Viennese School of Psychotherapy, Dr. Frankl first published in 1924 at the invitation of Sigmund Freud in the *International Journal of Psychoanalysis*. He has since published fifteen books —ten of which have been translated into Spanish, Italian, English, Japanese, Dutch, Swedish, Polish, Norwegian, Danish, French, Chinese, Hebrew and Portuguese—and has published extensively in psychiatry journals throughout the world. Dr. Frankl has been guest lecturer at the Royal Society of Medicine in London and in Argentina, Australia, Ceylon, India, Israel, Japan, Hawaii, Mexico and South Africa. He has made twenty-three lecture tours throughout the United States.

Name Index

Adler, Alfred, 122, 134
Agren, Alfred, 186 *n.*
Allport, Gordon W., 1, 7, 147–48, 160
Angel, Ernest, 48 *n.*, 65 *n.*

Baeck, Leo, 101
Bailey, Percival, 124
Bazzi, T., 159
Becker, Gerda, 94, 150
Beirnaert, Père, 129
Benda, Clemens E., 89
Berze, Josef, 124
Binswanger, Ludwig, 18, 65 *n.*, 73 *n.*, 133 *n.*, 134, 142, 147
Birnbaum, Ferdinand, 30 *n.*
Boss, Medard, 134
Brady, 39
Buhler, Charlotte, 37, 45, 46
Buhler, Karl, 81
Burton, Arthur, 88

Chambers, J. L., 183 *n.*
Corsini, R. J., 157 *n.*
Coué, Émile, 206, 208
Cronbach, L. J., 192 *n.*
Cushing, Harvey, 124

David, Jorge Marcelo, 157, 159
Davis, John M., 22, 66
Darwin, Charles, 114
Descartes, René, 80
Dienelt, K., 161 *n.*
Dreikurs, Rudolf, 80, 81 *n.*
Dubois, Paul, 158

Ebel, R. L., 185 *n.*
Einstein, Albert, 93 *n.*
Elkin, H., 45
Ellenberger, Henri F., 48 *n.*, 65 *n.*
Erikson, Erik, 9

Fabry, Judith and Joseph, 165 *n.*
Farnsworth, 90
Felder, R. E., 186 *n.*
Fleischmann, Karl, 100–101, 117

Frank, Waldo, 130
Freud, Ernst L., 20 *n.*
Freud, Sigmund, 7, 8, 18, 20, 37, 44, 59 *n.*, 72 *n.*, 99, 114, 118, 119, 142
Freyhan, 113
Fromm, Erich, 6, 45
Fromm-Reichmann, Frieda, 45
Furst, Paul, 109

Gebsattel, V. E. von, 153 *n.*, 208 *n.*
Gerbel, Gisa, 108
Glenn, John H., Jr., 18
Goethe, Johann W. von, 12, 17, 18 *n.*, 22, 113
Goldstein, Kurt, 44, 45
Gutheil, Emil, 119, 156, 157

Hartmann, Heinz, 9
Heidegger, Martin, 32, 48, 73 *n.* 135, 147
Hirschmann, 113
Hoelderlin, 165
Horney, Karen, 45
Husserl, Edmund, 2, 73

Isenberg, Sidney, 186 *n.*

Jaspers, Karl, 9, 78, 82, 103, 133
Jauregg, Wagner, 109
Johnson, Paul E., 28 *n.*
Jonas, Rabbi, 101, 117
Jung, Carl, 40, 45

Kaczanowski, Godfryd, 29 *n.*
Kant, Immanuel, 40, 80, 93, 114
Keen, Ernest, 9
Kierkegaard, Soren, 91
Knickerbocker, J., 37
Kocourek, Kurt, 26, 149, 153 *n.*, 160, 205
Kotchen, Theodore A., 22, 83 184, 187
Krantz, Heinrich, 115

La Mettrie, Julien Offray de, 123, 144

Lazarsfeld, Paul F., 97
Leibniz, Gottfried W., 83 n.
Lipton, Harry R., 186 n.

Mann, Thomas, 97
Maslow, Abraham H., 38, 45, 54
May, Rollo, 48 n., 65 n., 78 n.
McCourt, William F., 22, 66
McGregor, D., 37
Meehl, P. E., 192 n.
Meerloo, Joost A. M., 156 n.
Milner, 39
Murelius, O., 37

Nardini, J. E., 124 n.
Niebauer, Eva, 151, 153 n., 154,
    160, 205
Nietzsche, Friedrich W., 45, 103,
    165, 219
Olds, 39

Pascal, Blaise, 111
Piotrowski, Z. A., 44, 45 n.
Polak, Paul, 66 n., 133 n., 153 n.,
    158, 161 n., 220 n.
Putnam, James Jackson, 83

Rapaport, 37
Rappaport, Martha, 109
Rogers, Carl R., 45, 78, 79 n.
Rosenberg, Ernst, 109
Scheler, Max, 40, 73
Scher, Jordan, M., 65 n.
Schopenhauer, Arthur, 122
Schroeder, Pearl, 22

Schultz, J. H., 102, 153 n., 159,
    168, 208 n.
Schweitzer, Albert, 107
Shivers, Ed, 186 n.
Skobba, Joseph, 186 n.
Solomon, Philip, 22, 66
Spinoza, Baruch, 99
Standal, S. W., 157 n.
Stern, Karl, 118
Straus, Erwin, 11, 48 n., 65 n.

Thomas Aquinas, 35, 63
Toll, N., 215
Tweedie, Donald F., Jr., 1, 11, 28,
    66 n.

Ungersma, Aaron J., 1
Utitz, Emil, 96, 97

Valéry, Paul, 111
Von Eckartsberg, Rolf, 9
Von Orelli, 115

Weinke, 113
Weisskopf-Joelson, Edith, 15, 31,
    77, 84, 133 n., 152, 157 n.
Werner, 39
Whitaker, Carl A., 186 n.
Wisser, R., 37 n.
Wolf, Dr., in concentration camp
    102, 117
Wolpe, Joseph, 77, 211

Zeisel, 97

Subject Index

Activism, 31, 89, 90
Adaptation, 38, 68
Adjustment, 38, 45, 68, 194
Adlerian psychology, 5, 72, 119,
    122, 130
Agnostic convictions, and logo-
    therapy, 13
Agoraphobia, 5, 77
Allport-Vernon-Lindzey Scale of
    Values (A-V-L), 188, 191, 192

Anankastic substructure in phobic
    symptoms, 153
Animal psychologists, 126
Animals: biological and psycho-
    logical dimensions of, 137; in
    stinctual security of, 19, 42
Antianxiety medication, 217
Anticipatory anxiety, 3, 76–77-
    145, 146, 155, 158, 160, 163,
    200, 205, 210

Antidepressant medication, 217

Anxiety, 79, 94, 113, 163, 217; of aging and dying, 15; anticipatory, 3, 76–77, 145, 146, 155, 158, 160, 163, 200, 205, 210; attitude toward, 28

Anxiety neuroses, 161

Arbitrariness, 90

Archetypes, 119; motivation, 8; of one's collective unconscious, 64

Artificial psychosis, of LSD, 2

Atheistic patients, and logotherapy, 13

Atom bomb, fear of, 117, 120

Attention: excessive, 145, 160; forced, 160

Attitudinal values, 128

Authoritarian approach of therapist, 211–12

Autogenic training, use of, in therapy, 102, 159, 168

Automatic drawings of surrealists, 168

Automation, 123, 124

Autonomic-endocrine substructure in phobic symptoms, 153

Autonomic nervous system, 146, 199, 207, 218

Barbed-wire sickness, 95

Behavior: aim of, 41, 68; intended to impress, 126; moral, and stimulus of bad conscience, 42; and satisfaction of needs, 37, 68; and self-determination, 35, 61; and traditions, 43; unpredictability of, 63

Being: analysis of, 1; basic trust in, 57, 156; illumination of, and daseinsanalysis, 133; logotherapy's concern with, 1; meaning of, 57; relation of meaning to, 12

Being-in-the-world, 44, 55, 134; unity of, 135

Biological conditions of existence, 3

Biological dimension, 137, 141

Biologism, 123

Blushing: and anticipatory anxiety, 200; fear of, and paradoxical intention technique, 208

Boredom, 122–23, 183

Cartesian dualism, 48, 80

Causes, commitment to, 38–39, 56, 82

Character, reshaping of, 61–63

Choices: as to doing and being, 51; free, 3, 59, 82, 83, 90; in potentiality actualization, 46–47; responsibility of, 46–47; in role-playing concept, 9; value problem in, 47

Claustrophobia, 77, 203

Cognition: duality of subject and object of, 48–49, 135; and self-expression, 50; and self-transcendence, 50; and subjectivism, 50

Collective guilt, 111

Collective neuroses, of the present day, 17, 113–31

Collective unconscious, 64

Collectivism, 14, 119, 120

Community, 119

Complexes, psychological, 119, 122, 126, 199

Compulsions, obsessive, 147, 162, 163

Computer, and the human mind, 123

Concentration camps, 23, 25, 35, 80, 85, 116, 117, 123; group psychotherapeutic experiences in, 95–105; "In Memoriam" for heroes who died in, 107–111

Concept of man, 53, 61, 74, 123

Conditioning: and freedom of choice, 60–61; by social circumstances, 53

Conflicts, 43, 67, 211, 218; emotional, 91; instinctual, 76; in marital situation, 211; moral, 67, 122; power, 119; unconscious, 199

Conformism, 14, 20, 119, 120

Conscience, 3, 13, 64; bad, stimulus of, 42; good, 41–42; psychodynamic interpretation of, 42

Consolation: in suffering, 16, 91–94; as task of psychotherapy, 32

Creativity, 14; and meaning of life, 15, 24, 56, 127; and mental disease, 165

Daseinsanalyse, 133

Daseinsanalysis, 133–36

Daseinsgestalten, 134

Death, 15, 30, 84, 87, 88, 103, 109, 128; as aspect of finiteness, 24; fear of, 15, 56, 84

Decisions: freedom of, 30, 60 127; making of, by camp prisoners, 99; on mode of existence, 33–34, 35; as necessity of reality, 35; on potentialities to be actualized, 46–47; on responsibleness, 13

Defense mechanisms, 20, 38, 72; values as, 10–11

Defiant power of the human spirit, 99, 135

Defocusing attention from symptoms, 202, 212

Delirium tremens, treatment of, 208–9

Delusional ideas, 115–16

Demand quality: of existence, 21; of meanings and values, 64

Depersonalization of man, 63, 65, 100

Depression: endogenous, 20 *n.*, 23, 75, 137 *n.*; masked, 115; medication for, 217; neurotic, 23–24, 137 *n.*; noögenic, 137 *n.*; PIL as indirect measure of, 193–94; psychogenic, 137 *n.*; psychotic, 76

Depth-psychology, 18, 21, 118, 199, 205

Dereflection, 46, 160, 162

Despair: consolation in, 91; existential, 67, 92; and meaning, polarity of, 27

Detachment: noö-psychic, 75; scientific, 144; sense of, toward neuroses, 147, 157, 163 *see also* Self-detachment

Determinism, 3

Deterministic philosophy, 2

Devaluation, of the neurotic, 118

Dialogue: Socratic, in psychotherapy, 58; the Thou of, 104

Dimensional ontology, 75, 136–42

Dimension: biological, 137, 141; noetic, 3, 4, 43, 63, 73, 136, 138, 157; noölogical, 3, 63, 73–74, 75, 86, 136, 137, 141, 142; psychic, 43, 136, 138; psychological, 74, 75, 137, 141; somatic, 136, 138; spiritual, 73, 74, 208

Dipsomania, 125

Disease: fear of, 116; incurable, 24, 91–94; patient's attitude toward, 83–84, 91

Displeasure, avoidance of, 40

Doctor-patient relationship, in therapy, 78, 143–44

Dreams: interpretations of, 119; use of, in therapy, case history, 168–77

Drives: conflicts between, 43; goal of, 44; instinctual, 53, 55, 64; of psychoanalytic theory, 6, 7

Drug treatment, 81, 137 *n.*, 204 213, 217

Dynamics: existence interpreted in terms of, 59, 68; existential, 21, 22; of human volitions, 7 *see also* Psychodynamics

Dynamism, and mechanism, 59 *n.*, 63

Education, relation of, to existential testing, 194–95

Ego, 43, 68, 76

Ego psychology, 9

Electroconvulsive treatments (ECT), 23, 137 *n.*, 204, 213

Electro-shock treatment, 159

Encounter, psychotherapeutic, 78, 79, 80, 81, 144

Endogenous depression, 20 *n.*, 23, 75, 137 *n.*

Entrance-shock of prison camp life, 95–96, 101

Environment: economic, 118, 123; holding self above influence of, 99; as means to self-actualizing ends, 45; transcendence of, 136

Ephemeral attitude toward life, 117, 120
Equilibrium: bio-psycho-sociological, 68; inner, 7, 8, 55; maintenance of, 37, 38, 44 *see also* Homeostasis
Escapism, 15, 24, 47
Essence: of human existence, 13, 30, 44, 65, 74, 82, 90, 136; objective, of world objects, 38
Executive's Disease, 125, 126
Existence: analysis of, 1; boomerang as symbol of, 8–9; decision quality of, 35; demand quality of, 21; essence of, 13, 30, 44, 65, 74, 82, 90, 136; existential approach to, 74; "How" and "Why" of, 33; of human beings, uniqueness of, 44; illumination of, and daseinsanalysis, 133; instinctual aspects of, 87; and logotherapy, 53–58; and maintenance of homeostasis, 37; meaning of, 21, 22, 44, 57, 68 72, 73, 124, 136, 161; and polarity between the self and the world, 55; polarity between what is and what should be, 10, 47, 48; resubjectification of, 65–66; and risk of error, 13; self-transcendence of, 12, 49; somatic and psychic determinants of, 3; subjectivity of, 65–66; tragic triad of, 15, 24, 56, 87, 88; transitoriness of, 15, 30, 32, 47, 56, 88, 89
Existential analysis, 1, 83, 130, 133–42, 162, 220
Existential commitments, 47, 84
Existential communication, 78
Existential crises, 122
Existential despair, 67, 92
Existential dynamics, 21, 22
Existential facts of life, 87, 88
Existential frustrations, 17, 42, 43, 71, 76, 83, 122, 124, 125–26, 130, 183, 184, 185, 187–88, 192, 196, 208, 217
Existential guilt, 23, 75–76
Existential philosophy, 12, 48, 87, 183

Existential psychotherapy, 28
Existential psychiatry, 1, 87
Existential rationalization, 11
Existential reorientation in paradoxical intention, 157
Existential self-analysis, 131
Existential vacuum, 17, 19, 21, 35, 42, 43, 66, 67, 68, 71, 76, 77, 122, 125, 130, 162, 184 *n.*, 208, 217
Existentialism, 44; definition of, 42; experimental study in, 183–97; writers in field of, 72 *n.–* 73 *n.*
Experiencing: and meaning in life, 15, 24; subjective mode of, 134
Experimental study in existentialism, 183–97

Facts: attitude toward, 28; reverence before, Freud on, 7
Failure: as aspect of finiteness, 24; and success, polarity of, 27
Fallibility of man, 15, 30
Fanaticism, 85 *n.*, 120
Fatalistic attitude, 17–19, 120, 166
Fate, attitude toward, 128
Father image, and religious concepts, 29, 64 *n.*, 118
Fear: of aging, 15, 31, 84; of atom bomb, 117, 120; attitude toward, 28; of death, 15, 56, 84; of disease, 116; flight from, 161; of poverty, 116; removal of, 201; of suffering, 31
Finiteness of man, 24, 30, 32, 47, 57, 59, 84, 86
Follow-up studies on neurotic patients, 77–78, 211, 218
Frankl Questionnaire, 187–88, 191, 192, 197
Free associations, 119, 152
Free choice, 3, 59, 82, 83, 90 *see also* Choices
Freedom: becomes responsibleness, 12; to change, 61, 209; to choose, 3, 59, 82, 83, 90; of decision, 30, 60; fear of, and flight from, 121; and self-detachment, 28; to take a stand

toward conditions, 25, 59, 61, 75; of will, 2–5; within limits, 3, 60
Freudian orthodoxy, illus'ons of, 156
Frustrations, 18; existential, 17, 42, 43, 71, 76, 83, 122, 124, 125–26, 130, 183, 184, 185, 187–88, 192, 196, 208, 217; of meaning, 17; sexual, 121, 126; will to meaning, 42, 43, 66–67, 71, 122, 125, 130, 184 *n.*

Gerontopsychiatry, 124
God: belief in, and divine grace, 29–30; belief in, and psychotherapy, 33; concept of, 29; as a father-image, 29, 64 *n.*, 118; relationship to, among camp prisoners, 99–100; responsibleness to, 13; as the ultimate Thou, 104 *see also* Religion
Grace, divine, 29–30
Group psychotherapy, 26, 33, 206, 215; in concentration camps, 95–105
Guilt, 15, 23, 24, 30, 56, 75–76, 87, 88, 90, 109, 111, 115, 116, 117, 128, 173, 176, 212; collective, 111; existential, 23, 75–76; sexual, 216

Hallucinations, during sensory deprivation, 22, 66
Happiness, pursuit of, as self-contradiction, 41, 162
Hedonistic philosophy, of Epicureans, 41
Height-psychology, 18, 21
Hidrophobia, 146
Homeostasis, 7, 8, 21, 37, 38, 42, 44, 50–51, 68, 83; as neurotic phenomenon, 47–48
Homunculism, 118, 123, 127, 131
Humor: as attribute of deity, 147 *n.*; and neurotic symptoms, 201, 202, 209, 219; and self-detachment, 4, 147
Hyperhidrosis, 146
Hyperthyroidism, 76
Hypnosis, 168

Hypochondria, 41, 115

"I am" phenomenon of existence, 53–54
I-thou relationship in therapy, 79, 81
Iatrogenic neuroses, 202
Id, 43, 68, 76, 127
Ideals, as the stuff of survival, 18
Identity concept, of Erikson, 9
Incurable disease, 24; case history of therapy in, 91–94
In-der-Welt-sein (Heidegger), 135
Individual psychology, 72
Industrialization, and existential vacuum, 19
Inferiority, sense of, 122, 126
Initiative, lack of, and neurosis, 19
Inner equilibrium, 7, 8, 55
Insomnia, 145, 159 *n.*, 160
Instincts, in psychoanalytic theory, 7, 8
Intellectualization, in obsessive-compulsive neuroses, 158
Intention: direct, 6, 8, 41, 42, 45, 146; excessive, 145, 160; forced, 158, 160; paradoxical, *see* Paradoxical intention
Interest, loss of, and neurosis, 19
Interpretations: of psychoanalysis, 118, 119, 216; and psychodynamics, 11, 63, 65, 73, 88, 141

Jungian psychology, 7–8, 64, 119

Kaleidoscopic epistemology, 49–50

Language, theory of, 81
Laughing, at neurotic symptoms, 147, 201, 203, 219
Libido, 126
Life: meaning of, *see* Meaning of life; worthwhileness of, 30
Likert technique, 187
Lobotomy, 23, 154, 204, 216
Logodrama, 33
Logos:, logotherapy's concern with, 1; meaning of, 74; objec-

tivity of, 66; as world of meanings and values, 64

Logotherapy: and existence, 53–58; and existential frustration, 42, 43; and freedom of will, 2–5; and meaning of life, *see* Meaning of life; meaning orientation concept of, 22; as nonspecific therapy, 77; paradoxical intention technique, *see* Paradoxical intention; and patient's decision on responsibleness, 13; patterns of response toward neurotic problems, 161–62; philosophical foundations of, 1–18, 130, 183; psychogenic, 122; and psychotherapy, 74, 76, 77, 103, 122, 130, 134, 142, 216, 217, 218; and suffering, 84, 87–94; techniques of, 3–4, 5, 21, 28, 46, 143–64, 199; therapeutic orientation of, 1, 28; three basic assumptions of, 2; versus psychoanalysis, 11; and will to meaning, *see* Will to meaning

Love: of fellow human beings, 14, 56, 127; and otherness of beings, 135 *n*.

Lysergic acid diethylamide (LSD) 2

"March to Miltown," 23, 77
Masked depression, 115
"Mass murderer of Steinhof," story of, 62–63
Mass, submergence in, 119
Masturbation, guilt feelings about, 212
Materialism, 27, 75, 114
Meaning: concept of, and mental health, 83; confrontation, 10, 12, 17; and despair, polarity of, 27; frustration of, 17; fulfillment of, 6, 8, 9, 11, 12, 40 illumination of, and existential analysis, 133–34; logotherapy's concern with, 1, 87; objectiveness of, 16–17, 64; relation to being, 12; subjectiveness of, 17; ultimate, 33–34, 84, 92, 104 122; in the world, 44, 55

Meaning of life, 2, 11, 14–18, 20, 21, 24, 25, 33, 43, 64, 127, 128, 129, 185; and creativity, 15, 24, 56, 127; objectivity of, 44; in prison camps, 102–3; and procreation, 32, 85, 93; and stand toward fate, 15; in terms of experiencing values, 15, 24

Meaning orientation, 10, 17; life-prolonging and lifesaving effects of, 22–23; logotherapeutic concept of, 22; and mental health, 22, 23, 68; and pacemakers, 12 *see also* Will to meaning

Meaninglessness in life, 17, 27, 32, 67, 88, 121–22, 126, 162

Means-end relationships, 6, 37, 45, 56, 80, 120

Medical ministry, 90–91, 115

Mental health: and acceptance of finiteness, 47; and concept of meaning, 83; and existential concepts, 184–85; and fulfilling meaning of existence, 69; and homeostasis, 83; and meaning orientation, 22, 23, 68; and religion, 33; and tension, 21, 67

Mental well-being, 10, 67, 83

Minnesota Multiphasic Personality Inventory (MMPI), 188, 191, 193, 196, 197

Monadologistic view of man, 37, 39

Monadology, definition of, 38 *n*

Monism, 75, 135, 136

Moral conflict, and noögenic neurosis, 67, 122

Morality, and moral behavior, 42

Mortality of man, 15, 30, 88

Motivation, 38, 44, 183; logotherapeutic concept of, 71–72; psychoanalytic theories of, 5, 6, 7, 8; unconscious, 30

Motorization, 126

Mrs. Executive's Disease, 125–26

Narcissism, 114
Neurology, 115, 138, 139
Neuroses, 19, 77, 88, 113, 115, 116, 122; anxiety, 161; collec-

tive, of the present day, 17, 113–31; of early childhood, 152; etiology of, 145; iatrogenic, 202; monosymptomatic, 153; noögenic, 43, 67, 76, 122, 183–97, 209, 217; objectivizing of, 206; obsessive-compulsive, 118, 147, 153, 158, 159, 161, 163, 199–200, 212; patient's attitude toward, 153, 200, 209; and patient's fatalism, 28–29; phobic, 153, 155, 156, 161, 162, 199 203, 212, 214; psychogenic, 43, 76, 77, 217; sexual, 6, 39, 40–41, 88, 127, 145, 160, 161; somatogenic, 76, 210, 217; Sunday, 125; and trauma, 152; treatment of, by existential analysis, 135, 184 *n.*; of unemployment, 124

Neurotic depression, 23–24, 137 *n.*

Neurotic problems, patterns of response toward: right activity 162; right passivity, 162; wrong activity, 161–62; wrong passivity, 161

Nihilism, 118, 121, 127, 131

Noetic dimension, 3, 4, 43, 63, 73, 136, 138, 157

Nonspecific therapy, 77, 152, 153

Noödynamics, 49, 68, 83, 135

Noögenic depression, 137 *n.*

Noögenic neuroses, 43, 67, 76, 122, 183, 209, 217; psychometric approach to, 183–97

Noölogical dimension, 3, 63, 73–74, 75, 86, 136, 137, 141, 142

Noölogism, 75

"Nothing but" evaluation of man, 65, 72, 123, 127, 138

"Nothing-butness" of human phenomena, 72–73

Objectification of existence, 65

Objective world of meanings and values, 51, 55

Objectiveness of meaning, 16–17, 64

Objectivity: of meaning of life, 44; in meanings and values, 65; of the object, and cognition, 49

Obligative quality: of fulfillment of meaning, 55; of realization of responsibility, 64; in meanings and values, 65

Obsessive-compulsive neuroses, 118, 147, 151, 153, 158, 159, 161, 163, 212; treatment of, using paradoxical intention technique, 199–200

Oedipal situation, 11, 119, 199, 216

Oneness, in man, 74–75

Ontoanalysis, 1, 65, 134

Ontological analysis, 136

Ontological difference: in dimensions of being, 114, 136; between the noetic and psychic, 74

Ontology, dimensional, 75, 136–42

Ontos, logotherapy's concern with, 1

Optimism, 31, 32, 89, 90

Orgasm, ability to experience, 40, 145, 161

Pacemakers, and meaning orientation, 12

Pain, 15, 24, 87, 88, 110 *see also* Suffering

Palpitations, and paradoxical intention, 149–50

Pandeterminism, 28–29, 59, 88

Pansexualism, 59

Paradoxical intention, 3–5, 28, 46, 75, 76, 143–64, 199–220; case histories of, 4, 146, 148, 150–51, 153–54, 201–2, 203–5, 208–9, 209–11, 212–14, 215–16; reports on, in the literature, 159

Partners, participation with, 39, 56

Past, logotherapeutic attitude toward, 32, 84, 88, 109

Pastor, former role of, 72, 90, 115

Pathologism, 74 *n.*

Pathology of the *Zeitgeist*, 105, 142

Peace: of mind, 41; of soul, 41–42

Peacemakers, and meaning confrontation, 12

Personality: changes in, and therapy, 78; in a community, 119; and conformism, 120; dimensions of, *see* Dimension; fulfillment of, 46; in a mass, 119; and modes of reducing tension, 38; neurotic, 47; unpredictableness of, 61

Persuasion, in therapy, 158

Pessimism, 31, 87

Phenomenological analysis, 8, 12 14, 63, 141

Phenomenological approach, 2, 49, 73

Phenomenology, definition of, 2 *n.*

Philosophy: deterministic, 2; existential, 12, 48, 87, 183; hedonistic, of Epicureans, 41; of life, and the psychiatrist, 73; of logotherapy, 2, 130; quietistic, of Stoics, 41; reductive, 118

Phobias, 146–47, 162, 163, 204 205, 207, 216, 217; as displaced hostile impulses, 211; reversal of patient's attitude toward, 146; somatogenic, 77

Phobic neuroses, 153, 155, 156, 161, 162, 199, 203, 212, 214; treatment of, using paradoxical intention technique, 199–220

Physical-psychic collapse of camp prisoners, 97–98

PIL, *see* "Purpose in Life" Test

Pleasure: and meaning fulfillment, 6; as side effect, 146; and task achievement, 40

Pleasure principle, 5–7, 20–21, 37, 40, 44, 72, 102, 146

Politics: and fanaticism, 120; and means-end relationships, 80

Potency, demonstration of, 40 145, 161

Potentialism, 46, 47

Potentialities, 53, 88; actualizing of, 30–31, 46, 89; development of, 9–10; meaning and values of, 46; pursuit of, 46; realization of, 53, 68

Prayer, 175, 179

Prestige consumption, 126

Priest, former role of, 72, 90, 115

Prison psychoses, 95

Procreation, and meaning of life, 32, 85, 93

Progressivism, 88

Provisional existence of camp prisoners, 97

Psychiatry, 23, 115; existential, 1, 87; goal of, 33; impact of logotherapy on, 220; and man's quest for meaning, 71–86

Psychic determinants of existence, 3

Psychic dimension, 43, 136, 138

Psychic epidemics, 105

Psychic traumata, 122, 151–52

Psychoanalysis, 65, 77–78, 91, 118 152, 218; Freudian, 9, 64, 71, 130, 156, 220; logotherapy versus, 11; pandeterminism of, 59; pansexualism of, 59

Psychodrama, 26, 33

Psychodynamics: and inner equilibrium, 7; interpretations and, 11, 63, 65, 73, 88, 141; and paradoxical intention, 5; and religious interpretation, 30; underlying, 199, 205; and will to pleasure or power, 6

Psychogenetic interpretation of meaning and values, 65, 73

Psychogenic depression, 137 *n.*

Psychogenic neuroses, 43, 76, 77, 122, 217

Psychogerontology, 124

Psychohygiene, 124, 127

Psychological analysis, 74

Psychological conditions of existence, 3

Psychological dimension, 74, 75, 137

Psychological illnesses, 43

Psychologism, 74, 75, 123

Psychology: Adlerian, 5, 72, 119, 122, 130; animal, 126; of camp life, phases of, 95–100; depth-, 18, 21, 118, 199, 205; ego, 9; height-, 18, 21; individual, 72; Jungian, 7–8, 64, 119; pandeterminism in 28–29

Psychometric approach to noö-

genic neurosis, *see* Experimental study in existentialism
Psychonoëtic antagonism, 157, 163
Psychopathology, 184, 197; of prison camp life, 95
Psychophysical condition, rising above, 136
Psychophysical make-up of man, 118
Psychophysical problem in man, 137
Psychoses, 115, 129; artificial, of LSD, 2; and daseisanalysis, 135; paradoxical intention in, 155 *n.*; prison, 95; somatogenic, 75; toxic, 208
Psychosexual disturbances during childhood, 77
Psychotherapeutic need, 115
Psychotherapy, 1, 20, 21, 53, 57, 58, 81, 83, 122, 127, 130, 137 *n.*, 138, 142; deep analysis in 218; existential, 28; in existential frustration, 43; goal of, 32–33; group, 33, 95–105, 206, 215; logotherapeutic techniques of, 3–4, 5, 21, 28, 46, 143–64, 199; and logotherapy, 74, 76, 77, 103, 122, 130, 134, 142, 216, 217, 218; psychoanalytically-oriented, 199, 204, 213; and religion, 32; short-term, 79–80, 155, 156, 160, 163, 218; teaching and learning of, 143; techniques of, 1, 79, 81, 144
Psychotic depression, 76
Purpose in life: existential definition of, 185, 197; "Purpose in Life" Test (PIL), 186–87, 188–90 (*table*), 191–97 *see also* Meaning in Life

Quietistic philosophy, of Stoics, 41

Rabbi, former role of, 72, 90, 115
Rationalizations, 72; existential, 11; of instinctual drives, values as, 10; in obsessive-compulsive neuroses, 158; secondary, 20, 55, 64

Reaction formations, 10–11, 55, 72
Realism, 18 *n.*
Reality, 8, 38, 139; ambiguity of, 34; of being human, 141; decisions a necessity of, 35; principle, 7, 72 *n.*
Receptivity, 14
Reductionism, 72, 142
Reductive philosophy, 118
Reification, 63, 65
Reinterpretation of the human being, 53
Religion: and camp prisoners, 99–100; case history of neurosis involved with, 165–82; and divine grace, 29; and freedom of decision, 30, 84; and logotherapy, 13, 85, 93; and mental health, 33; as obsessional neurosis, 118, 142; and psychotherapy, 32; relation of concepts of, to father image, 29; salvation as goal of, 33
Reobjectification of *logos*, 66
Repentance, 128
Resistance of patient, 199
Responsibility, 127, 185; in choice of potentialities to be actualized, 46–47; fear of, and flight from, 121; freedom to take, 64; to fulfill meaning of existence, 69; of patient in paradoxical intention technique, 203; for self-determination, 61; sense of 22
Responsibleness, 12–13, 17, 30, 61 *n.*, 75, 90
Resubjectification of existence, 65–66
Retirement, psychological crisis of, 124
Role-playing concept, 9

Satisfaction of needs, 37, 38, 39 40, 53, 55
Schizophrenia, 2, 72 *n.*–73 *n.*, 124, 199, 213
Science, and man's predicament, 88, 141
Scientism, 88

Secondary rationalizations, 20, 55, 64
Security, 19, 42
Self: Jung's conception of, 45; projection of into world, 44; and the world, polarity of tension between, 55
Self-accusation, 23, 76
Self-actualization, 8, 44, 45, 46, 50–51, 53, 54–55, 68
Self-analysis, existential, 131
Self-centered interest, 46
Self-concept, change in, 79
Self-consciousness, 3
Self-construction, 61
Self-detachment, 3–4, 28, 75, 147, 157, 163
Self-determination, 35, 60–61
Self-expression, 10, 16, 34–35, 44, 45, 49, 50, 55, 64
Self-fulfillment, 127
Self-judgment, 3
Self-management, of neurosis, 148
Self-observation, compulsion to, 145, 146, 160
Self-preservation, 38, 96
Self-realization, 8, 45, 127
Self-reproach, 115
Self-stimulation, 39
Self-stupefaction, 125
Self-thwarting quality of direct intention, 6, 8, 41, 42
Self-transcendence, 12, 46, 49, 50 61, 67, 74, 82, 90, 135 *n.*, 136, 138–39
Self-understanding, 2 *n.*, 21
Sense of humor, in paradoxical intention technique, 4, 147, 201
Sensory deprivation, hallucinations during, 22, 66
Sexual frustration, 121, 126
Sexual neuroses, 6, 39, 40–41, 88, 127, 145, 160, 161
Shock treatment, 23, 62, 81, 137 *n.*
Short-term therapy, 79–80, 155, 156, 160, 163, 218
Sleeplessness, 158–59
Sociological conditions of existence, 3
Sociologism, 123

Somatic determinants of existence, 3
Somatic dimension, 136, 138
Somatic epidemics, 105
Somatogenic neuroses, 76, 210, 217
Somatogenic phobias, 77
Somatogenic psychoses, 75
Somato-therapy, 56
Specific therapy, 77
Speed, craze for, 126–27
Spirit of the age, 118, 126
Spiritual aspirations of man, 21, 74 *n.*, 87
Spiritual dimension of being, 73, 74, 208
Spiritual distress, 67, 72
Spiritual-moral attitude of camp prisoners, 98–99
Spiritual problems, and noögenic neuroses, 67, 76, 122
Spiritual resources, therapeutic use of, 85, 93
Spiritual struggle, and logotherapy, 72, 165
Spiritual therapy, 77
Spiritualism, 75
Spirituality of man, 63
Stress, 21, 68, 83, 116
Stuttering, and paradoxical intention, 148–49
Subjectification of meaning and values, 65
Subjectiveness of meaning, 17
Subjectivism, and cognition, 50
Sublimations, 55, 64
Success and failure, polarity of, 27
Suffering, 15–16, 31, 56, 83–84 103, 110, 116; as aspect of finiteness, 24; choosing stand toward, 25; fear of, 31; and logotherapy, 84, 87–94; and meaning in life, 15, 24, 25, 26–27, 33, 56, 87, 127
Suggestion, in therapy, 158, 206 208, 211
Suicide, 23, 76, 116; and prison camp life, 95–96, 102, 104, among students, 17
Sunday neuroses, 125

Superego, 8, 42, 43, 64 *n.*, 68, 76, 127

Super-meaning, and total existence, 57

Symptomatic therapy, 153

Symptoms: change of attitude toward, 147, 151, 163, 200–01, 203, 209, 218, 219; of collective neuroses, 113, 115, 117–21; defocusing attention from, 202, 212; persistence of, in unsuccessful analytic therapies, 218; responsibility for attitude toward, 75; strengthening of, through fighting against, 147, 212

Task: achievement of, and pleasure, 40; completion of, 90, 124, 127

Technique: of dereflection, 46; logotherapeutic, 3–4, 5, 21, 28, 46, 143–64, 199; of paradoxical intention, 4, 28, 46, 76, 143–64, 199–220; of persuasion, 158; psychotherapeutic, 1, 79, 81, 144; of suggestion, 158, 206, 208, 211

Tendentious apperception, 134

Tensions, 8, 10, 11, 12, 21, 37, 40, 44, 47, 48, 49, 50, 55, 67, 68, 83, 144

Tetanoid pseudoneurosis, 210

Therapeutic relationship, 81–82

Therapy, theory underlying, 2

Thou, of intimate dialogue, 104

Time: conception of, 84; sense of, 97

Tolerance, 85 *n.*

Toxic psychoses, 208

Traditions, behavior supported by, 43

Tragic triad of existence, 15, 24, 56, 87, 88

Tranquilizing drugs, 23, 41, 77, 204

Transcendence: beyond self, 12; as characteristic of existence, 136; of world, 25, 61 *see also* Self-transcendence

Transference relationship, 79, 81

Transitoriness of existence, 15, 30 32, 47, 56, 88, 89

Traumata, psychic, 122, 151–52

Trembling of hands, and paradoxical intention technique, 208–9

Trust, basic, in Being, 57, 156

Truth: through delusion, 3; and religion, 13 *n.*

Ultimate meaning, 33–34, 84, 92, 104, 122

Unconscious, the, 21, 64, 167; collective, 64

Unemployment, neuroses of, 124

Unity: of being-in-the-world, 135 of man, 136, 137, 138

Values, 10, 57; actualization of, 64; collisions between, 43; realization of, 40, 68; in role-playing concept, 9

Wholeness, of man, 68, 74–75, 136, 137, 138

Will, freedom of, 2–5

Will to meaning, 2, 5–13, 16, 17, 20, 40, 66, 67, 72, 73, 103, 121, 124, 127, 183; frustrations of, 42, 43, 66–67, 71, 122, 125, 130, 184 *n.*

Will to pleasure, 5, 6, 40, 72, 103, 121, 125, 127

Will to power, 5, 6, 20–21, 40, 72, 103, 121, 125, 127

World, concept of, 55

Zeitgeist, pathology of, 105, 142